DATE DUE		

The *Ultimate* Parrot

Barrett Watson and Mike Hurley

Howell Book House

New York

Photos by Barrett Watson, Michael Hurley, Amanda Bulbeck, Keith Allison and David Tyler, and courtesy of *Parrots* Magazine. Illustrations by Viv Rainsbury. The authors' thanks go to Alison Hurley for typing the original manuscript.

HOWELL BOOK HOUSE
IDG Books Worldwide, Inc.
An International Data Group Company
Foster City, CA • Chicago, IL • Indianapolis, IN • New York, NY • Southlake, TX

ISBN 0-7645-6102-2

Library of Congress Cataloging-in-Publication Data
available on request

Manufactured in Singapore

10 9 8 7 6 5 4 3 2 1

CONTENTS

AUTHOR PROFILES

CO-AUTHORS

Barrett Watson

Born in America in 1961 before eventually moving to England, Barrett kept and bred a wide variety of birds and mammals as a child, including budgerigars, cockatiels and lovebirds, which fashioned his interest in the parrot family from an early age.

Pursuing a career as a professional show jumper and eventer, he found that the keeping and breeding of parrots combined well with his equestrian activities.

Knowledge and experience has been gained in the breeding and rearing, both by hand and naturally by the parents, of many species. These include members of the pionus, amazon, macaw, cockatoo, eclectus, African Grey, and poicephalus families, some to second and even third generation.

Having studied the artificial incubation and rearing process for many species, Barrett now encourages as much parent-rearing as possible, and is proud to have reared many of the difficult species (e.g. Moluccan Cockatoos) who are in danger of dying out in captivity if solely hand-rearing continues unabated.

Barrett will continue to breed and hand-rear a proportion of the more common species, which make wonderful pets. Hopefully, this will lessen the pressure on imports. He also hopes to increase the numbers of endangered species (with captive breeding and parent-rearing) in the hope that they and their habitats can be saved.

Michael Hurley

Michael lives on a smallholding in Suffolk, shared with his family and a large number of parrots and a smaller number of dogs, cats, horses and sheep.

He has held a variety of health-related posts, both within higher education and in clinical areas, and is currently working as a health service manager.

Ever since he was a boy he has been fascinated by birds, keeping finches and injured birds in outside barns. In later years, he progressed to keeping cockatiels and many differing breeds of Australian parrakeets. Parrots soon became a natural step and over the last sixteen years Michael has successfully kept and bred many species.

He has a great love of the parrot and a deep interest in their care and conservation.

CONTRIBUTORS

Ron Rees Davies, BVSc., CertZooMed., MRCVS.

Ron Rees Davies qualified as a vet from Liverpool University in July 1994. He has a strong interest in 'Exotic pet' medicine, and has kept parrots, birds of prey, exhibition budgerigars, hamsters, hedgehogs and a five-foot green iguana. He gained his RCVS Certificate in Zoological Medicine in 1998 and currently treats a wide range of first-opinion and referral parrot, raptor, rodent, rabbit and reptile cases.
Chapter Two, What Makes A Parrot A Parrot?

Annette De Saulles

Annette is a writer and editor, and currently edits *Parrots* magazine. The conservation of wild parrots and their habitats, as well as their proper care in captivity, is her particular concern.
Rescue Parrots (see Chapter Four, Purchasing Your Parrot); If Your Parrot Escapes (see Chapter Five: Bringing Your Parrot Home); Safeguarding Your Parrot's Future – Wills and Trust Funds (see Chapter Six: Caring For Your Parrot); and Conservation Projects (see Chapter Thirteen: Rare and Endangered Parrots).

1 INTRODUCING THE PARROT

Dazzlingly beautiful, charismatic and intelligent creatures – we have long been captivated by the charm of these unique birds. Since Roman times, the parrot has been the constant companion of mankind. Sadly, its very beauty and ability to mimic has resulted in much abuse over the years, mainly due to ignorance.

It is only in the last 20 years or so that a greater understanding of the parrot's significant intelligence and emotional being has come about, enabling us to provide them with a better quality of life and even to encourage captive reproduction – a remarkably recent occurrence with many species.

With more than 320 species of parrot on record, this is a rich and diverse family of birds. Included amongst its members are the familiar budgerigars, lovebirds and cockatiels. Also recognisable to most people are the macaws and cockatoos, flamboyant amazons and African Greys. This extensive family also extends to the almost unknown Kakapo and night parrots.

In between these are a wide spectrum of varieties both familiar and unfamiliar. Some are so abundant and free-breeding that they have become notorious pests to agriculture, whilst others are extremely endangered – including a species of macaw with only one known survivor in the wild. Unfortunately

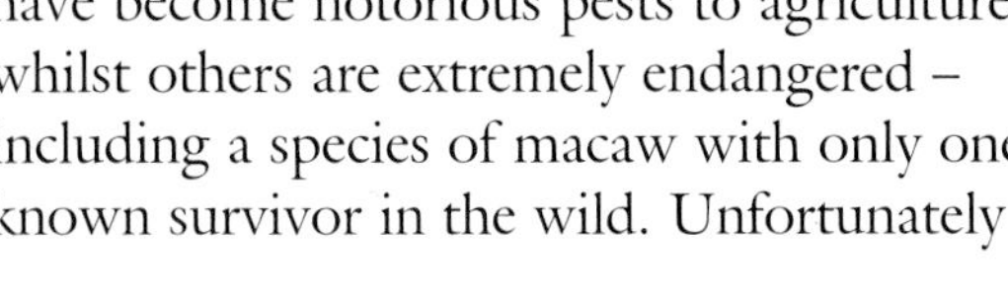

Opposite page: Blue and Gold Macaw.

The parrot family is a diverse group. Pictured: the Twenty Eight Parakeet.

there are several species which are just teetering on the brink of survival due to habitat destruction, commercial trade and hunting among their many opponents.

So, what makes a parrot a parrot? All parrot species have in common a hooked upper bill with an undershot lower one, which in conjunction with their muscular tongue can be used with great dexterity. They are also all distinguished by being zygopedal – that is, they have two toes pointing forward and two back. Another defining feature of the parrot tribe is that they all lay eggs with white shells. Beyond this, there is great variation in colour, size, feather-quality and diet across parrot species. One significant feature, which sets them apart from other birds, is a great intelligence with a huge capacity for learning. This is demonstrated in the wild by the ability of some species to exploit food sources in a hostile environment with great success.

UNDERSTANDING PARROTS

In captivity, countless pet parrots show word-association and cognitive ability in the home, and this has been further demonstrated by Dr Irene Pepperberg's great scientific work with her African Grey, Alex (Vines, G. 'Listening to Alex', *New Scientist*, 2000, No. 2221, pp 40-3). Dr Pepperberg has proved beyond reasonable doubt, and by scientific methods, that it is possible for parrots to understand and react to verbal commands, and also to be able to solve problems and make choices.

In observing both wild and captive parrots playing with each other, and with inanimate objects, it is immediately apparent that they do this with joie de vivre, the adults indulging in play just as willingly as the juveniles do. This is something that needs to be remembered if you are lucky enough to have one of these captivating creatures in your home or aviaries – they need entertaining or they soon become bored.

In some ways, the recent progress made in our understanding of parrots has given us the realisation of just how easy it is to abuse these intelligent creatures. Those of us who keep parrots must ensure that they are given the stimulation and affection which is so necessary to keep them well adjusted. If we fail to do so, our parrots can develop behavioural problems such as bouts of screaming, feather-plucking or other similarly distressing behaviours. Once these behaviours have become established, they can prove very difficult to eradicate. However, there is a positive side. Parrots which are well cared for make remarkably good pets and friends, keen to share many aspects of their owners' lives with them.

CLOSE COMPANIONS

Interestingly, it is those parrot species which have very close relationships with one another that also tend to make the best companions for humans. Some examples include the macaws and cockatoos, which form strong pair bonds throughout their

With gentle handling, parrots can become very loving pets. Pictured: Senegal Parrot.

Members of the Macaw family generally have good relationships with each other and with humans. Pictured: Hyacinthine Macaws.

lives, and are therefore also likely to become very bonded to their human companions; whereas parrots which have a rather stand-offish relationship with one another, such as eclectus parrots and the Asiatic ringnecks, are also not going to show much affection to their keepers.

Finally there are the species, such as the amazons, who become both very bonded to their partners in the breeding season and also very territorial: with their mercurial temperaments, they may react rather unpredictably around humans.

Records of longevity in parrots abound, some well-documented and others doubtless a little exaggerated. However, it is common knowledge that parrots are on the whole quite long-lived birds, and one can certainly expect some of the larger varieties to live into their 70s and 80s, with amazons and Greys often reaching 50 years of age, and so on downwards with the size of the birds. It is not unusual for the humble Cockatiel to reach the age of 25.

The advantage in this is that there are very few pets which can live with us as our companions for such long periods of time. However, with this comes the responsibility of being aware that it is quite possible for our pet parrots to outlive us! If this is likely to be the case, then it is only sensible to make some provision for your pet after your departure. Although parrots generally don't like disruption in their lives, they are quite capable of being rehomed very successfully if the move is undertaken with care and sensitivity. This says much for their adaptability, both from a psychological and physical point of view.

PARROTS IN THE WILD

Wild parrots are found on every continent in the world with the exception of Antarctica and Europe – although with an ever-increasing population of feral ringnecked parakeets in the south of England this may be set to change.

Popular belief leads many people to think of all parrots as inhabitants of tropical rainforests. This habitat does indeed house many wonderful species of macaws, amazons

This Blue-fronted Amazon is pictured in the wild in the Mato Grosso region, Brazil.

A flock of Hyacinthine Macaws in the wild, Brazil.

and conures. The well-documented destruction of this habitat has led to the decline of many species – due mainly to the loss of potential and existing nesting-sites, as well as depleted food supplies and constant human disturbance.

In the pockets and larger tracts of rainforest that are left, even the gaudily-coloured large macaws are hard to see, being wonderfully camouflaged against the leafy and shadowy background. Sometimes pairs and small flocks may be seen flying noisily overhead. The best way to view parrots in this habitat is to visit the great clay licks such as the one found in the Manu National Park in Northern Peru, where large numbers of various species of parrot congregate daily to take mouthfuls of the clay. This is thought to contain a lot of valuable minerals and perhaps allay the effects of some of the poisonous plant material that they ingest in the course of a day's foraging.

Many parrots can be seen to fly from their roosting sites to a fruiting tree at first light, and will spend an hour or two greedily eating, before embarking on a further journey to the next feeding area. By midday, fully satisfied, they will often sleep during the heat of the afternoon before engaging in another feeding frenzy in the afternoon and returning to the roosting area at dusk.

A far cry from the dense tropical rainforests are the open and often arid savannahs of Africa and Australia. There is no shortage of parrot varieties in these areas. Longtailed parakeets, budgerigars, cockatiels and cockatoos abound in the Australian outback, lovebirds and poicephalus parrots in the Savannah of Africa. Here, the battle to survive takes on a never-ending search for the dried seed-heads of grasses, weeds and shrubs. Huge flocks congregate where the feeding is good, and also at the few waterholes in the desert regions. These flocks of parrots normally take to a nomadic

Moluccan Cockatoo: many parrots live in treetops, though others are ground-dwelling.

existence, flying to the food source and, when that food source is depleted, flying on to the next.

When the pickings are good and less time is needed for the search for food, play will occur among the adults and youngsters alike. Macaws and amazons will often swing by one foot on palm fronds and twigs, play-fighting and squabbling while hanging upside down. Cockatoos will play with stones and twigs on the ground, rolling over on their backs whilst doing so.

Wild parrots live at varying distances from the ground. Kakapos, a very rare species, live amongst the tussocks of grass in the New Zealand mountains. These – the heaviest of all parrots – feed, court and breed both at ground level and below it in burrows. The aptly-named ground parrot inhabits a similar habitat. Conures of different species are often found in dense foliage and shrubs just above ground level.

Amongst the branches of the higher trees live many species – well camouflaged against the mosaic of leaves and dappled sunlight, where even the most spectacularly coloured parrots can disappear when motionless. Above the canopy, the larger macaws will feed on the ripe succulent fruits and risk predation by eagles when flying from the feeding sources. Every level has been exploited by some species filling an ecological niche.

Many of the world's rarest amazons inhabit the islands of the Caribbean. They cling to survival by a thread – a whole species can be wiped out by a hurricane at any time in this unpredictable region. The Tahitian and ultramarine lories could also suffer the same fate.

Some parrot species have become well adapted to living in closer proximity to man. Both Galahs and ringnecked parakeets can now be found living and breeding in highly populated areas, and many more varieties of parrots choose to visit bird-tables and parks.

FEEDING HABITS

Parrots in the wild exploit a wide variety of foods. Fruits form a large part of many species' diets. Palm drupes are popular with many macaws, especially the blue species. African Greys and Red-bellied Macaws are thought to rely almost entirely on the oily seeds of palm fruits. Hyacinth Macaws can be seen picking undigested seeds from the droppings of cattle.

Figs are a highly popular food for many species, the more obvious being the fig parrots, who rely on the substance they obtain from them to satisfy their high vitamin K demands.

As an adaptation to the agriculture now taking over huge tracts of their former habitat, Amazons will raid plantations of bananas, oranges and apples. In addition to these, wild mangoes, guavas and the like are eagerly consumed by those birds fortunate enough to find them.

Cereal crops are sometimes devastated by huge flocks of cockatoos in Australia. Although the Australian cockatoos are viewed by the public as a pest species, the growth in their numbers is in all probability due to man's intervention. As man colonised the country, vast areas were turned over to the growing of cereals, and other areas had water piped to them not only to irrigate the crops but also to water livestock. This has given rise to ideal conditions for the proliferation of cockatoos – a ready supply of food and water.

A number of insects are consumed along with the portions of fruit, and some parrots, such as the Black Cockatoo, will actively seek out grubs under the bark of trees. Parrots will also investigate and ingest any carrion that

Palm fruits enjoyed by parrots. Top right: Coconut palm (cocos nucifera). Remaining photos: Queen palm (syagrus romanzoffiana) at various stages of maturation.

they may come across. Keas – large long-billed parrots from New Zealand – will also actively seek out and kill the young seabirds hidden in their burrows and eat the flesh and fat from them. One of the biggest consumers of insects is the lories – many insects are ingested along with the nectar and pollen taken from flowers.

Some parrots can be seen as having specialist feeding equipment for their dietary requirements. Lories and lorikeets have tongues with a cluster of papillae at the end, forming a brush-like structure. This is used to lift pollen and nectar from the inside of flowers. Slender-billed Cockatoos and Slender-billed Conures have elongated upper mandibles, which they use to dig up roots and tubers. The Slender-billed Conure is also one of the few birds which can use its bill to extract the nuts from the monkey-puzzle tree.

Both Red-bellied Macaws and Hyacinth Macaws are known to supplement their diet with freshwater snails. The Golden-winged Parakeet has a slender beak that is hooked at the end: in the wild they regularly feed on freshwater snails and algae, and it has been suggested that the hook on the end of their beak may be an adaptation for removing the snail from its shell.

The diet of parrots in the wild is a far cry from the presumed fruit and seeds that the layman assumes to be all that parrots eat. Studying the habits of wild parrots can be a great asset in providing the omnivorous diet which most parrots need in captivity in order to thrive.

SOLITARY OR GREGARIOUS?

The majority of parrots in the wild seek out the company of other parrots, even outside the breeding season. They may form small groups or enormous flocks, presumably finding safety in numbers. Huge numbers of parrots will often congregate at a food source, or at water holes and clay licks.

Safety in numbers: flocking gives protection against predators. Pictured: Conures in the wild.

Parrots will also roost in large flocks. Roosting together in this way has both advantages and its disadvantages. It can be seen as useful in respect of safety in numbers, a mass of birds being a much more confusing target to a potential predator then a single victim. The disadvantage is that infectious diseases can be rife in parrots who will naturally cuddle up to one another at night, and whole flocks can be wiped out if the infection is fatal.

DISPLAYS

The unusual Kakapo, which lays claim to a solitary existence for much of the time, finds the males forming leks and booming to advertise their presence in the breeding season. Amazons will dilate their pupils, fan their tails and strut up and down on the branches whilst displaying to a mate. Some lories hop up and down on the branch, bob their heads and flap their wings vigorously whilst trying to impress a potential mate. Cockatoos display by raising the chest and strutting up and down. Many parrots will also use regurgitated food as an attraction, as well as a bonding reinforcement, for mates.

NEST SITES

It is often the cock bird who will seek a nest

Blue and Gold Macaw: the parrot feathers of some species are highly sought-after.

site and prepare its excavation for the awaiting hen. The majority of parrots use hollow branches or tree trunks in which to lay their eggs, gnawing slivers of wood from the sides to make a base on which to lay them. The nests are usually in existing splits or holes in old trees, modified by the parrots' strong beaks. One of the biggest problems now facing parrots in the wild is a lack of mature trees with cavities large enough to accommodate them.

Some parrots, including the aptly named Rock Parakeet and the Bahama Amazon will nest in the crevices between rocks. Lear's Macaws will investigate and nest in similar crevices in the faces of cliffs, while the Patagonian Conure prefers to excavate tunnels in sandy cliff faces in which to nest.

Some lovebirds and conures even tunnel into termite mounds, laying their eggs in the cosy temperature-controlled environment within. Some of these birds, along with others like the Golden-shouldered Parakeet, are extremely difficult to breed in captivity unless we can successfully replicate these conditions for them to nest in.

Although Galahs will line their nests with leaves and twigs, the only true nest-builder of the parrot family is the Quaker or Monk Parakeet. These small South American parrots will use twigs to communally build massive structures with many nesting chambers within. These enormous constructions are used year after year, and added to as needed, until eventually the supporting tree can bear the weight no longer and all or part of the nest falls to the ground.

DANGERS

Incubating females, eggs and chicks are highly vulnerable to predation. Some snakes will seek out and take all three. Rats, which have colonised every corner of the world, will disturb nesting females and eat the eggs and chicks. Any other climbing predator, such as cats, stoats and mink, will plunder every nest they encounter. Long-legged raptors will feel for the chicks inside their nesting hole and drag them out, whilst airborne attacks from the same will take adults and fledglings alike.

Research has suggested that in some parrot species the mortality of fledglings before the chick leaves the nest is very high. On occasions, this has very nearly led to the extinction of some parrot species – both the Red-fronted Kakariki and the Kakapo fall into this category, where it would appear that feral cats and rats were the main culprits.

Parrots are also predated upon by humans – both as food and for their feathers, highly prized by some tribespeople as adornments for dancing costumes. Of course, many parrots are captured for the pet bird trade, and sadly the mortality rate of these is high both in capture and in transit. However, probably the greatest threat to parrots is the destruction of their habitat and in particular the nest sites.

WHAT HOPE FOR WILD PARROTS?

Despite what seems to be a never-ending barrage of problems faced by parrots living in the natural habitat, some are very resilient and adapt well to their changing environment. However, we have already lost the likes of Paradise Parakeets, Mascarene Parrots and Ara Tricolours. There are a good number of dedicated and truly remarkable people devoting much of their time and energies to protect and preserve those parrots facing extinction. It must be remembered, however, that all animals can be vulnerable, no matter how numerous they are. A case in point is the passenger pigeon, which when flocking in their millions would virtually eclipse the sun at the beginning of the 20th century. The last one died in 1932. So we should never be complacent about the survival prospects for any species.

Protection measures already taken in some cases include the elimination of introduced predators on previously predator-free islands. Sometimes birds are relocated to safe islands, as has been done with the Kakapos of New Zealand. A simple yet effective method of preventing predators gaining access to nesting sites is a policy of tinning the trees. This involves nailing a wide strip of tin around the trunk of a nesting tree thereby preventing predators from gaining a foothold. Even such agile climbers as snakes and large lizards cannot overcome this simple obstacle.

Many conservationists construct and erect nestboxes to make up for the lack of natural nest sites available to the parrots. These are unfortunately also attractive to other creatures, such as bees, which colonise hollows and may attack parrots that investigate. Other more aggressive birds may also utilise them, driving the parrots away. However, a percentage of the boxes are successful, so the effort and expense involved will be rewarded.

Another method employed to support parrots in danger is the provision of supplementary feeding in those areas where the natural food is in short supply. As an example, liluri palms are being planted in the area in which the Lear's Macaws live, in a bid to boost the dwindling population.

2 WHAT MAKES A PARROT A PARROT?

Parrot-like birds are easily distinguished from other bird groups by almost everyone, but, when asked, people often cannot explain why. In this chapter, a number of the defining features of parrots are discussed, along with some of the general peculiarities that distinguish birds from other vertebrates (animals with backbones) such as mammals and reptiles.

A small amount of knowledge of the anatomy (sizes and shapes of things) and physiology (how things work) of parrots helps greatly in understanding how best to look after a bird, to prevent disease, to give it a long healthy life, and perhaps to persuade it to breed.

Characteristic features distinguishing birds from other vertebrates:

- Feathers
- Horny beak and no teeth
- Air sacs and fixed lungs
- Pneumatised bones
- Produce uric acid and urine
- Lay eggs.

Features distinguishing parrots from other birds:

- Curved, rounded upper beak, covering smaller cup-shaped lower beak
- Thick, prehensile tongue
- Craniofacial hinge
- Large, broad head
- Short neck
- Zygodactyl feet
- Powder-down throughout the plumage
- Intelligence
- Mimicry.

Opposite page: Sun Conure.

HEARING

Although they are hidden out of sight beneath the feathers, birds do have ear openings. The small holes on either side of the head behind the eyes lead to an ear-drum and middle ear similar to that of mammals, and the sense of hearing is very acute.

SIGHT

The eyes of a parrot are comparatively much larger than our own, but otherwise quite similar in structure. Birds need good eyesight in order to pick out predators, food and mates across large areas of forest or desert. Parrots have been shown to have good colour vision. It is believed they see far into both the ultraviolet spectrum and the infra-red – what looks like a very plain bird to our eyesight may appear to have bright, gaudy patterns to another bird!

External Features

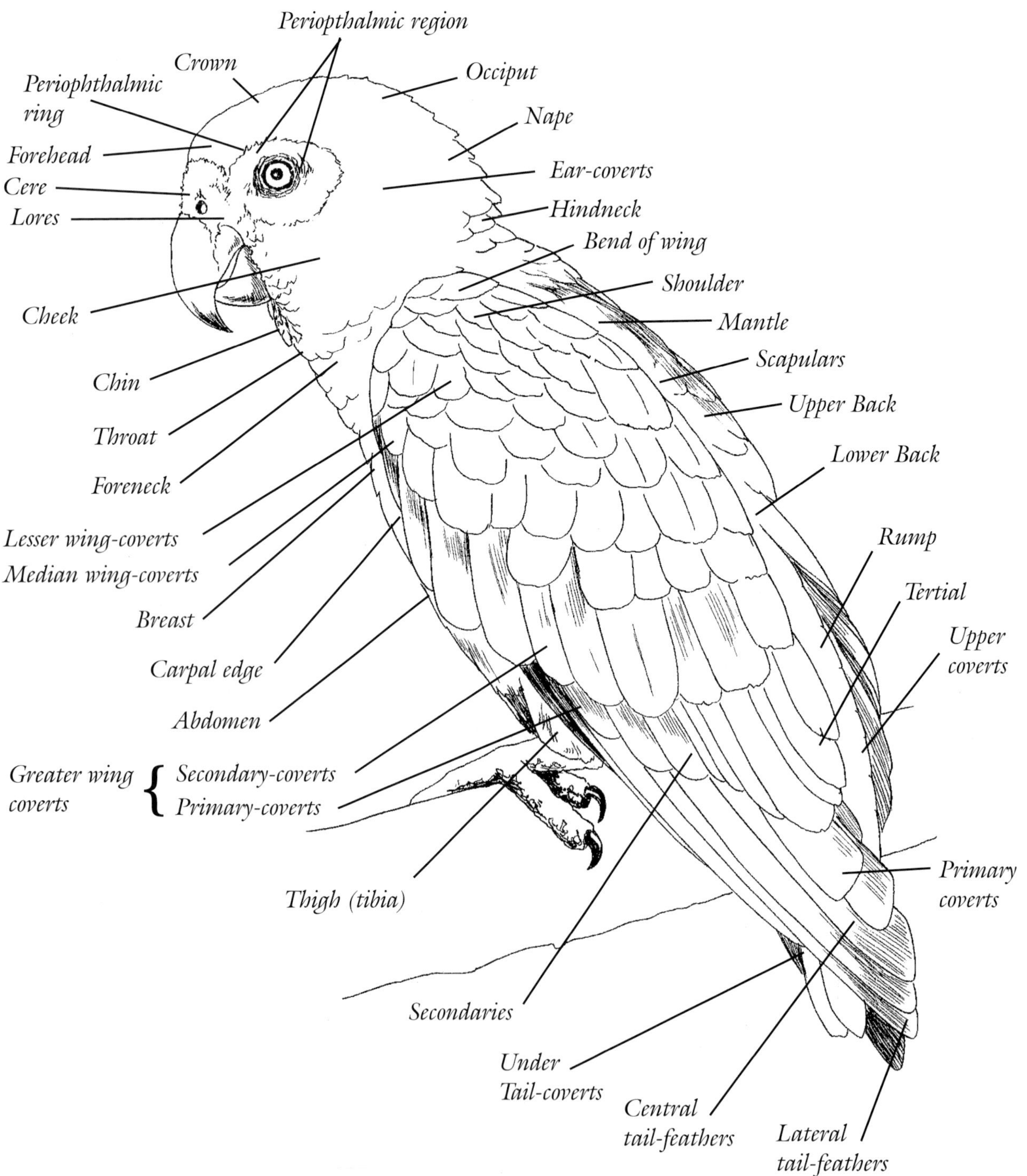

SMELL
In parrots, as in most birds, the sense of smell is very poorly developed or even absent.

TASTE
Parrots have much lower numbers of taste buds than mammals. Those they do have are situated on the roof of the mouth, the floor of the mouth and in the throat, but there are few on the tongue itself. However, parrots can taste very well, as anyone who tries giving medicines to birds will know. Despite having a solid horny beak, parrots also have very well-developed touch sensation within their mouth, which allows them to cleverly manipulate seeds into the perfect positions for cracking and dehulling.

SKELETON

The skeleton of birds is, of course, radically different to that of mammals, although it is still made up of the same basic components.

SPINE
The spine is made up of many small bones called vertebrae. Despite the size difference, there are actually more vertebrae in the neck of a parrot (10 or more) than in that of a giraffe (7 or 8). The presence of many small bones is what gives a bird's neck such flexibility. In contrast, most of the vertebrae in the thoracic (chest) region are fused together. The same is true of the vertebrae in the area of the pelvis.

In between, there is usually one free vertebra. This seems to be a weak spot in the spinal column, since birds which have suffered relatively minor trauma (e.g. flying into a window) can develop fractures or dislocations at this site and the bird becomes paralysed. Even if there is no immediate problem, the bruising that can occur after such an incident leaves the area prone to infection, which, over a period of days or weeks, can develop into an abscess for which there is no cure. Any bird that has had an unusually hard crash should be taken to the vet even if it seems unhurt.

WINGS
The bones that would develop into the front legs in mammals have been adapted in birds into the wing. The bones of the shoulder (scapula, clavicle), upper arm (humerus) and forearm (radius and ulna) are, surprisingly, little different from those of a mammal, although an extra bone – the coracoid – is necessary to counteract the pull of the powerful flight muscles. The 'hand' has been lost almost completely – only small remnants of two or three 'fingers' remain.

In the thoracic (chest) region there are several major changes to allow for the development of flight. The pectoral muscles provide the power for the downstroke of the wing. In order to provide the tremendous force needed, the muscles are massive, and attach to a bony plate called the sternum. A bony strut called the coracoid is necessary to keep the shoulder and sternum separated.

In mammals the sternum is a small, rod-like series of bones attached to the ribs on the front of the chest. In birds it is massive, extending half-way around the body and having an outward projecting ridge called the keel which extends several centimetres in front of the chest and provides support for the muscles.

The keel-bone can usually be felt running down the front of a bird's chest – in a normal bird, you should just be able to feel it. It is a good indicator of a bird's general health state, since any weight loss will make the keel stand out much more prominently, while in an obese bird it is difficult to feel at all.

The power of flight requires vast energy expenditure in order to lift the bird into the air in the first place, but once aloft, flight is a much more efficient mode of transport than walking or running. This is why birds can

The Skeleton

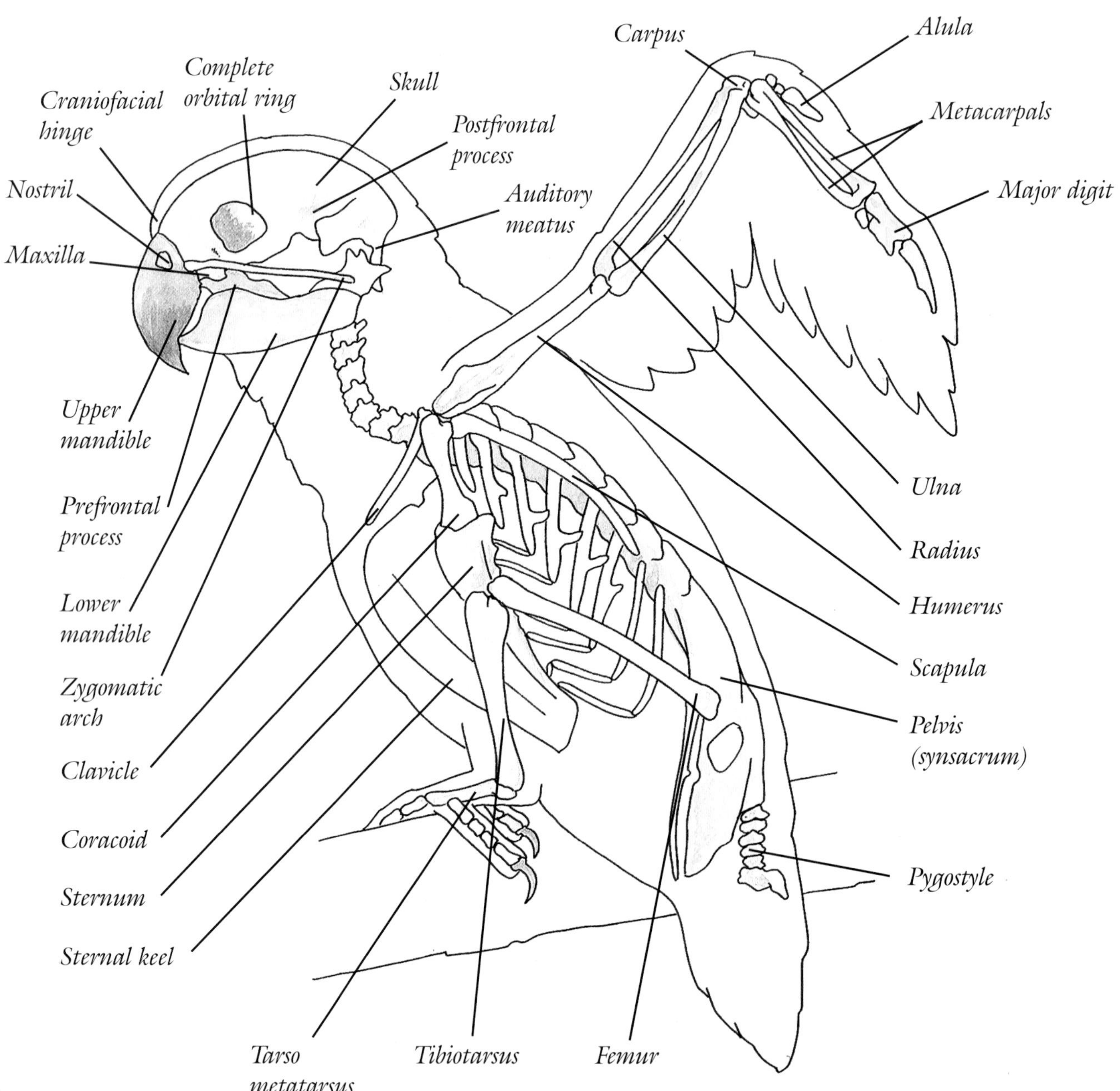

cover distances of hundreds of miles a day while a mammal of the same body size would struggle to cover a few miles.

PELVIS AND LEGS

The pelvis of a bird is formed from the same bones as in a mammal. The major difference is that whereas in mammals the pelvis forms a rigid closed ring, in birds the 'floor' of the pelvis is open, since it would be impossible to pass an egg if the ring were complete.

The leg of a bird again has similarities to that of mammals. The thigh bone and shin bone are much the same, although several small bones around the ankle joint have become fused together. The ankle joint of a bird is actually the one a few centimetres up the leg and not at the ball of the foot itself.

The tendons in a bird's leg are arranged in a special manner. When a bird falls asleep, its own weight pressing downwards causes tendons to tighten. These in turn cause the toes to clench, and so the bird can sleep standing up gripping its perch.

The toes of a parrot have what is termed a 'zygodactyl' arrangement. While most birds have three toes pointing forward and only one pointing backward, zygodactyl birds (such as parrots, toucans, woodpeckers and a few others) have two toes pointing each way. This gives a much greater degree of dexterity and allows parrots to use their feet for holding things when eating, playing and climbing.

SKIN

The skin is obviously one of the main areas of difference between birds and other animals. No other type of animal has developed true feathers, and no bird is completely without them.

Compared to mammals and reptiles, the skin itself (excepting beak and feet) is very thin. When wetted slightly it becomes almost transparent. Over the legs, the skin becomes thicker and forms scales, which protect the feet from rough perches and are easier to clean food and dirt from than feathers.

There is also featherless skin around the face. The amount varies depending on the species of parrot, from a small rim of skin around the beak, nostrils and eyes of many varieties, to the large facial patches of the macaws. Some birds have a large fleshy mound surrounding the nostrils called the cere. In budgerigars and some other species this area of skin is sensitive to reproductive hormones and changes colour depending on the sex of the bird and the stage of the reproductive cycle.

The females of many species of parrot have a specialised area of skin on their front. When the hen is preparing to lay, the skin in this area loses its feathers, becomes thickened and develops a greater blood supply. This is the 'brood patch' or 'incubation patch' and is used to maximise the transfer of heat from the hen to the eggs while on the nest.

PREEN GLAND

Another specialised area of skin in some parrot species is the 'preen gland' ('uropygial gland'). It is very well developed in some parrots (Green-winged macaw; budgerigar) and present but less well developed in most other parrots; in a few species (Hyacinth macaw, most Amazons) it is completely absent. It is a small mound-like area over the rump which has an opening surrounded by a tuft of hair-like feathers. The glandular tissue secretes a type of oily wax, which can sometimes be expressed from the opening. The bird uses this wax during preening to condition the feathers and make them insulating and waterproof. The secretions of the preen gland are also thought to have antibacterial properties – simple skin infections are very rare in birds. They are also involved in the alteration of vitamin D_3 to an active form via the action of ultraviolet light.

FEATHERS

Feathers come in several different types, and overall contribute five to ten per cent of a parrot's bodyweight. They grow from small pockets in the skin called follicles. At the base of each follicle is a small mound (the dermal papilla). Once a feather has been lost, this mound produces a long quill full of blood-vessels within which the new feather grows. This is called a 'blood feather' or 'pin feather'. At this stage, the feather is very vulnerable to damage, and if not protected by its adjacent feathers (e.g. in a badly clipped wing) the feather can be broken and will bleed profusely. Once the formation of the feather is complete, the blood vessels die back, the outer layer of the 'pin feather' disintegrates and falls off and the newly-formed feather unfurls.

Some feathers, such as the body feathers, will be regrown straightaway if they are lost. Others, such as the flight feathers, may not regrow until the bird is ready to moult, which may only be every year or two. Some birds undergo a set period of moulting. Exhibition budgerigars will usually moult as a flock over a few weeks of September or October. Other birds, especially housebound pets with artificially controlled day-length and temperature, and therefore fewer seasonal influences on their life, will moult continuously or very irregularly.

Growing new feathers is a tremendous drain on the bird's resources – it has been estimated that a bird's metabolic rate must rise by 30% during a moult. If a bird is subjected to illness or undue stress during the period when the feathers are actively growing, it does not have the reserves to allow normal feather growth. Lines across the vanes of the feathers may appear when they unfurl days or weeks later, and these 'fret marks' or 'stress bars' are a point of weakness where the feather will be prone to breakage.

Points of a Feather

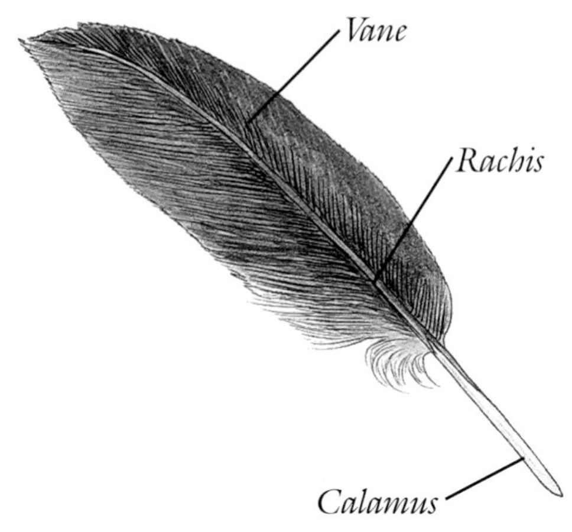

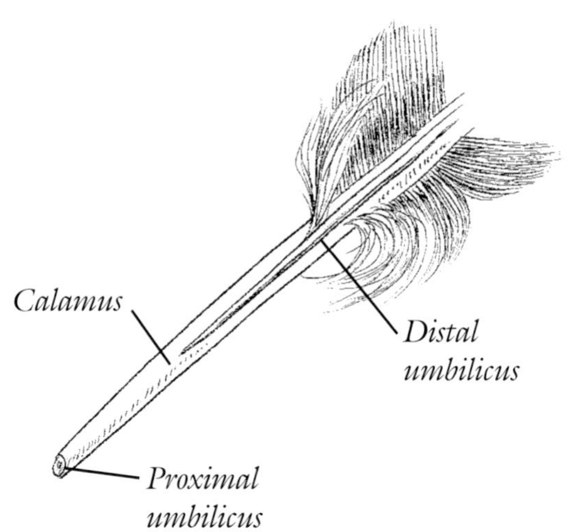

Down feathers provide much-needed insulation.

Structure of a Feather

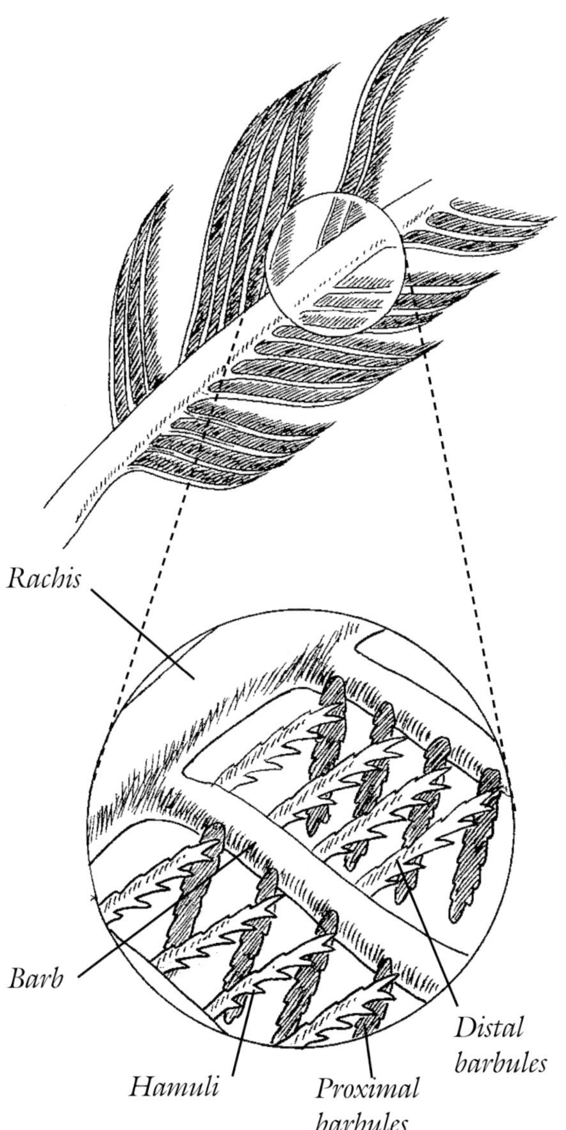

CONTOUR FEATHERS

'Contour' feathers are the most conspicuous type. These are the feathers covering the surface of the bird and giving it its general colour and shape. Those on the body tend to be round to oval in shape and have a small soft quill. The flight feathers ('remiges') are modified contour feathers and are elongated in shape with a strong thick quill. Covering the quills of the flight feathers are an intermediate type of contour feather called 'coverts'. Other types of contour feathers include 'ear coverts' over the ear opening, tail feathers ('rectrices') and crest feathers in some species.

Contour feathers are a miracle of natural engineering – despite many years of research there is still no man-made material with the ability to repair itself in the way a feather vane can. The main shaft of a feather (the rachis) runs up the middle and gives off smaller 'barbs' on either side. The barbs themselves branch into tiny barbules which themselves are covered in tiny hooks (hamuli). When pressed closely together, the hooks of one barbule engage those of the adjacent barbule and the whole structure becomes a single piece of material called the 'vane'. When a vane becomes damaged on an obstacle, rather than being irreparable, as would be the case with a man-made parachute or kite, the bird simply has to groom itself and the hooks re-engage and the vane is mended.

The vane is strong enough to allow the bird to fly, and once covered with the fine layer of wax during preening is very waterproof. In order to help control the bird's body temperature each of the body feathers can be raised and lowered by its own tiny muscle to trap more or less air as an insulating layer around the body. This is why a cold or sick bird looks 'fluffed up', while one which is overheated looks 'drawn in'. Some birds, and most notably the crested cockatoos, can raise or lower certain feathers as a display of emotions.

DOWN FEATHERS

The next feather type of importance is the 'down' feathers. These provide much of the insulation of the bird against cold. The skin is thin and usually lacks the fatty layer found in mammals, so a bird would rapidly lose its body heat if it were not surrounded by its own 'feather duvet'. The down feathers are small, fluffy and white. They lack the barbules and hooks of the contour feathers so they are not waterproof and are of no use when flying. They remain hidden away under the body feathers, protected from becoming wet.

Oily substances can damage the waxy layer on the contour feathers so they lose their waterproofing, and also make the down feathers sticky so they lose their fluffy, insulating character. Birds with oil on their feathers therefore have tremendous difficulties in regulating their body temperature and can quickly succumb to overheating or hypothermia. Oil-based medications or creams should never be used on a bird unless specifically under the instructions of an avian veterinarian.

'Powder down' is a term given to feathers whose prime purpose is to disintegrate to produce dust. This dust is thought to mix with the wax from the preen gland and further add to the waterproofing properties of the contour feathers. In some bird species the powder down feathers are absent or just present in a few localised patches. The parrot family is different in this respect in that powder down feathers are scattered throughout the plumage.

Powder down is particularly noticeable in the cockatoos and African Greys, where it is responsible for the greyish sheen of a healthy bird's beak and feet. Reduced production of powder down feathers is often the first sign of problems in birds infected with the Psittacine Beak and Feather Disease (PBFD) virus – a shiny beak and black feet in a cockatoo are highly suggestive early signs of this devastating disease.

Various other types of feathers have been noted, and are usually described depending on their structure or function. One type worthy of attention is the so-called 'guide feathers' surrounding the vent. The vent is surrounded by a circle of well-defined feathers which are thought by some to guide the male and female's vents together during mating.

COLOUR

Although some birds have dramatic colouring to their non-feathered skin – e.g. the bright yellow facial skin of Hyacinth Macaws, and the orange-yellow legs of some of the lories, lorikeets and hanging parrots – it is the range of gaudy feather colours which is more notable. Feather colours can be divided into two separate forms – pigmentary colour and structural colour.

Pigmentary colours are those formed by the presence of a substance acting as a dye within the feather. The most common are:

- Melanin colours, responsible for blacks, browns and some yellows.
- Carotenoid colours, responsible for some yellow, orange and red colours

The colouring and markings of some parrots is very dramatic. It is easy to tell why this bird is called the Moustached Parakeet.

Different Types of Parrot Beak

The small compact bills of some of the parakeets (above), designed to remove grass seeds from their stalks and husks. Cockatiel (above left) and budgerigar (above right).

The relatively larger beaks of Amazons (pictured) and Greys for tackling a variety of fruits and seeds.

The long thin bill of the Kea which is used to probe for insects.

- Porphyrin colours, responsible for some greens and reds.

The carotenoids are obtained from the diet and lack of sufficient of the appropriate materials in the food can lead to a fading of the plumage colour.

The production of many of these pigmentary colours is regulated by the liver, and a number of different diseases – including vitamin A deficiency, Chlamydia infection, zinc poisoning and many others – can alter this process. Commonly seen abnormal colours due to these problems include red feathers appearing on African Greys and amazons in 'unusual' places, and yellowing, bronzing or unusually dark edges to the feathers of amazons.

The second form of colour found in feathers is termed 'structural colour'. The structure of the feather can be such that it acts either as a mirror for certain wavelengths of light, producing iridescent sheens, or as a filter, only allowing certain wavelengths to show. The most important of the structural effects in parrots is 'Tyndall scatter': when light hits a feather it is scattered so that only blue light is reflected. Most blue colours in birds are due to Tyndall scatter, and many green birds are actually showing a combination of the blue effect of Tyndall scatter and yellow from carotenoid pigments – the yellow and blue colours combining to give green.

White-coloured feathers reflect and refract all the wavelengths of light that reach them. They contain no pigments, and this lack of pigments also makes the feathers much less resistant to wear than coloured feathers.

DIGESTIVE SYSTEM

The digestive system is the group of organs that enable a bird to get its food, process and absorb the nutrients within it, and get rid of the waste.

The massive nut-cracker beak of the macaw family. Pictured: Green-winged Macaw.

BEAK AND MOUTH

The first part of the digestive system is involved with collecting food materials. It comprises the beak and tongue and is probably the most characteristic feature of the parrot family. Despite a wide range of soft, hard and even liquid foods, all parrots have a characteristic large curved – or even hooked – upper beak, sitting over a smaller cup-shaped lower beak. The tongue is generally fleshy and highly mobile and takes a very active role in manipulating the food (it is 'prehensile'), and this is a distinction from most other birds, which generally have much more delicate and less functional tongues.

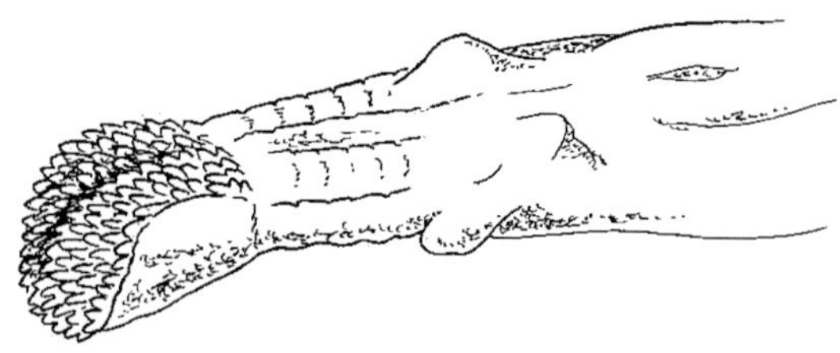

The tongue of a lory. Note the brushes on the end for collecting pollen.

Some parrot species have made modifications to the general structure depending on the diet that needs to be consumed. For example:

- The small compact bills of some of the parakeets, designed to remove grass seeds from their stalks and husks
- The relatively larger beaks of Greys and amazons for tackling a variety of fruits and seeds
- The long thin bill of the Kea which is used to probe for insects and meat
- The massive nut-crackers of the macaw family.

Probably the most specialised parrot mouths of all are those of the Lories and Lorikeets. In many of these birds, the beak is long and slender, in order to reach pollen and nectar deep within flowers. The tongue has been adapted so that, instead of being thick and fleshy, it is longer, more slender and has 'brushes' on the end, enabling the birds to collect and swallow pollen grains as a large part of their diet.

The beak is quite a complex structure in its own right. It is formed of a horny outgrowth of the skin – similar to a human fingernail – which grows out to cover a strong bony framework. In most types of bird, the bones of the beak are attached directly to the rest of the head, but one distinguishing feature of the parrots is an extra joint between the upper beak and the skull (the 'cranio-facial hinge'), which allows a much greater degree of movement.

The horny layer of the beak is produced continuously by the skin around its base, and grows outwards to replace what is worn away during eating and chewing. New beak tissue takes about three months to migrate from the skin at the base of the beak to the tip of the beak and be worn away. Damage, such as chips or shallow cracks to the horny layer of the beak, will gradually move to the edge of the beak and disappear. Deep cracks may involve the bone underneath, and damage to the skin at the base of the beak can disrupt future horn growth so veterinary attention should be sought immediately. Modern veterinary techniques can allow some very impressive reconstructions, so even if part of the beak is lost, it can often be temporarily or even permanently replaced.

Some diseases affect the growth of the horny layer of the beak. Psittacine Beak and Feather Disease (PBFD) and various nutritional problems can cause the beak to become flaky and crumbly, whilst many overgrown beaks are actually due to an undiscovered liver problem.

THE CROP

Once it has been consumed, a parrot's food, rather than passing straight to the stomach as in mammals, can be stored for several hours within a sac-like structure in the neck area called the crop. In baby parrots the crop is seen very easily, and one of the best indicators of the health of a baby bird is the speed with which the crop empties itself.

Not all types of bird have a crop. In addition to parrots, it is present in birds such as pigeons, chickens, hawks and finches, but absent in owls, gulls and penguins. Birds need a trickle of food entering the stomach at all times, so having a crop enables them to eat a large meal in one go and then let it pass in small amounts down to the stomach.

THE STOMACH

From the crop, the food passes to the stomach, which has two separate parts in parrots. The first part is a glandular stomach called the 'proventriculus'. This is a thin-walled organ, which secretes the digestive juices ('enzymes') necessary for the food to be digested.

The second part of the stomach – the 'ventriculus' or 'gizzard' – is equally

Internal Structure

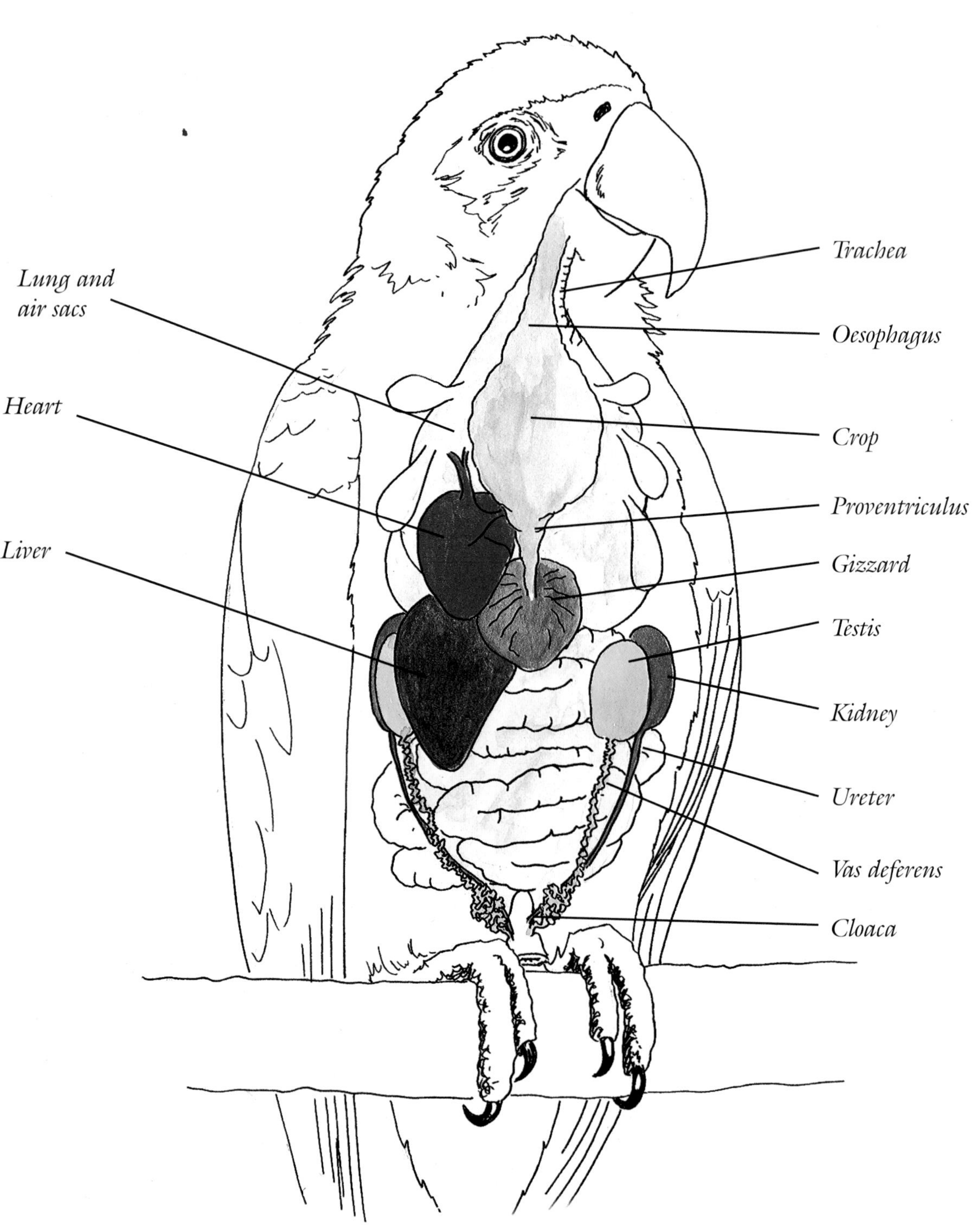

important. Many parrots eat hard seeds and it is only once these have been ground up that they can be digested. The gizzard is a very muscular organ with a hard, rough lining that grinds down the seed into a paste.

There is considerable debate on whether or not grit is necessary for the gizzard to function properly. Some wild birds certainly eat grit in small amounts. Once in the gizzard, grit will stay there for many months or even years and usually does not need replacing regularly.

In captivity, birds have been known to overeat grit, especially if they are ill for some other reason, and the gizzard can become blocked ('impacted').

Much of the rest of the system – the intestines, liver and pancreas – are the same in birds as in mammals. Food passes from the gizzard through to the intestines. The pancreas secretes more digestive enzymes that are added to the food as it passes through the intestine.

Once fully broken down, the food is absorbed and processed or it is stored by the liver. The indigestible wastes are passed out through the vent ('cloaca') as the faeces (the dark part of the droppings).

The vent itself is a complex structure that receives faeces from the intestines, liquid urine and white urates from the kidneys and also the eggs or sperm from the reproductive tract. It is composed of three vaguely sac-like compartments which manage to keep all these different products separated until they are voided.

RESPIRATORY SYSTEM

The respiratory system is the group of organs involved with breathing, smelling and talking. The respiratory system of birds is tremendously different to that of humans and mammals in a number of ways.

SINUSES

While many of us will have suffered headaches from 'blocked sinuses' in the past, we are actually fairly lucky. Human sinuses extend only a little way up the forehead and behind the nose. The sinuses in the head of birds extend down into the beak, up on to the forehead, around, behind and beneath the eye, around the ear, down the neck and even down into the jawbones.

Sinusitis can be a very serious disease indeed for a parrot, particularly because many of these sinuses are below the level of the nose: if fluid builds up there, it cannot drain out as it would if our own sinuses were inflamed. Many birds that seem to have 'conjunctivitis' or other eye problems, actually have an infection of the sinuses surrounding the eye.

VOICE PRODUCTION

This is very different in birds in general to mammals. Man and other mammals use the larynx (the 'Adam's apple' at the back of the throat) and lips to make sounds. In birds the larynx is further forward and can sometimes be seen at the base of the tongue. However, the larynx plays little or no role in noise production in birds.

Birds have a structure called the 'syrinx' deep within the chest cavity at the point where the windpipe splits off to the left and right sides. The syrinx is a very complex combination of muscles, membranes and folds that alter in size, shape and tension to produce the voice. Many types of bird possess a complex syrinx allowing them to sing, whistle and chirp.

The ability of a parrot (and other birds such as mynahs and starlings) to mimic sounds (including the human voice) which birds such as canaries cannot do is thought to be more a product of the brain-function controlling the syrinx than a peculiar feature of the syrinx itself.

The Respiratory System

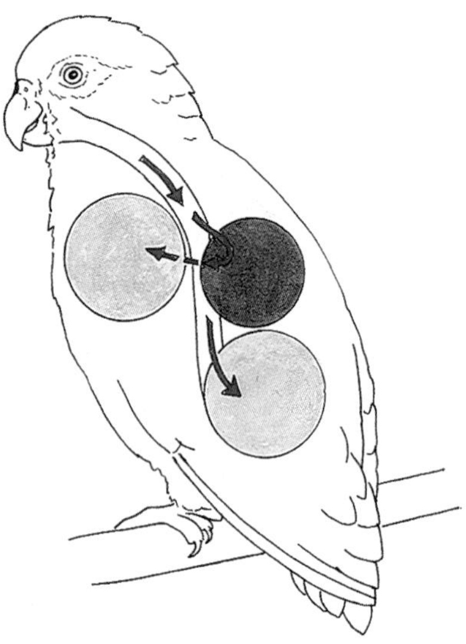

During inspiration (breathing in) fresh air passes down the windpipe to fill the 'caudal' (rear) air sacs without passing through the lungs. At the same time fresh air is also drawn through the lung into the 'cranial' (front) airsacs.

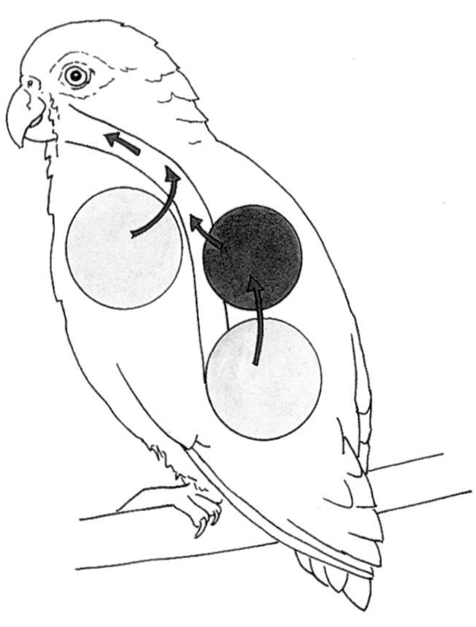

During expiration (breathing out) stale air is expelled from the cranial air sacs without passing through the lung, whilst fresh air is pushed through the lung from the caudal air sac and directly out through the windpipe. This means that, during both stages, fresh air is passing through the lung tissue.

The complexity of the syrinx, and its position at the narrowest part of the respiratory system, unfortunately leaves it vulnerable to diseases. In particular, the syrinx is one site where the Aspergillus fungus can take a hold, and any bird which appears to 'lose its voice' suddenly should be examined by an avian vet as soon as possible, as any delay could be life-threatening.

LUNGS

When flying, a bird burns up a tremendous amount of energy. This level of energy consumption in turn requires vast amounts of oxygen, and if a bird had the same lung design as a human, flying would be impossible.

The respiratory system of birds is far more efficient than that of mammals. When we breathe in, fresh-air flows into the lungs and oxygen is absorbed. When we breathe out, however, there is no fresh air reaching the lungs, so half the cycle is wasted.

Birds have developed a system to avoid this. Instead of having lungs that inflate and deflate, sucking in and blowing out air as they do so, birds have a system of 'air sacs' which act as two pairs of bellows. A valve system regulates the flow of air so that when a bird breathes in, the air is sucked through the lungs to the air sacs of the head and neck; when the bird breathes out, the air is pushed through the lungs from the abdominal air sacs behind. This keeps fresh air flowing across the lungs all the time, giving the bird twice as much oxygen as a mammal could get.

The extra efficiency, however, makes birds more susceptible to toxic gases. This is why canaries were used to detect gas in coalmines. It is also one reason why parrots are so susceptible to poisoning by fumes from Polytetrafluoroethylene (PTFE or Teflon™). Anyone with a parrot should avoid using non-stick cookware, newer heat-resistant paints and many other heat-, cold- and stain-resistant fabrics, which contain this substance, as, when hot, the fumes are released and can kill a bird within minutes.

One advantage from a veterinary point of view of having the air sacs is that it becomes possible to look inside a bird using an endoscope. In a mammal, fat and intestines would obstruct the view of the internal organs; in human medicine, keyhole surgery relies on inflating the body cavity with sterile carbon dioxide to create an air space. In a bird the presence of air sacs means that it is a relatively simple task to make a tiny hole and with the endoscope look directly at the testes or ovary for sex determination, or at the lungs, liver, kidneys, spleen and many other organs to look for signs of disease.

FLYING LIGHT

Another problem with flying is that 'excess baggage' is always a hindrance. Birds need to reduce their body weight to as little as possible to enable them to get airborne. Some of the tissues in the body are actually not really necessary, and in particular the inside of the bones (the marrow) in mammals is composed mainly of fatty tissue.

In some of the major bones, birds have managed to do away with marrow altogether and instead replaced it with pockets of the air sacs which extend in many birds as far as the elbow, the knee and even into the spine.

URINARY SYSTEM

Birds have a need to eliminate waste products via the kidneys in the same way that mammals do. Birds excrete urinary wastes in two different forms – liquid urine (the watery part of the droppings) and solid uric acid (the white part of the droppings).

The use of solid uric acid in this way in both birds and reptiles allows the embryo to develop within a solid eggshell without becoming poisoned by its own wastes. It also provides a means of conserving water for birds living in desert environments, and this is why the droppings of many larger fruit-eating parrots are quite wet, while those of budgerigars and cockatiels are very dry with very little of the watery part.

KIDNEYS

The kidneys themselves are found embedded in hollows within the bony pelvis. Several of the major nerves to the legs pass between the kidney and the bone, or even through the kidney itself. One result of this is that any disease affecting the kidneys – infection, inflammation, tumours etc. – can also cause a paralysis of the legs.

REPRODUCTIVE SYSTEM

FEMALE

The female reproductive system of birds is somewhat of an oddity. Most female animals have two ovaries, which are served by a branch of the uterus on each side (though the uterus then often joins in the middle). In most birds the ovary and uterus on the right side are completely missing.

When inactive, the reproductive system comprises a tiny ovary the size of a pea, and a thin tube that can be further divided into oviduct, uterus (shell gland) and vagina.

When the female becomes ready to produce eggs, all these components increase dramatically in size. Follicles on the ovary 'mature' into the yolk portion of the egg. This yolk is released from the ovary and falls into the open end of the tube (the 'infundibulum').

If, for any reason, the yolk cannot enter the tube, or the developing egg passes backwards up the oviduct, the egg material is released into the body cavity. At best, this means that the egg never gets laid so the hen may be infertile. At worst, the egg white can set up an inflammatory reaction known as 'egg-peritonitis' which can lead to life-threatening infections.

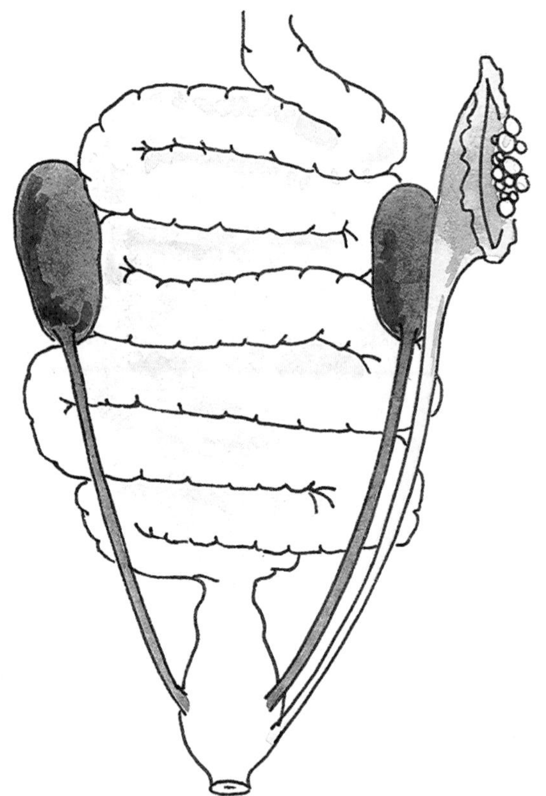

Reproductive system of a non-active female.

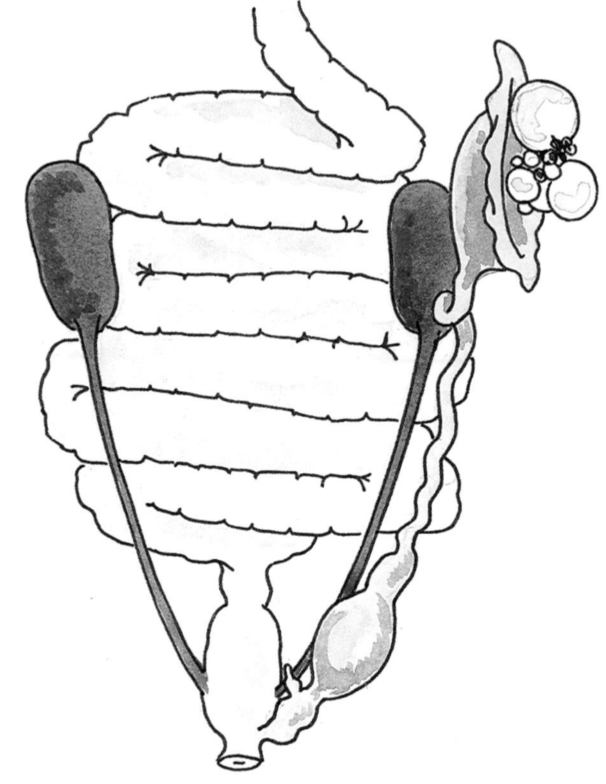

Reproductive system of an active female.

If the yolk does successfully pass into the infundibulum, it is passed down the oviduct to the uterus where much of the albumen (the white of the egg) is added and finally the calcified shell. The egg then remains in the vagina until the hen is ready to lay. In larger parrots the egg's journey from ovary to nest takes between 36 and 56 hours.

In some female parrots, the urge to breed is very strong. Once a bird feels it is in a stable relationship – whether that is with another bird, the owner or even a toy – it may proceed to lay eggs.

Birds such as lovebirds, cockatiels and budgerigars will quite commonly proceed to lay multiple clutches of eggs which puts a tremendous drain on the body's resources and greatly increases the risks of 'egg-yolk-peritonitis' and 'egg binding'.

In other psitticines, the continual hormonal stimulation of the ovary leads to a weakness of the muscles of the body wall and the bird develops a hernia. Although behavioural and dietary techniques help these birds, in some of these cases it can be necessary to surgically remove the oviduct and uterus so that the reproductive system shuts back down.

MALE

As with the female, the male's reproductive tract varies tremendously in size depending on the breeding season and sexual activity of the bird. In the non-breeding season the testes are a pair of tiny organs situated deep

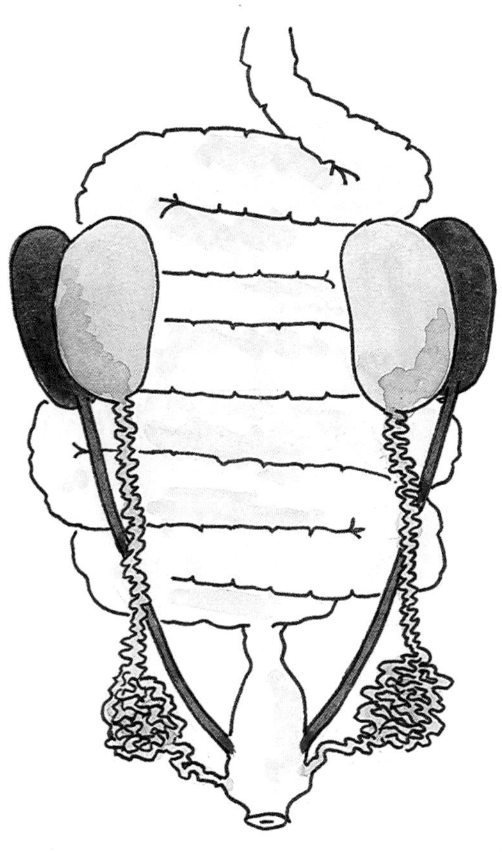

Reproductive system of a male.

in the roof of the abdomen near the kidneys. As the breeding season approaches the testes increase in size by several hundred times!

MATING

Mating takes place, often following an extensive courtship, by the male bird 'mounting' the female. He usually stands with one foot on the perch and the other over her back. The female raises her tail, exposing her cloaca (vent) and the male bird bends his tail around underneath so their vents meet. In most parrots there is no 'penis' structure – the vents simply touch and sperm is transferred.

Vasa parrots (*Coracopsis vasa and C. nigra*) are an exception and both male and female have a prominent enlargement of the cloacal region during the breeding season which can hang several centimetres below the body of the bird, although the exact function of this structure is not known.

After mating has taken place, the sperm travel up the oviduct and fertilise the egg. There is evidence in some cases that a single mating supplies enough sperm to fertilise an entire clutch that may be laid over a period of many days.

3 *SETTING UP HOME*

When contemplating the owning of a parrot or parrots, one of the first considerations is accommodation. Much will depend on whether you intend to keep a pet companion parrot, or if you would like more than one parrot in an aviary in the garden with the possibility of breeding in the future. Another important consideration is the species of parrot which you intend to keep. Parrots vary considerably in size and strength and it is important that the accommodation which you supply is strong and large enough for the purpose. Some of the larger parrot species such as macaws, cockatoos, amazons and African Greys will benefit from a stand as well as a cage if kept in the home.

PARROT STAND

These can vary from quite straightforward 'T' bar constructions to quite ornate metal ones. However, the essential components include a wooden perch, which is replaceable. It is important that the parrot has permission to chew its stand: this is controlled chewing which is helpful to the owner and gives the parrot an opportunity to indulge in what is very natural behaviour.

Another essential is food and water dishes. Usually these are situated one at each end of the stand and in practice this would appear to be the most effective option. Many parrots appear to delight in 'dunking' food into their water dishes. This is no problem in the short term; however, food rapidly degrades in

Blue and Gold Macaw. Your parrot must be allowed to chew his wooden perch.

Opposite page: Greater Sulphur-crested Cockatoo.

A bowl fixed to the cage by a screw-thread should prevent your parrot from removing it.

moist, warm conditions and is quickly colonised by bacteria. This may threaten your parrot's health, so it is important to give consideration to hygiene. The dishes themselves should be metal and easily detachable, as this makes them easy to clean. Metal dishes are also less likely to be damaged by the parrot's destructive tendencies.

Another important consideration is the mechanism by which the dishes are held in place. Parrots are naturally curious and intelligent and, unless the dishes are held in place securely, your parrot will quickly learn how to get the dishes off the stand and scatter them and their contents all around. The usual method of keeping them secure is by using a screw-thread, which appears to work well.

The parrot stand should also have a collecting tray. This collecting area may be part of the way up the stand or form part of the base. The purpose of the tray is to collect droppings and uneaten food. Parrots will frequently take food items out of the dishes and eat only a part of them before discarding the remainder, which hopefully will be collected by the tray. It is more convenient if the tray area can be covered by newspaper; it is then an easy matter to remove and discard a sheet when it becomes soiled.

The height and weight of the stand is another important consideration. If you feel that it is likely that you might want to move the stand regularly from room to room, then it is important that it is not too heavy to lift and carry. However, most people tend to keep the parrot's cage in one room and the stand in another, so it is only the parrot which is transported from place to place.

The stand has a value in allowing the parrot more space and opportunity to move, allowing a change in scenery that helps to prevent boredom, and also in giving the owner another designated parrot area. It is essential that the parrot has a cage in addition to the stand, as it is not recommended that a parrot should be left on its stand unattended. An unwatched parrot is more than likely to leave the stand and involve itself in all manner of mischief.

When choosing a stand, the height needs to be considered, as one can purchase stands of different heights. Most are intended to sit directly on the floor, but some of the shorter ones are best suited to being placed on a sideboard or some other furniture.

Although the height at which a parrot perches is quite important in relation to training and dominance, a parrot will feel quite insecure if it is too low and near the ground. In this situation the most natural thing for the parrot to do is to attempt to climb higher which, if given a low stand, will invariably involve it getting off the stand to climb or fly to a higher perch. A compromise to this situation is often a stand that is at least 4'6" (1.4m) high.

Another important factor when buying a stand is that you find it pleasing to look at. Parrots can live for many years, and it is worth considering that the stand may share your home for an equally long period.

For those who would prefer a smaller member of the parrot family, a cage is the most important piece of equipment needed.

There are, however, small 'play-stations' available, which have been specifically manufactured for the smaller members of the parrot family. These will usually have a perch, as well as a swing and toys. Because of their small size it is also a simple matter to transport them from room to room.

CAGE

Whether you have made the decision to own a larger or a smaller member of the parrot family, it is always preferable to get the largest cage that you can accommodate. If you have chosen a larger parrot, then the cage size must reflect the larger proportions of that parrot. If the parrot chosen is the size of one of the larger macaws or cockatoos, then it is probable that the cage will need to be one of the larger free-standing ones. In this case, unless you live in a large house, careful consideration will be needed as to where you are going to 'house' your parrot.

Parrots are naturally gregarious and many are also territorial. This means that a parrot will want to be caged in an area where it will have easy access to attention, but also in a place where it can have its liberty and choose to sit on top of its cage. A place often selected for this is the kitchen, but unfortunately this is an area where parrots most definitely should not live.

The hazards to parrots in a kitchen are numerous. Not only are there the easily seen ones, such as sinks full of water and boiling/hot food on the cooker, but there are also less obvious dangers. These include non-stick pans, which when burnt give off highly toxic fumes which can be fatal to birds within

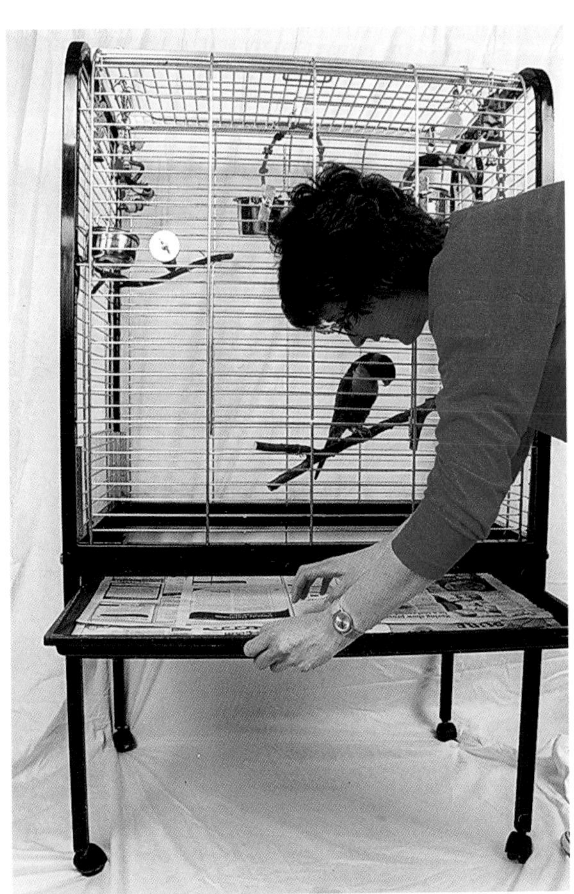

A tray is needed to collect droppings and wasted food.

A parrot playstand is enjoyed by many parrots. It is advisable to replace a plastic perch with a wooden one.

Remember that you will have to live with the cage too, so consider your own personal tastes as well as the parrot's needs.

a short space of time. When windows are opened in the kitchen to allow steam to dissipate, if the parrot isn't in its cage, there is the danger that it will fly out. There is also the possibility that cats will come in through the window, with the obvious risks associated with this.

CAGE LOCATION

Wherever you do accommodate your parrot in the house, there are some common considerations. Parrots need attention; they are highly intelligent and can easily become bored and depressed if not given something to concentrate on. This may result in behavioural disturbances, such as regular bouts of attention-screaming or feather-plucking. This means that the locations you select for keeping your parrot should be in places where they can easily interact with others.

The location for your parrot needs to be light and airy. Some access to sunshine is beneficial, but there must also be shade, as the parrot must always be able to get out of the direct sunlight. Parrots enjoy looking through the window, although if they can be seen from the outside, you must always be mindful of the danger of your parrot being stolen. It is important that you ensure that the area in which you have your parrot is free from draughts and not closely situated to a heat source such as a radiator, as this will cause discomfort and dry the plumage. Parrots can cope with cool conditions if extremes of temperature are avoided.

There are some dangers associated with the cage area. Parrots are naturally destructive; this is not to say that this is deliberate vandalism, but it is again due to their highly intelligent and inquisitive nature. Their beaks are extremely strong and shaped in such a way as to enable them to dismantle many household items. It is important to ensure

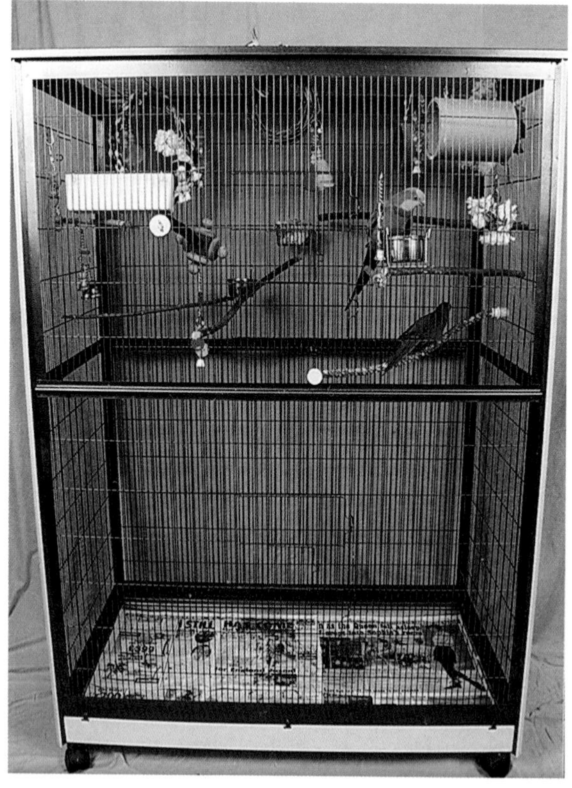

Parrots seem to prefer square or rectangular cages. Horizontal bars are also welcomed, as they give the opportunity to climb.

Hyacinthine Macaws: many parrots enjoy the space and companionship that an aviary can offer.

that it is not possible for them to gain access to items lying outside their cages.

It is especially important that all electrical wires and equipment are kept well away from the cage, as parrots are adept at grasping things by sticking a foot out of the cage. A hazard that is frequently overlooked is the curtains, as parrots will shred the material. Some curtains also have lead weights incorporated in the hem that can, if eaten by the parrot, cause heavy-metal poisoning. Pot plants are another item which parrots will make much effort to gain access to.

For the parrot's comfort, square or rectangular cage areas appear to give a greater sense of security. As parrots naturally climb a great deal, horizontal bars are preferable to vertical ones that are more difficult to climb. Some cages have tops that open to form a play area, and this has the added advantage of allowing the parrot more freedom and giving it a different place to play in.

Some particulary territorial parrots will become aggressive using this set-up, in which case it may be preferable not to utilise this facility.

In many cases, the keeping of a pet parrot may herald a new interest for the owner, which may well result in them wishing to find out more about the fascinating hobby of aviculture. When aviculturists use this term it usually means keeping birds in an aviary, which can be inside or outside the home. Most want to breed their birds, as this adds a new dimension to bird-keeping. Where parrots are concerned, this hobby is both challenging and rewarding.

AVIARIES

When contemplating keeping parrots in an aviary, the location is one of the first decisions that has to be made. For most, situating the aviary outside has the most benefits for the parrots; however, one needs to be aware of the dangers of theft. In recent years the number of parrot-like birds stolen has escalated. This has resulted in many people choosing to construct their aviaries within outbuildings, which can easily be secured, or inside the house in a spare bedroom, attic or cellar. All these options have their advantages and disadvantages; however, most parrots will benefit from having the opportunity to interact with another parrot and of having the extra space and freedom that an aviary offers.

If you are situating the aviary outside, it is of benefit to its future occupants if you site the aviary where there is some natural shelter from the elements. You may also want the aviary sited where you can easily observe the occupants from the comfort of your own home. As already mentioned, unless you live in a very remote part of the country, it is preferable to site the aviary where the birds cannot be observed from the road, to reduce the risk of theft. It is worth considering the likelihood of your wanting to develop further aviaries in the future. It will save you considerable time and money if the aviaries are next to one another; therefore you may want to site your aviary where there is room for you to expand in the future.

NOISE

Another major consideration is noise. Some parrots are noisy and, if you feel it is likely that any near neighbours will resent the clamour that they make, you will need to make plans on how best to reduce the noise

An aviary should be large enough for the parrot to fly freely.

and consequent irritation factor for others. The larger parrots do vary considerably in the volume of sound that they make, and some of the smaller species of conure such as the Quaker Parakeet (*Myiopsitta monachus*) and the Nanday Conure (*Nandayus Nenday*) can be extremely noisy.

Most, however, have two main periods in the day when they are at their noisiest, and this is usually at first light and at dusk. This can be relatively easy to manage if you can secure the parrots in a shelter before dusk and only let them out at a reasonable time in the morning. The other times when parrots are noisy are if they preparing to breed or are breeding, when they meet any perceived threat with much noise. Your near neighbours may be much more tolerant of the parrots if you involve them from the onset and take their feelings into consideration; this can have the added benefit of you then having someone who may be willing to help out with their care if you go on holiday.

ACCOMMODATING PARROTS

If a pair of parrots is kept, the aviary needs to be as large as possible. As a guide, it ought to be possible for the parrots to have sufficient room to fly freely. If you keep, or intend to keep, several pairs of parrots, it is sometimes possible to have one large communal aviary where the parrots can be housed collectively outside their breeding season. Then in the breeding season, individual pairs can be placed in much smaller aviaries.

If this method of accommodating your birds is chosen, all the birds that you intend to keep together should be placed in the communal aviary at the same time, to ensure that no parrots can map out a territory for themselves before another bird is introduced. It is wise to do this when you have the time to observe your birds, so that if serious fighting does break out you can quickly isolate the guilty party.

This method of accommodating parrots has proved to be very successful for many keepers. The extra space in the large communal flight allows the parrots to exercise to a greater extent and, as a consequence, they are in much better condition when put into the breeding situation. The second benefit is that it allows the parrots the opportunity to integrate as a flock, which is what normally happens in the wild. One must, however, emphasise that the communal flight must be large enough to enable those pairs, which do not want to socialise to be able to enjoy their privacy.

Also, under no circumstances should any nestboxes be available or serious fighting may ensue. The only exception to this rule is where a particular species is maintained together as a colony all year round, as is found fairly regularly with some species of conures and lovebirds.

Once a colony of birds has been set up, there can be tragic consequences if further birds are added to it. It is also important that the pairs that are put into the smaller aviaries for breeding are truly compatible. If not, there is always the danger that one of the pair could be attacked by the other, which may result in serious injury or even death.

CONSTRUCTION

When constructing or purchasing an aviary, it is necessary to have some idea of the types of parrot that you intend to put in it. This is essential because of the variation in size and strength of various members of the parrot species. If you intend to keep the smaller types of parakeets, then the construction of the aviary will obviously have to be far less robust than if you are going to keep some of the larger macaws.

Both the larger and smaller parrot-like birds will require the same overall plan, which includes a shelter where they can be shut in to protect them from inclement

WIRE-MESH GAUGE SIZES

The following gives an indication of the suggested wire-mesh gauge required for the various sizes of parrot-type birds.

Species	Gauge
Small parakeets, cockatiels, Lovebirds, small conures, large parakeets, rosellas, ringnecks	16g
Pionus, amazons, African Grey parrots	14g
Large macaws, cockatoos	10g/12g
Hyacinth Macaws	10g

weather conditions if necessary, and an outside flight which enables them to interact with their environment.

If you wish to keep your birds in an indoor enclosure, then a flight is all that is required. Some parrots do roost in their nestboxes each night, and for these it is essential that the nestbox be left in place all year round. If it is your intention to gain experience with a more common, easily bred parrot such as a cockatiel, and then to move on to a larger parrot, it perhaps is worth the effort to build the aviary so that it is suitable for both species.

Wire mesh used for parrot aviaries is available in various sizes, the most suitable being 1" x 1" (2.5cm x 2.5cm). By using this size you will eliminate most rodents and also prevent wild birds from entering the aviary. For the much larger parrots, such as macaws, many aviaries are constructed using 2" x 2" (5cm x 5cm) mesh.

Metal, ready-made aviaries need not be an eye-sore. With careful planting and attention to decor, they can provide a stimulating environment for your parrot.

An aviary should provide protection from the elements and from natural wildlife. Pictured: Salvins Amazon.

There are many firms who sell ready-made aviaries. It is worth going to one of the large parrot-selling days, which take place two or three times each year, as this will allow you to view the many designs which are available. Most ready-made aviaries are now produced in aluminium, and there are many advantages to these – including their ease of cleaning, being difficult for parrots to chew, durability, and their light weight making them easy to transport. The disadvantage is that they do seem rather industrial in appearance but, as with traditional wooden aviaries, careful selection of planting and the use of container plants can make a great difference. The bonus to this is that the birds also appear to be more secure when housed amongst living foliage.

Wooden aviaries have been utilised for many years, and many aviaries are still constructed in this way. The main disadvantage to these is that if the parrots can get to the wood then it is entirely natural for them to chew it, to the point where escape may become possible. This can be controlled by ensuring that there is no exposed wood available, which is usually accomplished either by covering all the exposed wood with sheet metal or by covering the wood with welded mesh.

If it is your intention to join more than one aviary, the aviary must be double-wired. This means that each aviary must have its own wire mesh, and that there is a need for a gap between the two wire meshes of about two inches (5cm). This is to prevent the parrots from coming into contact with one another. When parrots are in breeding condition they become very territorial and aggressive and will have no hesitation in attacking their neighbours. In this case, if the birds are not in double-wired accommodation, the result could well be serious injury, such as bitten toes and possibly torn mandibles.

It is also useful to part-cover the flight with opaque plastic roofing sheets, as this allows the parrots to still sit outside in the rain without necessarily getting wet. Most parrots will delight in bathing in natural rain.

When siting food and water dishes in the aviary it is important that they are placed in a position where they can remain dry. They should also be protected from contamination by natural wildlife, or by the parrots themselves, such as might happen if dishes are placed under a favourite perch. It is also extremely helpful if they are easily accessible for cleaning and replenishing.

SLENDER-BILLED CONURES: A CASE HISTORY

by Michael Hurley

I keep several parrot species which many people would regard as unpopular. Several of the larger conures appear to fall into this category. However, of the species of conure that I keep, the Slender-bill is a firm favourite of mine.

The reason for the apparent unpopularity of this breed is probably the beak, which, as the name suggests, is elongated and thin. Slender-billed Conures are usually classified within the genus Enicognathus, which they share with the austral conure (*Enicognathus ferruginea*). In appearance there is some similarity between the two, although the Slender-billed Conure (*Enicognathus leptorhynchus*), at 16 inches (40cm), is two inches larger than the austral. Also, the austral conure does not share the thin elongated upper mandible. It has been suggested that the Slender-bill's beak is adapted for extracting the nuts from the monkey-puzzle tree and for digging up bulbs and tubers.

EARTH FLOORS

My own Slender-bills are housed for the most part of the year in aviaries, where they can have access to earth floors. This would normally be regarded as unhygienic and hazardous to health. However, anyone who has seen the absolute pleasure these birds derive from digging up grass roots and any other roots and stones they encounter, would be hard-pressed to find a sufficient counter-argument in favour of depriving the birds of this pleasure. I do, however, attempt to minimise the hazards, by only feeding them in their shelter, to avoid contamination from uneaten food in the flight, and by carrying out a regular prophylactic worming programme (consult your vet for details).

After trying out various methods of administering this, such as directly into the crop via a crop tube and by mixing it with favourite items of food, I now simply drip the worming solution into the beak. This takes two people – one to hold the bird and one to drip in the solution – but it does avoid the danger of accidentally introducing the liquid into the air passages, which could prove fatal. It also ensures that each bird receives a therapeutic dose of the wormer. This regime has proved effective for several years.

PAIRING AND BREEDING

Some Slender-bills are maintained, and even breed successfully, within a colony system. I have personally found breeding results to be poor using this method, with many eggs being eaten or broken. The method I have found to be most effective is to maintain the birds in a large communal flight while out of the breeding season and then to transfer them to individual smaller aviaries for breeding. There appear to be several advantages to this. The birds can socialise as a flock and have the opportunity to exchange partners if they wish. It also brings them into peak fitness prior to the breeding season.

Although my own partners have always paired up with the same partners each year, the pair bond is almost non-existent outside the breeding season. During this time individuals integrate freely with other members of the flock. Preening of others is carried out freely by all individuals and all birds behave in an extremely affectionate manner towards one another.

FOOD FANATICS

The diet I feed my Slender-bills is varied. Mixed, soaked pulses are the main constituent, to which are added fresh fruit and vegetables. Half to one dessertspoonful of hulled sunflower kernels is given to each pair of birds daily, and the fat content of the food is slightly increased when they have young and in winter, when pine nuts and peanuts are added. Slender-bills adore their food, and I do make the effort to give them a wide variety which includes different coloured and textured foods. Their excitement at feeding time never fails.

These birds will become obese if given a diet too rich in fats, and this can lead to other problems, such as egg-binding and lethargy if not addressed.

PARENTING SKILLS

Slender-bills usually become sexually mature at about two years of age. However, hand-reared young, in common with other hand-reared parrot species, mature earlier, and I have had personal experience of a hand-reared cock fertilising eggs at the tender age of nine months. Several of my own birds have taken a few years to get their parenting skills established – playing football in the nest box with the eggs, and eating them, appears to be a fairly common trait amongst this species.

However, in my view it is important to allow them to make these mistakes as, if all the eggs or young are removed for hand-rearing, the parents may never develop the necessary parenting skills. With those parents that I know to have poor parenting skills, I tend to remove some of the clutch for hand-rearing and integrate these with parent-reared young when weaned, to enable them to socialise with the parent-reared birds.

KEEPING HOUSE

My Slender-bills breed in aviaries which have an inside cube-shaped cage of 1m square (3' 2"), to which the nest box and food and water-containers are attached. It has a pop-hole leading to an outside flight 2.5m (8") long, 1m (3' 2") wide and 2m (6' 4") high. Upright nest boxes are provided which are 60cm high and 30cm square.

The usual clutch consists of between four to six eggs, and these are incubated for about 26 days. When the young are being reared by the parents, it is important to change the nest litter at regular intervals as the parents make no attempt to keep the nest clean, which results in debris and faecal matter collecting and drying on the inside and outside of their leg rings. If the ring is not then removed, the end result may be that the blood supply to the leg is cut off. This may damage the leg to such an extent that amputation is the only viable option to save the life of the bird.

COMICAL CHARACTERS

The chicks are hatched with white down, which is later replaced by thick, grey down. Interestingly, hand-reared young tend to wean much earlier than their parent-reared siblings do. The young, like the adults, are very inquisitive, and it is my belief that because of this, the hand-reared young will explore and try food at an early age. In my experience, this is before they have even lost all their secondaries and a few weeks before they can fly. This is not suggesting that they still do not require attention, as at an early age they still need to be put near the food, and hand-rearing food still needs to be offered at regular intervals. My birds will often start exploring food from about six weeks.

The young leave the nest box at between nine to ten weeks and are normally weaned about two weeks after this. Hand-reared young are an absolute joy to be with, being extremely mischievous and fearful of nothing. Although they don't particularly like being touched, they make up for this by soon learning to say some simple phrases. Their mannerisms, like those of the adults, are most amusing, with head bobbing, eyes blazing and an upright stance when investigating something really interesting.

Slender-billed Conures are quite strong-willed and resent anything being taken away from them. In our own household this has resulted in them stealing and flying off with the children's small toy cars, much to the annoyance of the toys' rightful owners.

A GOOD CHOICE

It is unfortunate that, with the limited popularity of this species, fewer birds are being aviary-bred. As aviary subjects they can be noisy, especially when someone they don't know is in the vicinity. However, the noise does reduce considerably if the birds feel secure. They do very little damage to the aviary framework, but door catches do need to be very carefully chosen, as these birds are absolute masters at figuring out how to undo things. If you are interested in parrot-like birds that have intelligence, inquisitiveness and character in excess, Slender-billed Conures are the birds for you.

SAFETY CORRIDORS

It is well worth the investment in ensuring that you have a safety corridor adjoining either the flight or the shelter door. This will enable you to go into an area that can then be securely shut before you enter the aviary proper. If a bird then flies out as you are entering, it will still remain secure in the safety corridor. This will also give you a good access point for feeding and watering.

FLOOR

There are various materials that can be utilised for the floor to your aviary, the most common being concrete. There are several advantages to this – it prevents access by rodents, it prevents parrots from finding an escape route, and it can easily be cleaned. The main disadvantage would appear to be its rather hard and barren appearance. If you do decide upon a concrete base it is useful to plan this with a slight tilt to enable water used for cleaning to drain into a gully, which can then, if necessary, be directed to a drain. This will make the cleaning of the aviary very straightforward and efficient.

Another material which is commonly utilised as flooring is shingle, both small and larger grades. This is often used for the lory family where, because of their liquid faeces, it is important that the floor can easily drain. In this case, the shingle can be cleaned with the use of a pressure-washer or hose.

For some birds, an earth floor can be used, although one has to accept that there are several disadvantages to this. The greatest disadvantage is the difficulty in maintaining adequate hygiene. This can be overcome in part by placing paving slabs underneath the places where the parrots most often sit, thus collecting the droppings that can then be removed out of the aviary. It is also important in this case that measures are taken to prevent rats and mice from burrowing into the aviary. This can normally be managed by ensuring that the wire mesh is buried vertically for at least 18 inches (45.5cm) around the perimeter of the aviary. The advantages to an earth floor are that it appears to be a much more normal habitat for the birds, and they really do seem to enjoy the different textures available to them. Some parrots will spend many hours feeding on seeding grass heads. With parrots with a long upper mandible, such as the Slender-billed Conure and the Slender-billed Corellas, you will find they will spend much time on the floor extracting various roots from the growing plants, as they would do in their wild habitat.

Some aviculturists use bark chippings, which aesthetically is very pleasing. Unfortunately the use of bark carries a high risk of contamination with fungal spores in warm humid conditions, which can prove harmful or even fatal to parrots.

Parrots can be incredibly destructive to the aviary and for this reason it is useful to get into the habit of regularly checking for any damage. This does need to include the floor, as some parrots will burrow, and also the nestbox, as it is entirely normal for parrots to chew both the inside and the outside of the box.

PLANTS FOR THE AVIARY

It is possible to use plants in some parrot aviaries, although this is somewhat contrary to popular belief. It is possible to have aviaries which have small trees, plants and shrubs growing in them, and aviaries with natural earth floors can have a variety of seeding grasses and native wild plants growing. This is much easier to accomplish in larger aviaries, but once parrots are accustomed to living with plants they do appear less destructive when placed in smaller aviaries with plants.

To see parrots acting in a natural way with plants in an aviary is an extremely satisfying sight. We have literally spent hours watching Lesser Vasa parrots nibbling and eating the seeds from large seeding grasses. These parrots sunbathe a great deal, and will adopt all sorts of postures to ensure that the sun reaches their hidden parts. When given the option of a grass floor – ours used the floor a great deal for this and appeared to luxuriate in this new-found bedding, going from sunbathing to nibbling the seed heads. Their plumage took on a lustre and richness of colour that we had never observed before. When the pair went into breeding condition, their behaviour and appearance could only be described as robustly healthy.

There is no clear way of accomplishing the planting of an aviary, and much will depend upon a trial-and-error approach and the individual habits and characters of the parrots. Parrots that live in a planted aviary seem to have a more contented and secure appearance, and from an aesthetic viewpoint, a planted aviary can be very attractive. It has been observed how parrots have become more relaxed in a planted aviary, and on a few occasions it has been seen that parrots in the habit of feather-plucking cease almost immediately when given this enriched environment.

INTRODUCE GRADUALLY

As a first step, it is useful if the parrot can be exposed to the greenery in a staged way. If done in this way, it doesn't have quite the same level of novelty value. It is important to remember that parrots are naturally inquisitive and will therefore appear to be destructive towards the plants, and all you can do is to attempt to manipulate this behaviour until the desired outcome is reached.

There are some things the keeper can do to ease the transition into a planted situation. Having an earth floor with grass growing is a good start. If there are some native plants such as plantain and dandelion present, so much the better. (Buttercups are thought to be poisonous.) Care must be taken to ensure that no poisonous plants are available to the parrots, as there may well be a tendency for

If they are not used to plants in the aviary, parrots may destroy them. However, they would not be able to cause very much damage in an aviary this size.

Garden tubs can be put outside the aviary to recover from any chewing inflicted on them.

the parrots to attempt to nibble and even eat everything that is growing. Experience has shown that this behaviour will decrease the longer the parrots are exposed to the greenery.

Using an aviary where one or more trees, shrubs and climbing plants are growing against the side of the aviary is another option. Ideally these plants will have grown through the mesh and therefore will have encroached upon the interior of the aviary space. Again one must expect the parrots to nibble, eat, and denude the plants of their leaves, which is natural behaviour.

The next step is to attempt to grow small plants in the aviary. These will ideally be plants that have the capacity to grow large. The advantages to this are that the plant will have a faster growth which will help to compensate for the wear and tear from the parrots, and that, being small to start with, it will not have the same immediate novelty value, so will hopefully be untouched. As the plant grows larger and stronger, it will be possible for the parrots to sit on the branches and camouflage themselves among the leaves.

PLANT TUBS

It may also be possible to grow plants in tubs. These can then be rotated, so that some tubs are always out of the aviary recovering, and can be put back later. When you are growing plants in an aviary containing parrots, it is wise to always expect the loss of the plants, and not to feel irritated when a lovely-looking plant that might have been in the aviary for several months is suddenly destroyed in a matter of hours. The owner of the parrots can take delight in the fact that the parrots probably gained tremendous satisfaction from this activity.

Parrots are highly inquisitive and intelligent, and it is quite normal for them to be destructive when exploring the plants. The less bored the parrots are, the healthier they are likely to be, both from a mental and physical perspective. Another good time to introduce small plants into the aviary is in the breeding season; at this time the parrots will have other things on their mind and the plants may well be left alone.

When considering plants for the parrot aviary it is important to find out if the plant is poisonous, and this information isn't always easily available. If you are not sure, it is worth noting what plants have been used around aviaries in zoos and bird gardens. It is not worth the risk of using plants which are poisonous.

AESTHETICS

Even if you don't want to go to the trouble of introducing plants to the aviary, it is a good idea to have plants and shrubs around the aviary site. The benefit of this is that it will give the birds a feeling of security, as it is quite natural for most parrot species to live amongst leaves and trees. Another advantage is that you can use shrubs and hedging to act as a windbreak in windy exposed sites. In addition to these benefits, a well-planted site can add to the attractiveness of your garden.

Some aviculturists use hanging baskets on the outside of their aviaries. These do add to the attractiveness of the aviary, but can also cause some anxiety to the parrots. When it is windy it causes the hanging basket to rock and in some cases even to knock against the aviary, which can cause distress to the occupants. An easy way to overcome this, while still having the benefit of the hanging baskets, is to use rigid half-baskets which fit directly on to the structure of the aviary with the aid of screws.

Ponds and pools can be used on the inside of an aviary and can look extremely attractive; however, one has to be aware that there are dangers attached to this. The water will undoubtedly be used by the parrots for bathing and drinking, so the water does need to be replenished at regular intervals to ensure that it is fresh. The pool also needs to be located where it is less likely to be fouled by the parrots' droppings, or to have uneaten food dropped into it. It is also important that the depth is only a few inches, to minimise the risk of drowning.

If your aviary is reasonably large it is quite possible to landscape it using different textures and colours. The materials used should ideally be those which can stand up to the attention of the parrots. There are a variety of coloured and various-sized shingles that can be used to make attractive designs. Paving slabs too are available in a variety of colours and shapes. Tree trunks laid on their sides will add interest to the interior of the aviary and give much amusement to the occupants. If you have used an earth floor, you can also lay turf. Depending upon the types of parrots that you keep, this may last indefinitely. Cement can also add interest, as it can be used to mould different levels and shapes. Some parrots also appear to gain much satisfaction from nibbling at concrete, which will also assist in keeping their bills in shape.

PLANTS WHICH CAN BE USED IN AND AROUND THE AVIARY

LAVATERA ARBOREA (tree mallow)

This can grow up to 6 feet (1.8m) or more. It is fast-growing and roots rapidly from cuttings. It isn't long-lived, frequently dying after 3-4 years, and is said not to be hardy in cold, exposed sites. The leaves are lobed and soft. The flowers are 2 inches (5cm) across, purple with dark veins, and appear throughout the summer. The plant prefers a sunny location with protection from a wall. Other colours are also available.

We have found this plant to be one of the most successful for parrot aviaries, both grown inside the aviary and also grown against the mesh on the outside, where the stems soon invade the interior. The plant is very free flowering, and parrots find this an added bonus, as they appear to like the taste of the flowers. These stain the beak dark purplish-red, and this can be quite disconcerting until the cause is identified.

SAMBUCUS NIGRA (elder)

These can reach heights of 12 feet (3.6m) or more unless cut. It can easily be cut and shaped to the size needed. The leaves are toothed, and the wood in the stems is soft until the plant is older. It will grow easily from seed. We were first introduced to this plant when some of the elderberries that we feed fresh in late summer fell to the ground and germinated. We have found that our parrots will frequently leave these small plants untouched for very long periods, until they become small trees, then suddenly discover that they like the taste and destroy most of the plant very quickly.

Plants and trees around the aviary offer protection against the elements.

POLYGONUM BALDSCHUANICUM
(mile-a-minute vine)
As the name suggests, this is one of the most rampant of all climbers. If you use this near or against the aviary, there is a need to ensure that this vigorous climber doesn't damage the mesh or the structure of the aviary. However, the positive aspect of this is that it can take a large amount of abuse and return even stronger. Parrots appear to take delight in nibbling it, especially when they are first introduced to an aviary where the plant is established. When in flower, the vine is covered in sprays of tiny white flowers, which adds to the attractiveness of the aviary. This plant can be used to soften the harsh appearance of aviaries and is very useful for providing shade in the summer.

Providing natural protection can prevent stress in the aviary inhabitants. Pictured: Green Amazon.

SALIX (willow)
Of all the plants that can be utilised for parrots, the willow must surely be the one that is used more than any other. Willow branches are extremely useful for perches, as they are normally available in a variety of different widths, from small 1-inch (2.5cm) diameter branches to those that are several inches thick. This is useful in the aviary, as it gives the parrots' feet and toes exercise and helps to keep them flexible.

There are several different varieties of willow, most of which can become very large trees, and for this reason they shouldn't be planted against the walls of buildings where their roots could damage foundations and drains. If you do feel that you can plant some willow, 25 feet (7.6m) away from the house is the usual distance that is recommended. It is very easy to propagate willow, as it will literally sprout if left in water or moist earth. It is more likely to succeed if it is not allowed to dry out in its first year of life, when it will still be putting down roots.

If you have a large garden with a moist area away from the house, it is worth planting some willow as you will then have an endless supply of fresh perching material. We have never managed to grow willow in the aviary, as the parrots appear to find it irresistible, and this also includes willows that have been grown on the outside.

4 MAKING THE CHOICE

When considering a parrot, it is always preferable to see the parrot before agreeing to the purchase. Within the hobby of parrot keeping, it is not that unusual for parrots to be bought without first being seen. This is usually because the parrot or parrots are located many miles away, and it is a fairly simple process to arrange for the transportation of the birds via one of the national carriers. In some instances this does work well; however, at other times this can be fraught with problems.

It is also useful to be able to see at first-hand the conditions in which the parrot is kept, and to find out as much information as possible about your intended purchase. Because parrots have a long life-span and very few carry documentation or passport information with them, this historical data is often only passed on by word of mouth.

If the sellers are agreeable, it is also useful to see the condition of any other parrots they may have, as this may give an indication of any captive-related conditions, such as vitamin deficiencies or psychological problems. Many owners of parrots, although bestowing much care and affection on their charges, do not always closely observe their parrots, and it is sometimes possible to find various physical abnormalities which the person selling the parrot really isn't aware of.

It is also useful to see documentation in relation to sexing and registration if the parrot is endangered. Leg rings, tattoos and microchip information can also be seen.

OBSERVATION OF THE PARROT

If possible it is always preferable to see the parrot in its usual accommodation. The behaviour which is then observed is likely to be as near to normal as possible. A healthy parrot, which feels secure in its environment, is a joy to behold; however, there is a need to make a closer assessment than just a general observation.

FEATHERS

All feathers should be present, and they should be glossy in appearance.

Possible areas of concern:

Some of the feathers may be ragged in appearance; this is quite common in birds, which have been recently imported and are just out of quarantine. Some hen parrots can look quite bedraggled after rearing young.

If there are bald patches, or areas of down poking through, this may suggest feather-plucking. If the parrot is alone the plucking is only in areas where the parrot can reach; however, if the parrot is housed with another parrot it could be caused by the other parrot plucking it.

Opposite page: Great-billed Parrot.

Feathers should be glossy and none should be missing. Pictured: Chattering Lory.

If parrots have been through a stressful episode, their larger feathers become barred horizontally. These are known as stress bars, and can sometimes be seen in young birds. One could assume that they might have been caused by too early weaning, or perhaps too early removal from the parents.

It is important to remember that poor feather quality is not necessarily an indication of poor health, and it is quite amazing how quickly feather condition can improve when the parrot is cared for correctly.

The main concern in relation to poor feathering is a disease known as Psittacine Beak and Feather Disease (PBFD). If you suspect this, you would be unwise to purchase the parrot unless it is vet-checked. Some disease processes such as liver disease will cause a colour change in feathers, and this needs formal investigation by an avian vet.

EYES

The eyes should be bright and clear, and the parrot should behave in a way that suggests their vision is not impaired. When young parrots are said to be black-eyed, this means that the eye appears black. Unless very closely observed it is difficult to differentiate between the pupil, which is the dark centre of the eye, and the iris, which is coloured muscle surrounding the pupil. As the parrot matures, the eyes become lighter. In adult parrots the eye is often used as a form of expression which allows for extra communication. Some species of parrots use this more than others and are referred to as 'blazing': the parrot will usually adopt an upright position with a very alert expression, and this may be accompanied by head nods. The eye blazing occurs when the iris of the eye is constricted and dilated in quick succession. This behaviour is quite normal when it occurs in healthy parrots.

Many cockatoos keep black eyes, whereas the hen's eyes take on a browner appearance; however, this sexing method in cockatoos is not infallible, and it is still wiser to have cockatoos formally sexed.

Eyes should be bright. Pictured: Moluccan Cockatoo.

Possible areas of concern:
There is normally an area of skin surrounding the eye known as the periophthalmic ring, and in many parrot species this is light-coloured. There should be no bumps in this, nor should there be any discharges from the eye. If the eyelids or the surrounding skin are red, or have sores or thickened areas, this may suggest previous trauma or vitamin deficiency.

Some imported parrots do have eye problems as a result of trauma, which in all probability was caused during capture or in the subsequent transportation or quarantine period. The eye may be missing altogether or be deformed. If the parrot appears otherwise healthy, it is a personal choice as to whether you wish to own a parrot with a deformity. Blindness in one eye doesn't appear to prevent some parrots from making good pets or prevent adult parrots from breeding and rearing their own youngsters.

Cataracts are relatively common in older parrots and appear as an opaque lens on the front of the eye. Although surgery has been attempted and carried out successfully on occasions, this treatment is rarely available.

NOSTRILS AND BEAK
The nostrils should appear clear, be of equal size and in a central position to the beak. The beak should be smooth and the upper mandible should fit neatly on top of the lower mandible.

Possible areas of concern:
A discharge from the nostril may indicate a bacterial infection or sinusitis. If this has occurred recently, the feathers around the area may be stained, and of poor quality. In very chronic conditions, the discharge may even cause a furrow down the beak where the discharge has drained downwards.

In older parrots the nostrils often become enlarged, but even then they should be clear and not plugged.

Vitamin deficiencies can cause pus-filled lesions to develop around the area of the nostrils, often seen in old African Greys. This may lead to permanent deformity and disfigurement in the area above the beak.

The beak should not show signs of scaliness. If this is evident, it may suggest an infestation of mites, known as scaly face.

In Psittacine Beak and Feather Disease, the beak often takes on a very glossy appearance.

The beak should be well-shaped. It is worth observing for areas of overgrowth that may suggest a previous injury; however, this shouldn't necessarily put you off purchasing an otherwise healthy bird. You will, however, have to take into account the stress caused to the parrot in having to trim the beak at regular intervals.

The area around the nostril should be clean, and the beak should be well-shaped and show no sign of infection. Pictured: Blue and Gold Macaw.

It is advisable to examine the bird carefully, and handle it as much as possible, before making a decision to buy. Pictured: A very unusual Cinnamon Blue-fronted Amazon.

FEET AND LEGS

The feet and legs should move normally, and demonstrate a range of movement. Parrots have two toes facing towards the front and two toes facing toward the back. The legs and toes are smooth but naturally scaled. A nail should be present at the end of each toe. If parrots are resting they normally rest on one foot only, although young parrots use both legs. The toes and legs are normally quite flexible and are used for holding food whilst it is being eaten.

Possible areas for concern:
Lack of movement or stiffness in the area of the foot or toes may suggest previous injury, arthritic changes or soft-tissue injury.

Nails that are overgrown may suggest a lack of different-sized perching and is not serious.

If the nail is missing, it suggests earlier trauma possibly caused by another parrot or by frostbite. If the site is not healed, it is worth asking the owner how the injury was sustained. Recent injuries to the feet or toes often cause swollen feet, which can be especially dangerous if the parrot has a closed ring. The swelling could then potentially prevent blood-flow to the foot, resulting in gangrene and subsequent loss of the foot.

If the scales are overgrown and elevated, it may suggest mite infestation.

WINGS

Ideally it is useful to see the parrot fly, as this can illustrate clearly its physical balance.

Possible areas of concern:
A dropped wing is characterised by one wing drooping compared to the other. There are varied levels of severity to this, going from a bird with a wing which will touch the ground when the parrot walks, with the parrot being unable to fly, to only a very slightly dropped wing which doesn't appear to have any bearing upon the parrot's flight capability. The usual cause is trauma, and, in some cases, old fractures.

Parrots with a dropped wing often manage very well, both as pets and as breeding birds. If the wing prevents flight, it is worth having a veterinary opinion, but many birds appear to manage very well without the power of flight in an aviary situation. In this case it is important that the perches are arranged in such a way as to maximise the parrot's ability to get around.

If the wing has been clipped, it is worth finding out when this was carried out, as this will give you an indication of when flight will be restored. It often takes a year to 18 months before the cut flight-feathers will be moulted out and be replaced with new feathers.

VENT AREA
This should be clean with no dried matter in the surrounding areas. The actual faecal matter is quite variable and dependent upon the parrot's diet. Parrot droppings consist of three main parts: faeces, urates and urine.

FAECES
This is the dark-coloured portion of the droppings, and will vary in colour and consistency depending upon what has been eaten. If large amounts of fruit and vegetable have been eaten, the faeces part is likely to be a lighter brown to green, with a bulky appearance. If mostly seed has been eaten, the faeces will be darker brown to green with a more tubular shape.

URATES
This is the light-coloured part of the stool and represents the solid waste produced by the kidneys; the urate part is wrapped around the faeces.

URINE
This is the clear liquid that is passed with the stool. The amount of this will also vary. If the bird is stressed, it is likely to pass more droppings with a greater than usual percentage of urine, producing a very wet dropping. There will also be a larger amount of urine if the parrot is eating a large amount of fruit and vegetables, and also in baby parrots when they are being hand-reared, as the hand-rearing formula will contain a high water content.

Possible areas of concern:
It must always be remembered that the parrot's diet will have a correlation with the appearance of the droppings. Cherries, for instance, will cause the urate part of the droppings to be pink in colour. However, features which do give immediate cause for concern include blood in the stools, greenish or greyish diarrhoea, or the passing of undigested food. If any of these symptoms occur or are apparent when you are intending to purchase a bird, it is important that the parrot has a veterinary assessment, as each of these symptoms could indicate serious illness.

WEIGHT OF THE PARROT
It is unlikely that you will have scales available to weigh a parrot on a visit; however, it is possible to make a rough assessment of its weight by picking the bird up if it will allow you to. If it won't, it is helpful to restrain the bird in a towel and gently but firmly feel the breastbone and the muscle either side of this. If you are new to parrot keeping, it is useful to have someone with you who is experienced. They will be

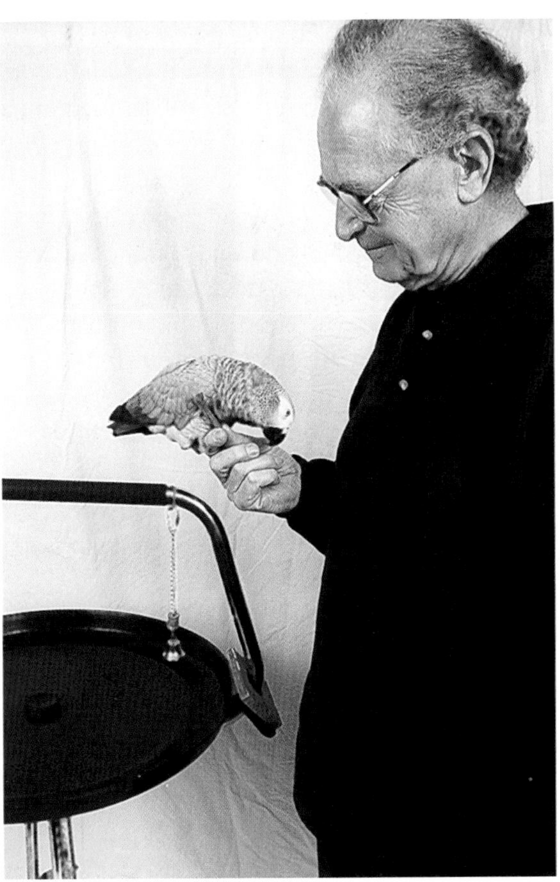

African Grey: assess the weight of the parrot by handling him.

able to make a judgement as to whether the breastbone is particularly sharp – this is a common observation in underweight parrots – and to how much muscle is present on either side of the breastbone.

While you have access to the bird, it is a useful exercise to feel gently over the body. This will enable you to ascertain if there are any lumps or bumps that might give rise for concern.

Possible areas of concern:
If the bird is underweight, it could be something as simple as the parrot requiring worming. It would be useful to find out the last time the parrot was wormed, and to note if the accommodation allowed access to worm eggs that could infect the parrot. Likely areas include earth-floors and flights that are open to the sky, thereby allowing birds to pass droppings into the aviary from the top. Some parrots are much more prone to worms than others. The conures and some Australian parakeets are particularly susceptible.

If worms are not likely to be the cause, attempts should be made to ascertain the age of the parrot, as older parrots are generally lighter than younger ones. Any lumps or bumps should be treated with caution; possible causes include infections, feather cysts, malignant and non-malignant lesions.

BEHAVIOUR DURING ACTIVITY
If it is possible to observe the parrot moving in its usual environment without feeling stressed, then you can pick up other abnormalities, such as slightly twisted necks and backbones. Some parrots will inform you of something wrong as they become excited. (An example that comes to mind involved a Roseate Cockatoo, which during its delight at being made a fuss of started breathing deeply. As it breathed, a large swelling appeared on one side of its upper chest. The keeper of the cockatoo was most surprised when this was pointed out. The cause turned out to be an air sac rupture, which in effect meant that air was collecting under the skin. When the cockatoo wasn't excited, the air dissipated, and it then appeared to be quite normal.)

Parrots have two toes facing forwards and two pointing backwards. Pictured: Cornelias Eclectus hen (extremely rare in aviculture).

A normal parrot will be inquisitive and active, unless, of course, you are observing it during one of its rest periods. Most parrots have routines that involve them resting after feeding and throughout other periods in midmorning, lunchtime, and again, late afternoon.

If you are new to parrot keeping, it is always a wise move to take someone with you who is experienced in checking a bird. If the parrot is an expensive one, it is worth asking for a vet-check before making a purchase.

RESCUE PARROTS

Annette De Saulles

It is a sad fact that there are many unwanted or neglected parrots in need of good homes. The following scenarios are all too common and explain why parrot rescue homes are always filled to capacity.

IMPULSE BUY

There is a cuddly white baby cockatoo sitting in a cage in a local pet shop. A young couple go into the shop, thinking of buying a pet. A kitten, maybe, or a budgie. They have never considered buying a parrot, but the cockatoo is irresistible – and so tame – and home they go with it.

Umbrella Cockatoo: many buy Cockatoos without realising they are highly intelligent animals that need attention and stimulation.

The baby cockatoo is so cute, the couple cuddle it and play with it all the time – although, of course, when they go to work it has to go into its cage. All day on its own. In its frustration it starts screaming for attention as soon as the family gets home in the evening. They let the bird out, but it starts to chew large chunks out of the dining-room table. It is put back in the cage again, where it begins plucking out its feathers.

Not the cuddly baby anymore, the adolescent bird sometimes nips. Afraid of that powerful beak, the bird's keepers leave it in its cage all the time now. Then they move the cage out to the garage because of the noise. Soon the cockatoo has a completely bald chest. Disillusioned (and anyway, there's a human baby on the way), the couple take the bird back to the shop. They feel very guilty, giving up on their pet, but don't know what else they can do.

This bird, confused, upset and deeply frustrated, will probably be passed from home to home for years to come. Lack of understanding of its needs will mean it is confined for hours in its cage, leading to more screaming, feather-plucking and biting. Cockatoos, like all parrots, are highly intelligent, sociable creatures. They crave attention and stimulation. So it is little wonder, if imprisoned alone in a sterile cage for long periods, that behaviour problems eventually set in.

CAUGHT OUT

The second scenario is that of the wild-caught bird that never becomes properly tame. Tempted by the apparently low purchase price of the African Grey at the bird auction, the unsuspecting purchaser thinks he has found a bargain. He does not ask to handle the bird out of its cage. When the parrot growls and backs away, the seller says it is just a bit nervous and will be fine once settled in its new home.

Observe the parrot in its usual home environment before deciding to buy. Pictured: African Grey.

The purchaser did not know enough to ask whether the bird was captive-bred or wild-caught – and his problems are only just beginning.

This 'bargain' bird turns out to be nothing of the kind. Traumatised by the journey from Africa and caged with other stressed birds for several weeks, it has fallen victim to a serious respiratory disease. Several visits to the vet and a period of intensive care have cost as much as the bird itself did.

It is completely wild and very frightened. When its keeper attempts to put a hand into the cage to remove the bird, it growls and flies about in panic. Then it bites. That's it – the cage door is firmly shut. A few weeks and more painful nips later, an advert appears in the local paper. The bird is sold on to another buyer who fancies owning a parrot but has not done his homework. The pattern is now set for a long line of disappointed buyers – and a very unhappy parrot.

THINK BEFORE YOU BUY

Until quite recently there has been little information available for prospective parrot keepers. The familiar image has long been of the lone parrot in its cage, content with a bowl of seed and a perch to sit on. Thankfully, this view is at last changing, if only slowly. Keepers are looking at the parrot's natural origins and finding ways of duplicating these as far as possible in captivity – the need for company, occupation, freedom to fly, the opportunity to bathe, branches to chew and food items that take time and ingenuity to open and eat.

Anyone thinking of taking on a parrot should consider whether they are able to provide a suitable environment for their bird. Is there someone home all day? Are you prepared to give a variety of fresh fruit and vegetables every day? Can you afford vet's bills? Adequate caging and toys? Do you have sufficient space for the species you are thinking of keeping? Would noise be a problem with neighbours? Will you still be in a position to keep a parrot ten, twenty, thirty years from now? What about other family members, children, pets? What will you do when you go on holiday?

Perhaps most importantly, what are your expectations of your bird? Do you look forward to interacting with it, having it as a permanent companion in its own right? Or is teaching it to talk the main attraction? Remember, not all parrots choose to mimic human speech, so this is not a good reason for buying one.

It saves a lot of heartache all round if these questions are carefully considered before parting with what is likely to be a considerable sum of money for your new parrot. It is the parrots bought on impulse that so often end up on the rescue circuit. The new keeper buys an African Grey because he has heard they can learn to talk. What he hasn't bargained for is feather dust and seed on the carpet, the occasional painful nip, and the screaming when he wants to watch television. Only one thing for it – put an advert in the local paper and sell the bird on.

Weigh up all the responsibilities involved in owning a parrot. Pictured: Yellow-fronted Amazon.

THINK BEFORE YOU SELL

The responsible breeder and seller of birds will take care to ensure that potential buyers are able to offer a good, permanent home for their new parrot – and that it will not soon be joining the many others on the rescue merry-go-round.

Ask questions before letting the bird go:

- Has the buyer kept parrots before – and what happened to them?
- Is there someone home all day?
- Is there sufficient room for the species being bought?
- Can they provide a good-sized cage, toys, a daily diet of fresh fruit and vegetables, an opportunity to bathe, fly and interact with the family?
- Would vet's fees be a problem?
- Who will look after the parrot when the family goes on holiday?
- What provision will be made for future care if the keeper predeceases the bird?

The genuine buyer will want to have as much information as possible before committing himself. A detailed information sheet and the offer of a back-up service in case of future problems are important.

TAKING ON A RESCUE PARROT

If you would like to re-home a parrot but don't feel you have the experience for one with severe behaviour problems, take care before committing yourself. Ask to see the bird out of its cage and make sure it can be handled safely by you. Ask questions. What does it eat? A bird that has been given nothing but sunflower seed may have serious health problems that are not immediately apparent. Does it have a preference for men or women? (It can happen that a bird never really takes to its keeper, but bonds with another family member instead. It is often the case that a female parrot will prefer male humans and vice versa.)

Observe the parrot's body language and follow your instincts. You can often tell early on if yours is likely to be a happy relationship. Ask for a vet's certificate of good health, or arrange a check-up of the bird yourself. Some obvious signs of illness are:

- A fluffed-up, lethargic appearance
- Laboured breathing
- Closed eyes
- Inability to perch
- Messy vent area
- Sharp breastbone.

Scarlet Macaw: ask as many questions as possible about the bird's background, health and needs.

A parrot that has been passed from one home to another will almost inevitably be confused and unhappy, and this can manifest itself in anti-social behaviour that will take some time to overcome. However, a frightened, nipping bird can, with care and patience, become tame and loving. If you feel you have the commitment to take on a damaged bird, the outcome can be very rewarding.

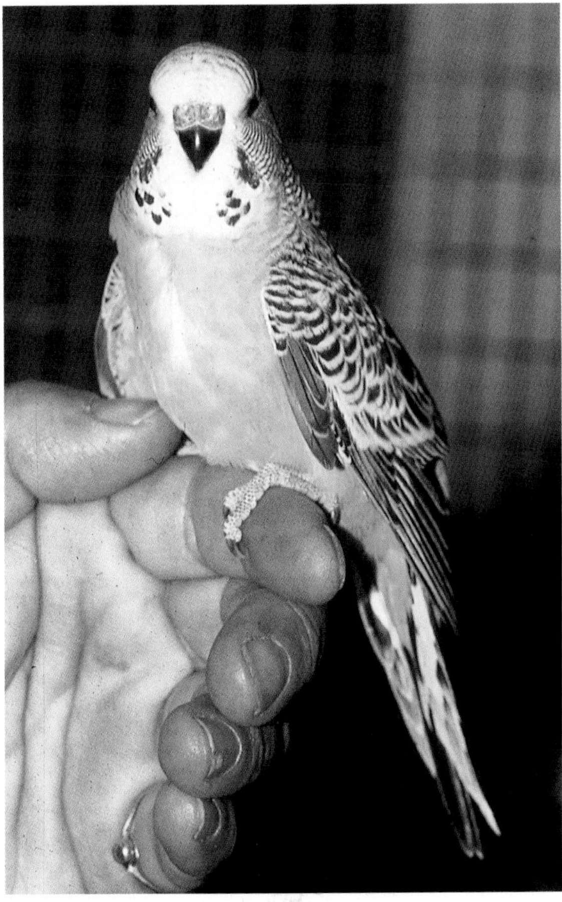

Patience and hard work can make an unsocialised bird into a tame and rewarding pet. Pictured: a young budgerigar (as evidenced by the black beak).

PARROT SANCTUARIES

With the current 'throwaway' mentality, there is a growing need for professional sanctuaries where unwanted and neglected birds can find the care they need, and perhaps live out the rest of their lives if they are not suitable for re-homing. It is also a fact of life that people become ill or die, or their circumstances unexpectedly change so that they can no longer care for their beloved parrot. Where there are no family members or friends to take on the bird, a knowledgeable rescue home is often the most suitable solution.

One such home in Colorado, USA, is The Gabriel Foundation. This non-profit organisation has its work cut out, caring for over 100 psittacines at any one time. Many are brought in with physical and psychological problems and need intensive medical attention. Calls come in every day from people all over the country wanting to get rid of their birds, always more than the space, time and funds available. Veterinary bills and medicines, food, housing and toys are funded by a mail-order parrot-goods shop and a sponsorship programme.

Education and increased awareness, through schools programmes, environmental groups and international avicultural conferences, educational literature and websites, is seen as the way ahead. People wanting to foster or adopt a parrot are asked to complete a detailed questionnaire, and are then given in-depth information and hands-on experience before taking away a bird. The message, finally, is the need for a lifelong commitment when taking on one of these highly intelligent and long-lived creatures.

5 ARRIVING HOME

What do you do when you arrive back home with your new pet parrot? The cage/aviary should be set up and furnished, ready to receive its new occupant. You should have inquired from the breeder or seller of your bird, what it has been fed on previously. Have a supply of this food ready even if you intend to change the diet eventually. Moving home is stressful enough, and changing the diet will only make matters worse. It is also an idea to add a probiotic such as Avipro to the water for a few days to help eliminate stress.

TRAVELLING HOME

A suitable carrier should have also been purchased in anticipation; this is a very useful item to have for moving your parrot around in the future. We find the plastic dog carriers with a metal grille at the front are ideal for this use. If you screw a perch halfway up and about a third of the length of the box back from the grille, the parrot will be able to sit on this and balance by holding on to the mesh with its beak when necessary.

When travelling short distances, it is not necessary to enclose food and water within

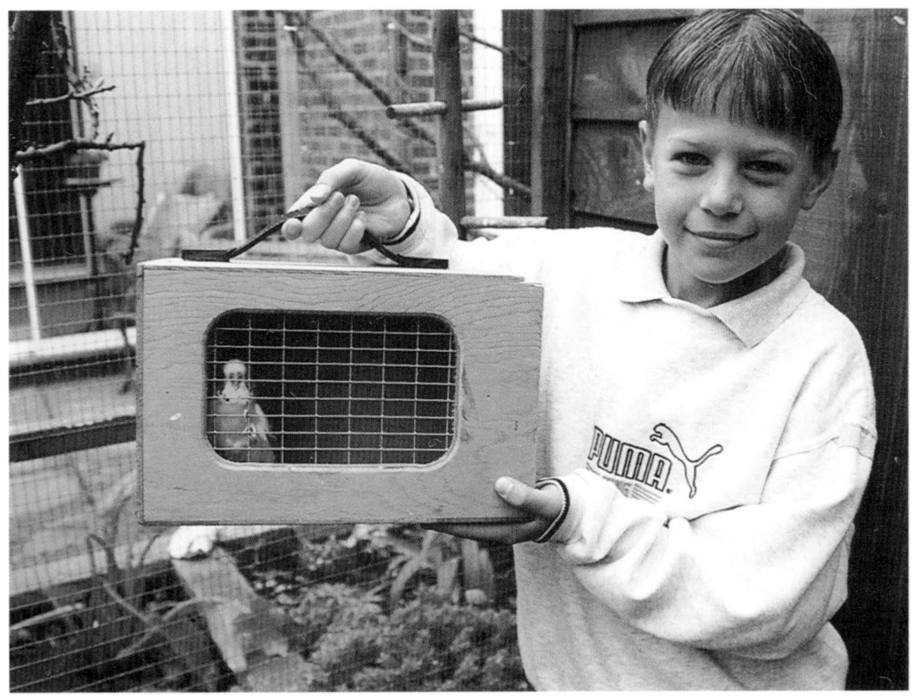

Make sure your parrot carrier is the correct size for your type of parrot.

Opposite page: Red-lored Amazon.

the carrier. However if long journeys are to be undertaken, hook-on 'D' cups can be hung on the mesh with water and food in them. Fruits and vegetables are the best travelling foods to help offset dehydration. The floor can be covered with newspaper, and a sheet at a time can be lifted when necessary to keep it clean.

FIRST DAY

Having got your parrot home, it is wise to place it in the cage or aviary and leave it in peace and quiet to accustom itself to its new surroundings. It is probably best to leave him quietly alone for the remainder of the day to relax and survey the surroundings.

Once you have brought your new parrot home, leave him to settle on his own for a while.

A hand-reared baby may cry and beg for food, even though it has been weaned for a number of weeks – many regress on being moved. These will take a handfeed for a few days, once each day, until it starts to feed itself properly. One hand feed a day is sufficient, and should only be given if the baby is really crying for it – never force the parrot to eat. Some babies will try to fool the feeder into thinking that it needs three or four feeds a day. A healthy baby of weaning age certainly does not need that, and will thrive on one top-up feed until it is eating sufficiently by itself. Ensure that food and water are easily accessible, particularly to babies and nervous birds, even if this means placing it right under their noses.

GENTLE APPROACH

The following day, warn the bird of your impending arrival by speaking quietly as you approach the cage or aviary. Even a hand-reared baby, no matter how tame, will appreciate a few words spoken in a gentle voice before you thrust your hand towards it. If you are trying to tame a parent-reared or wild-caught parrot then just sitting quietly by the cage for ten minutes, three or four times daily, and talking gently will be the first steps to gaining the parrot's trust. In the case of the wild-caught parrot, this stage may be fraught with difficulty and stress for both parrot and human.

It is a good idea to leave the hand-reared baby in the cage for an hour or two after you get up in the morning, so that it learns that you do not allow it out the moment you arrive in the room. This discourages restless or noisy attention-seeking behaviour. It is very important to start as you mean to go on – your parrot will settle down much more quickly if he learns and adapts to a routine.

Although the hand-reared baby can be allowed out for a play session after this period, the parent-reared bird should stay within the safe confines of the cage, as trying to return it to the cage once it has been removed at this early stage will only alarm it further. The time spent with these nervous birds can be gradually increased, as can the closeness of your body and hand.

Discovering as soon as possible your parrot's favourite treats will enable you to offer the treat by hand, and so show him that hands need not be threatening.

FAMILY INTRODUCTIONS

Introducing the new arrival to all members of the family should be done in the same manner – allowing the parrot to inspect them first through the bars of the cage, and if possible waiting for him to approach and solicit attention from the new person. The greater the number and variety of people he sees at this stage, the more social he will be in the future.

Both parrot and child must learn to respect each other. Pictured: Blue and Gold Macaw.

Children must be supervised and, prior to meeting the new pet, it should be explained that the children's excitement should be contained so as not to frighten the bird. Parrots of all ages can find the quick jerky actions of children quite disturbing, hence the need for constant supervision until both parties know how to behave towards one another. Without frightening the child, you should teach them to respect the potential danger of a parrot's beak, and also how easily the parrot could be damaged both physically and psychologically.

MEETING OTHER PARROTS

Similarly, pets should be introduced to each other with extreme caution. If there is already a parrot in the home, it could be jealous of a new arrival. It may be a good idea to place the existing parrot's cage in a different position or room, to prevent it regarding the space it is in as its territory. Even if it is planned to house the two parrots in the same cage – and this is sometimes possible – never introduce the newcomer into the resident's cage.

Place the two cages side by side so that the occupants can observe but not touch each other. When they have had a few days to get used to each other, they can be introduced in neutral territory. This meeting should be brief and supervised by you for its entire duration. The body language of the birds will tell you much. You can obviously break up any squabbles. A water spray may help if there is any serious aggression.

Birds of a similar size should be capable of avoiding serious injury, but if you are trying to introduce a large bird to a smaller one,

Move your parrot's cage to a new location (to avoid it being territorial) before placing the newcomer next to it.

then the risk is obviously greater. This is not to say that there are not many friendships between birds of greatly differing sizes. These periods of time spent together can be extended, until they eventually spend time sitting close or even preening. This is the time to try them together in a neutral cage, supervised once again. Common sense will tell you if this is going to be a harmonious relationship.

At this point, we must dispel the notion that a talking bird will stop talking if kept with another of its kind. We have found the reverse to be true: the second bird will often learn to speak from the first.

MEETING OTHER PETS

Introductions to other pets such as dogs and cats should be taken even more carefully. Even the most trustworthy of dogs could snap at this unfamiliar figure. Conversely, an inquisitive nose could be bitten badly by the bird. No matter how much you trust the dog or cat, never leave them alone with the

African Grey: cats and parrots are not always mortal enemies. Nevertheless, they should not be left alone together.

parrot – there are too many horror stories to risk it. Even caged, some parrots, especially the smaller ones, can be panicked into injury or even death by a teasing cat. However, after the initial interest, both parties will usually show a mutual respect, at a distance, for each other.

HOME HAZARDS

Dangers in the home should be considered, before the new acquisition discovers them first. Aquariums, toilets and any other water receptacles should be kept covered. Also windows, as well as being kept shut, should be covered with net curtains, venetian blinds or even strips of masking tape to make the parrot aware that a hard surface is there – not a gap to be flown through at speed. Tame birds can be held near windows and allowed to examine their structure with beak and tongue.

TEMPERATURE

Parrots, even youngsters, do not need the huge amount of heat many people believe. A comfortable temperature for you is usually comfortable for the parrot. However, a newly-arrived bird might appreciate a little extra heat to help combat stress.

WING CLIPPING

The practice of clipping parrots' wings is sadly all too common. If it is to be done, it is very important that a youngster is allowed to learn to fly first as, if in the future its wings are allowed to grow back, it may never have the courage or ability to fly. Early flying also aids in building the correct muscle structure.

Think carefully before undertaking a wing clip – as many have disastrous consequences. A badly clipped wing can irritate the recipient into chewing the mutilated feathers and even lead to plucking and denuding the body. A bad clip can also unbalance the bird, allowing it to fall to the ground, fracturing

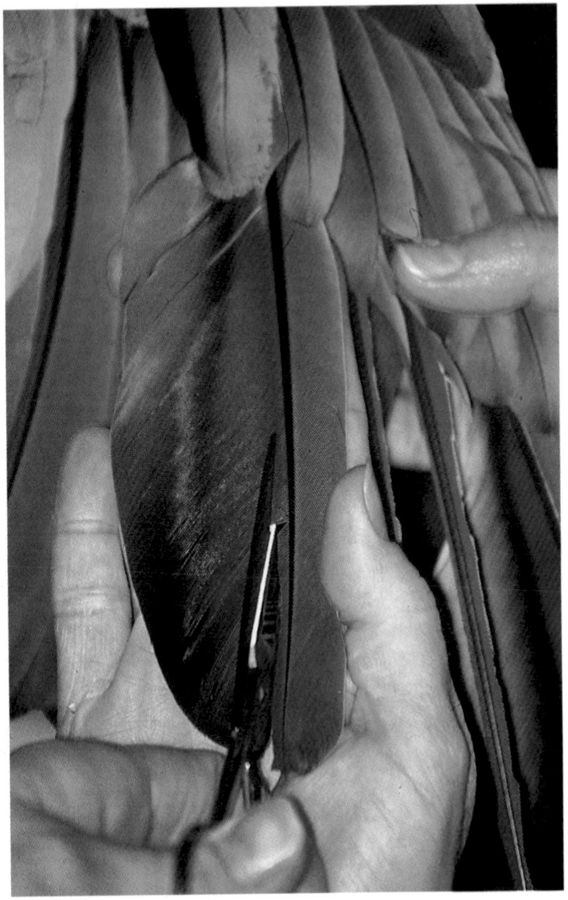

Strim the feathers gently.

A clipped wing, strimmed to leave the quill intact.

Toys can prevent the destruction and self-harm caused by boredom. Pictured: Blue-fronted Amazon.

limbs or the keel bone. These problems are usually associated with cutting the primaries straight across or through the quill.

A much better alternative, if somewhat time-consuming is to strim the wings. This involves leaving the quill intact, but trimming the feather either side of it. This allows the parrot some restricted downward flight, governed by the number of feathers that are clipped. A note of caution with this method is that some smaller parrots can still fly with a little wind behind them. All will still preen normally.

The reasoning behind clipping is that it should only be used as a temporary measure in the training of unruly parrots, or to temper aggression in a dominant cock bird of a pair – not to disable a bird for human convenience.

Bear in mind from the beginning, to start as you mean to go on with your new arrival. If a few simple rules are adhered to in the early days of training, you will be rewarded with a long-term well-behaved friend and companion.

TOYS FOR PARROTS

Parrots are playful, and as such should never be denied access to toys. One of our special memories is of watching Hyacinth Macaws at dawn in the wild. What was the first thing they did? Played amongst the palm fronds. They would hang upside-down flapping their wings vigorously. They would also slide down the leaves, falling off the end, then wheel and circle to return and slide again. Mock fighting would ensue with an equally playful neighbour. All of this took place before commencing the serious business of food-gathering, drinking and courting. Young macaws, both wild and captive, will find a stick or a stone on the ground and roll around with it in their feet. Cockatoos do the

Toys Suitable for a Parrot

Rope is durable and versatile and can be used to make swings, or toys to chew – see below.

A swing should be positioned in the cage where there is plenty of room for the parrot to swing freely.

A rope swing.

Softwood, coloured with harmless vegetable dye brightens up a cage/aviary and is great for nibbling.

A fun rope chew-toy.

Bells are enjoyed by parrots, but not necessarily by their owners!

same, and also enjoy recreational tree-chewing.

The mischievous Kea is well known for its antics of sliding down the roofs of houses, and also of dropping objects on to them just to enjoy the noise that this makes. Cars and other vehicles are fair game to this species, with the keas believing that windscreen-wipers, mirrors and tyres were put on cars solely for their amusement, and they are ready to remove or damage what they can.

Anyone who has seen a lory, amazon, or corella hanging upside-down, shrieking and then swinging upright again just to repeat the procedure, cannot fail to be impressed at the sheer joie de vivre this elicits. A simple shower of rain will send some parrots into an absolute frenzy of excitement. Knowing some of the antics performed by psittacines can help considerably in your choice of toys for the birds.

IMPORTANCE OF PLAY

Often caged birds are given a clutter of toys – often taking up valuable exercise space – whilst aviary birds are overlooked in their requirement for playthings. A little thought goes a long way in these situations, with perhaps one or two favoured toys being given to a bird in its cage, and a greater selection available on a play-stand. Several can be dotted around an aviary, giving the breeding occupants much-needed exercise and mental stimulation which can only improve their breeding success.

Too often pairs are kept in small breeding cages with only a perch and a nest box to break the monotony – and they do indeed reproduce. However, the long-term benefits of adequate space, plus stimulation from playthings, will become apparent when such well-kept birds carry on breeding after several years – not losing form like their bored counterparts kept in factory-farming conditions. It also has to be said that play and chew things go a long way towards preventing feather-plucking and chewing.

We find that if several weanling macaws are kept together, the tails and flights of the brethren become a target for chewing, which then leads to plucking. However, if they are given a quantity of chewable toys which are constantly replaced, this situation can be avoided.

TYPES OF TOY

What constitutes a toy and how do we differentiate between good and bad ones? Anything that the parrot finds interesting can be used as a toy if a little common sense is applied. Simple cardboard boxes, with any staples or sticky-tape removed, are great favourites, as are toilet-roll and kitchen-towel tubes. These are light, hygienic, and easily replaced when soiled. Most species will delight in making confetti out of these, and of any spare paper you choose to give to them.

Your imagination is the only limiting factor when it comes to these items. We found that a food treat inserted into one of these cardboard tubes, with the ends twisted to seal it in, elicited much excitement among the recipients. This is a simple toy that makes a noise, is easily destroyed and rewards the player with a treat at the end of it all.

FIR CONES

Fir cones are another great favourite and any number can be collected and kept in a cool dry place to be used at leisure. Again, these will be played with, chewed up and discarded. A food treat can be pushed into them to add even more interest. Aviary birds will derive great pleasure if the cones are laid on top of the flight and the birds can dismantle them from within.

TWIGS

Bunches of willow twigs hung from the roof will also provide the same sort of fun enjoyed by the wild Hyacinth Macaws on their palm fronds. As well as swinging and sliding on these, parrots will derive nutritional benefits from chewing the stalks, and also eating the buds and any insects attached to them.

Autumn berries, such as hawthorn and pyracanthus, left on the twigs will provide similar amusement as well as nutrition. You will notice that in the foregoing there is a theme involving a certain amount of chewed-up mess that accompanies playing parrots. This is the very nature of parrots – and surely a small price to pay for their happiness.

SOFTWOOD

Another easily obtainable and inexpensive item that can be used as a parrot toy is simple lengths of untreated softwood in various shapes and sizes. Many parrots will hold these like a corn-on-the-cob and nibble and whittle away at them with much relish.

If you are a creative type, you can drill a hole through the middle of several pieces of wood and thread them, kebab-like, on to a stout piece of wire to hang as a home-made toy from the cage or aviary top. Going a step further, the individual pieces could be dyed

Toys should be introduced gradually. African Greys are notoriously suspicious of anything new.

with a harmless vegetable dye to produce a rainbow of colours – parrots love colour.

Once again, you are only limited by time and imagination as to what you can produce. Going back to the food theme, holes can be drilled haphazardly over a length of timber, and food such as nuts inserted inside for the parrot to extract.

ROPE

Hemp rope is another greatly appreciated material, which can be used as horizontal perching, vertical swings or U-shaped swings. It has been used widely for parrots, and the varying diameters encourage healthy use of their feet. However, a note of caution: we once lost a weanling Blue and Gold Macaw through strangulation when it got its head stuck through a frayed length of rope and managed to twist it tight. Sadly, accidents can happen with almost anything, but this example is worth recording in the hope that it won't happen again: any frayed or stray bits of rope should be cut off, and the ends secured.

SWINGS

Talking of swings, these are a great favourite of many birds, cockatoos especially. Whether they are rope, wooden, or wood hung on wire, thought must be given to locating them where there is clearance, at full swing, of the tail in either direction. A recent innovation available to parrot keepers are the so-called pedicure perches. These are produced in roughened sandstone that helps keep the birds' nails in good condition, and when used on a swing seem to do a particularly good job.

BELLS

Bells have long been associated with parrot-like birds and cause great amusement to many psittacines. They should, however, be easily removable if the human inhabitants of the parrot area are not to be driven to distraction. The round bells with a ball in the middle are certainly not suitable for parrots, as they can get their beaks stuck in the holes, and the metal is often very sharp. The original bell shape, with a clanger hanging inside, is much more suitable, but care should be taken to ensure that no part of it is made of lead, as this will, of course, poison the bird.

HOOPS

We have found that hoops are great favourites. They should be large enough for the parrot's head to pass through them easily, and made of stainless steel, plastic or hard rubber. A single hoop hung around a perch will entertain for hours; or try putting a few on the 'T' stand, as parrots love throwing them off and hearing the thud as they hit the ground. The so-called Olympic rings, several hoops intertwined, also provide fun. We have heard of parrots becoming entangled in these, but if they are large and light enough this is unlikely.

YOGHURT POTS

Plastic yoghurt pots (with a little yoghurt still inside) are relished by many birds, who carefully lick it clean of the yoghurt and then proceed to dismantle the container. Care should be taken to ensure that there is no foil still attached as this can be ingested, with dire results.

ENCOURAGING PLAY

Some birds – notably African Greys – may be suspicious of new toys and if they suddenly appear in the cage this may cause a violent reaction from the bird. In these cases, if the toy is left near the cage where the bird can see it, and is gradually moved closer, this may elicit a more favourable response from the bird. Some birds find comfort in having a favourite toy near them at all times, whereas others have a low boredom threshold and need the stimulation of a constant procession of new toys. These should be a mixture of non-destructible and those that can be destroyed.

So far, having discussed toys for parrots, we should also think about playing with them (the parrots – not the toys). This may take the form of just shaking or rattling the toy to gain the parrot's attention. Some birds like to fetch toys in a dog-like manner, although rarely with such fervour as our canine companions. Some parrots also like to be rolled over, tickled and generally roughhoused. However, care must be taken not to go overboard and hurt the bird, or to encourage biting amid the excitement.

IF YOUR PARROT ESCAPES

Annette De Saulles

It is all too easily done. Your pet parrot spends so much time perched happily on your shoulder, you forget it's there – until you go into the garden just for a moment to put out the rubbish; or you answer a knock at the door. Then the sight of a neighbour's cat, a sudden noise, or strong gust of wind, and – disaster – your bird has taken fright and flown away.

Many parrot keepers do not realise that, even with clipped wings, their pet may still be able to achieve considerable height and distance in flight. Or they forget how long it is since the wing clip was done – and that the feathers have grown out again. Their bird may have got out of the habit of flying when in the safety of the home, but once outside in an unfamiliar environment, escaping from perceived danger remains instinctive.

Your bird did not intend to fly away from you, but it is now in a totally unfamiliar environment without a clue as to how to get back to its home.

Do not give up hope if your parrot escapes – there are many measures you can take.

PRACTICAL MEASURES

As you watch it disappearing over the tree tops, panic sets in. However, don't despair, as there is a lot that can be done. What is called for now are practical measures and being prepared for what may be many hours' determined searching, and – even when the bird has finally been located – waiting.

As your parrot flies off, keep a close eye on where it is going and head off yourself in that direction. The good news is that escaped territorial parrots do not usually go for many miles, but are often finally recovered quite close to home. Your confused bird will probably be unused to the exertion, and be

MAKING THE CONNECTION

A companion parrot that has a close bond with its keeper stands a better chance of being retrieved in the event of escape. A familiar communicating call or whistle can be very useful when trying to locate an escaped bird. And once located, a bird that will automatically step on to a hand or arm on command will be far easier to retrieve than one that has never been given this basic training.

MICRO-CHIPPING

Despite our best efforts, escapes or thefts do sometimes happen. Even after the bird is recovered, it is not always easy to prove it is yours. This has in some instances led to court proceedings over ownership.

Closed rings are one means of identification, although a micro-chip implant, which can be scanned for proof of identify, is the most satisfactory method, as it cannot be removed. Your avian vet will be able to advise on this.

looking for a place to perch. You may be lucky enough to see it land in a tree or on a roof. If not, make your way to where you saw the bird heading and scan any likely resting places. Call your pet's name and any other encouraging words, phrases or sounds it may recognise and respond to. You will probably get some funny looks from passers-by, but at least you'll be spreading the word that there is an escaped parrot in the neighbourhood.

Stay in the area and get someone to bring you a dish of your parrot's favourite foods, and maybe a familiar toy. Keep on calling, rattling the dish or toy, whistling – any sound you can think of that your bird will recognise. Get its favourite people to join you as you encourage it to respond. At this stage, it has been known for a very tame and bonded parrot to fly back down to its keeper. The chances are, though, that it is still too frightened at its unfamiliar surroundings to do anything other than sit silently in its tree. It may know you are there but be too confused to respond or know what to do next.

While you are attempting to locate your parrot by staying in its most likely landing area, get friends and family to inform neighbours of what has happened and ask

Moluccan Cockatoo and African Grey. Few keepers allow their birds outside to free-fly. A very close bonding should have been established before the idea is even considered.

Fitting a Parrot Harness

1. Place the harness collar over the lead.

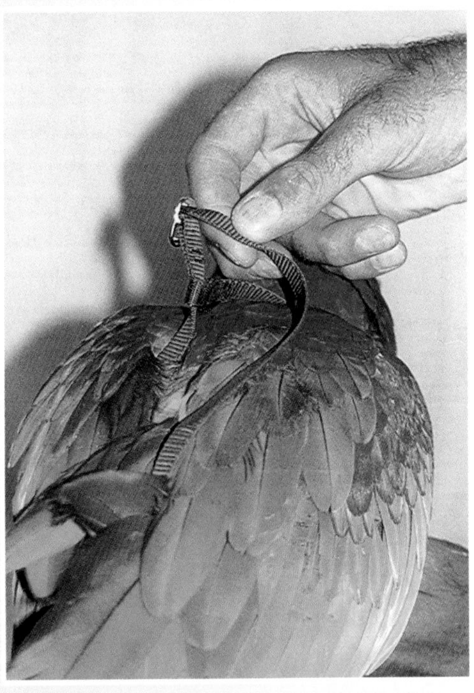

2. Place the second part of the harness under the wings.

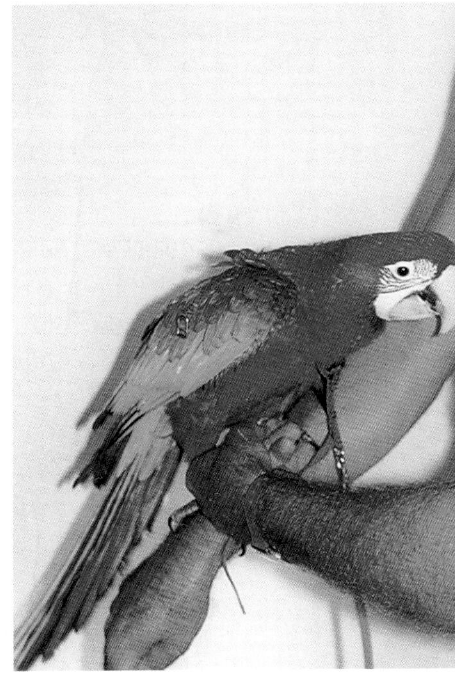

3. Place around the chest.

4. Fasten it together.

5. Finally, attach the lead to the bottom of the harness.

Pictured: Green-winged Macaw.

FREE-FLYING YOUR PARROT

There are a very few parrot keepers who allow their pet birds to free-fly. This can only be achieved where there is an exceptional level of bonding and communication between parrot and human. The bird is introduced to the outside environment in gradual stages, learning where its home boundaries are and of potential hazards, whilst remaining in close contact with its keeper at all times.

Some bird parks and zoos free-fly their large macaws. These birds are tame and bonded to their human keeper and will return for food. They are in less danger than, say, an amazon or parakeet, which might be attacked by crows or seagulls.

Please do not try free-flying your parrot unless you have a high level of experience and understanding of what is involved.

them to keep a close eye out. Post leaflets door to door, put up posters, inform the Police, local animal rescue sanctuaries, veterinary surgeries, local radio, TV stations and newspapers. Offer a reward – your parrot has a monetary value which might otherwise tempt the finder to keep it.

Parrots tend to be vocal at the beginning and end of the day. Even if your escaped bird has been silent all day, keep listening out for it. As the light fades, you may hear its distinctive voice above the sounds of the other birds. At this point, you may decide to stay up all night, watching and listening for your parrot, letting it know you are around.

At first light, you may well hear your bird, who by now is probably feeling hungry and might be more easily tempted with food.

CATCHING YOUR PARROT

Just when you'd given up all hope, there's that familiar call, some way away, high up in a tree in a neighbour's garden. What now? Calling in the fire brigade, or any other stranger with a ladder, is almost certainly guaranteed to frighten your bird away again. Patience is important now. Some people have had success by bringing the parrot's cage within sight, leaving bowls of tempting food inside and the cage door open. If this doesn't have results, be prepared – very slowly and carefully – to climb up to your bird.

Take food treats with you and make no sudden movements or sounds that may give alarm. Reaching the bird and recovering it may take some considerable time. As a last resort, it may be necessary to try catching it up with a net, but if you have taught your bird to step onto your hand on command, this could now pay real dividends.

Climbing down again and keeping your parrot secure at the same time presents a different set of problems. If it is familiar with a parrot harness, this is one possibility. Alternatively, a tame parrot may not object to being tucked inside a sweater or jacket.

Of course, your parrot may have disappeared without a trace when it flew off, and you have no idea where to start looking. Don't despair if this happens, but keep up public awareness of your missing bird. Leave its open cage in your back garden, with favourite foods and toys inside, go out calling at dawn and dusk, check local pet shops and notice boards. Parrots have been recovered after being missing for many days, so don't give up too soon.

HARNESSES

The advent of using harnesses on parrots has enabled us to take them with us when we are going out. This opens up a whole new avenue of enjoyment for the pet bird. Ideally, the harness needs to be introduced to baby hand-reared parrots as soon as they are large enough to wear it. Adults will become accustomed to them, but obviously this can be a little more stressful for them.

Babies can have them fitted every day and left on for an hour or two. In this way they quickly become accustomed to wearing them and don't object to having them fitted in the future.

Fitting them just involves placing the collar part over the parrot's head and then passing the second strap under the wings and around the body. This strap is passed through a loop and is then fastened. The harness should be comfortably snug-fitting, as, if it is too loose, it will chafe and annoy the bird and there is the possibility of trapping a toe or even a leg in the harness.

The lead then clips on to a ring either on the chest or between the wings on the back. It is prudent to fasten the lead by threading it through itself rather than just clipping it on. This way there is no chance of losing the bird if it is taken outside.

SAFETY MEASURES

If you have a suitable area to fly the parrot on the harness, then your only restriction is the length of lead that you attach to the bird. Obviously care must be taken to ensure that there is nothing for the parrot to get caught up on. Trees, barbed-wire fences and overhead cables are all potential danger zones. If two people are present, wonderful exercise can be given to the parrot by flying him between the two if he has been taught to fly to the hand.

Of course, harnesses should only be used under supervision and should be taken off if the parrot is to be left alone for any length of time. They certainly should not be left on, in the way a dog would wear a collar all the time. But with supervision, the harness is remarkably safe.

With the greater distribution of forces, the harness will not damage the parrot in any way, unlike the old-fashioned leg-chains. Thank goodness these are not in common usage these days. Many fractured legs and damaged ligaments resulted from the use of these chains in times past, not to mention the stress they caused to the poor wearer.

As with the leg chains, a parrot should never be tied to a fixed object by the harness. The resulting panic, if it did not damage the bird physically, would surely cause enough stress to create psychological damage.

6 CARING FOR YOUR PARROT

Parrots, if given conditions which maximise their potential, are very likely to live long and productive lives. There are husbandry techniques which will facilitate this and, although some techniques such as nail clipping may seem fraught with difficulty to start with, once the technique has been observed a few times, they shouldn't be beyond the capabilities of the majority of pet owners. If, for any reason, you don't feel confident with what you are doing, it is always preferable to seek the advice of either an experienced parrot-keeper or an avian vet.

Because parrots are both intelligent and emotional, it is extremely important that, when thinking of the care which they require, we don't just consider physical care. We need to include social care and psychological care, as these too are very important to parrots. Many people would argue that these two areas are more likely to give rise to concerns than the physical aspects – frequently the problem may manifest itself as a mixture of the three.

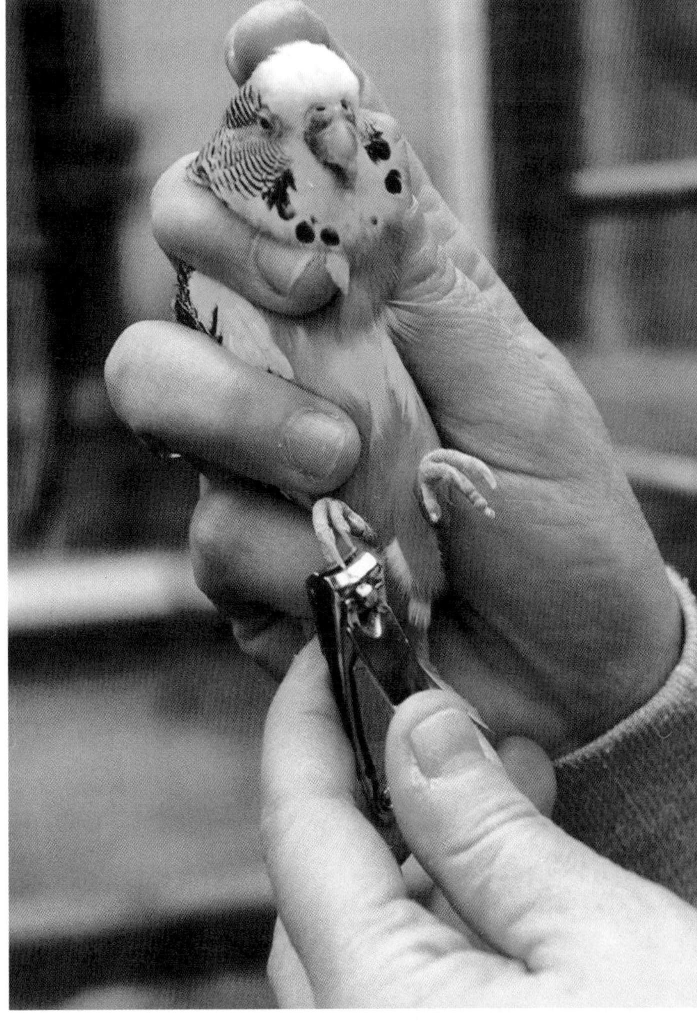

Clipping the nails of a tame budgerigar is considerably easier than when dealing with a much larger, and perhaps less co-operative, parrot.

HUSBANDRY TECHNIQUES

NAIL CARE

For parrots maintained in cages it is especially important to pay attention to the feet. Parrots benefit from grasping a range of different-sized perches. In cages this variety

Opposite page: Masked Lovebird.

of sizes is very restricted, and this can lead to callus formation where, because of the restricted perching areas, the foot has hardened areas of skin. Nails normally would be worn down by the variety of perches and surfaces, but in cages this doesn't happen, resulting in overgrown nails. If this isn't attended to, the nails can become caught as the parrot climbs, resulting in nail damage and in some instances in the total loss of the nail, which is extremely painful.

If you have a hand-reared young parrot, then it is wise to file the nails weekly whilst the parrot is on the stand, as this is a much kinder and stress-free way of dealing with the problem. Once this routine has become established even large parrots like macaws will offer their foot up for filing. It is only the sharp pointed ends of the nails that require filing. Once the pointed part has been removed the nail will wear down more easily as the parrot moves around. Having sharp nails can be quite painful for the owner, as the parrot naturally grasps for balance and sharp nails will easily penetrate human skin.

If your parrot's nails are long, and it won't tolerate filing, then you have no option but to clip the nails. It is always wise to be shown this procedure by an experienced aviculturist or vet. Normally one wouldn't expect any blood loss; if this occurs, too much of the nail has been removed. In some instances this may be what is required, perhaps for the collection of a blood sample for DNA sexing.

Equipment needed to cut your parrot's nails:

1. Catching net
2. Towel
3. Nail clippers
4. Bar of soap
5. Assistance of another person.

RESTRAINING YOU PARROT

The catching of the parrot needs to be as little frightening to the parrot as possible. If in an aviary, the parrot needs to be caught as quickly as possible using a catching net, with a padded rim to avoid injury. If the parrot is in a cage, it is preferable to catch it when out of the cage. If this is not possible, take the cage into a restricted area such as a bathroom.

The parrot should then be approached from behind with the towel, and the towel should quickly be placed over the parrot. One hand should grasp the bird's head to prevent the beak from moving and biting. The second hand should hold the tail and legs, and the towel should prevent the wings from flapping. If the parrot has been caught in the aviary with the net, the parrot needs to be taken out of the net and held in the towel as described above. It may be necessary to ask the assistance of another person to gently remove the toes from anything they may have grabbed, as it is quite a natural response for the parrot to make this grasping action.

NAIL-CUTTING

With the parrot firmly but gently restrained, it is useful to then use a table for a support. The assistant can lightly place the end of the towel over the parrot's head, as this will help the parrot to feel calmer. The assistant can then gently take one foot at a time and, using the nail clippers, remove the end of each nail. With birds with very overgrown nails, only a small amount should be removed as the blood vessels inside the nail will grow towards the end, and if a large amount is cut the nail will bleed. The longer nails will need to have further clipping at a later stage.

If a nail does start to bleed, the nail can be scraped against the bar of soap; this seals the nail and prevents bleeding. Occasionally the bleeding restarts an hour or so later when it

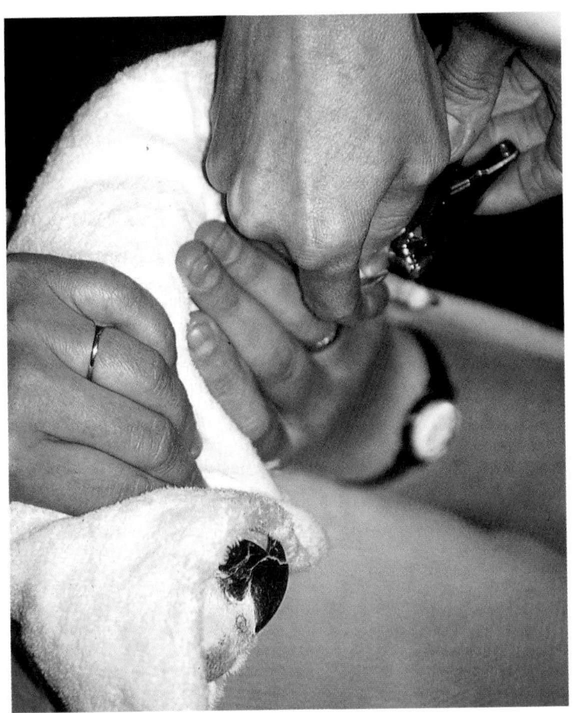

Gently restrain the parrot, and, with the help of an assistant, remove the end of each nail with clippers.

may be necessary to re-scrape the nail against the soap.

After both feet have been attended to, the parrot needs to be placed back into its normal environment as quickly as possible. If the parrot is a pet, a treat can be given which will help it to get over its ordeal.

If you need a blood sample for DNA sexing, there is a need to cut a nail slightly shorter. In this instance it is advisable to cut the nail 1/8 inch (3mm) at a time until bleeding starts. Do allow a short interval after the cut to see if the bleeding is starting. Nowadays it is possible to sex parrots using just three feathers, and this does seem much more preferable than sending blood samples.

When restraining parrots it is much better not to use gloves, as those that are thick enough to prevent pain from parrots' beaks are so thick that they don't allow enough sensitivity for you to know whether you are holding the parrot too tightly.

BEAK TRIMMING

Beak trimming shouldn't normally be required – if parrots are given sufficient toys and appropriate perches their beaks will remain at the correct length.

Some parrots that have had a previous injury to the beak may develop an area of the beak that overgrows. This is most commonly on the lower mandible. If left, the overgrowth can cause the lower mandible to scissor against the upper mandible, which can seriously restrict or even prevent feeding.

The procedure for beak trimming is very similar to that required for nail clipping, and again will require two people.

Parrots must be given the opportunity to chew – a wooden perch and durable toys should reduce the need for beak trimming. Pictured: African Grey.

The area of overgrowth should be gently nipped away using nail clippers. If the area is very overgrown, again only a small part should be removed at a time, which will prevent bleeding and pain. The ideal is to shape the mandible to the same contour as the part of the beak it should meet.

It is important that you supply perching and some wood which can be chewed, as this may prevent recurrence or slow down the overgrowth rate.

Overgrowth of the beak also sometimes occurs when parrots are old.

SPRAYING AND BATHING

All parrots benefit from bathing. Without opportunity for this, their plumage can appear dull and streaked. It is only fair to state, however, that some parrots seem to take a marked dislike to any contact with water on their plumage. In our experience, this dislike is overcome if a different technique is used, or if the bird is given time to get used to it.

Birds who do like bathing show their pleasure often in an extreme manner, vocalising and strutting about with their eyes blazing.

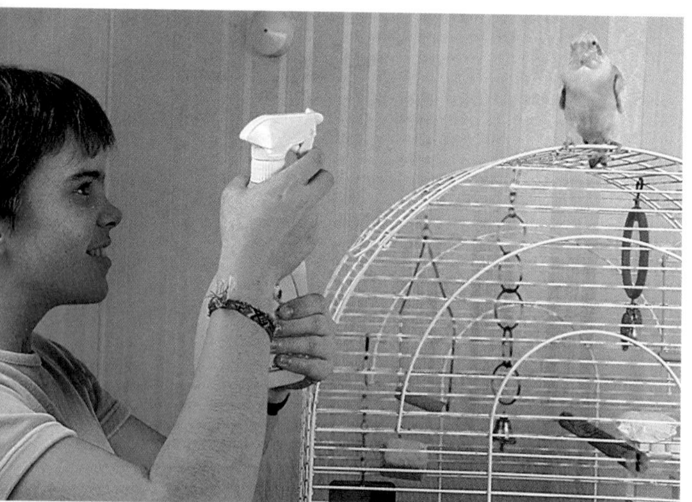

Cockatiel: regular bathing is necessary to keep the parrot's plumage in tip-top condition.

PET BIRDS

Pet birds really do benefit from bathing. The heating in homes produces a very dry atmosphere that can make feathers brittle and dry. If your pet is a young hand-reared specimen, it is quite an easy matter to mould their behaviour into what makes it easiest for the household. Some parrots prefer being sprayed with a spray bottle, and these can be obtained very cheaply from hardware stores. Others prefer a container, in which they can sit and bathe themselves.

We tend to teach our young parrots to bathe in the sink. We fill the sink with about an inch (2.5cm) of water, and then allow a small amount of water to run from the tap. Most parrots have tremendous fun in the water in this way, and it helps to prevent water from being distributed all over the place. We know of other pet owners who take their pet into the shower or bath with them.

The difference in the plumage of parrots that regularly bathe is really quite marked. The plumage appears much more colourful with a greater depth and lustre. Clean plumage allows the parrots to more fully utilise the feathers for regulating their temperature. Parrots that are at a comfortable temperature keep their feathers close to their body, but as the temperature goes down, they fluff up their feathers to keep an insulating cavity of air against their skin. Feathers that are clean and free from the grime of their environments can more easily move to accommodate fluctuating temperature changes.

When either spraying or bathing in containers, it is preferable to use water of approximately 70-75° F (21-24°C). For those parrots unused or not keen on the prospect, it is better to spray them gently on their stand, as this gives them some added security. Most parrots quickly get used to being sprayed and accommodate this by opening their wings and offering any dry bits for spraying.

A Blue and Gold Macaw after bathing. Note the nictating membrane – the third eyelid – over the eye. This membrane helps to protect the eye from dust and grit.

As already stated, this is usually accompanied by vocalising and much posturing. As a word of warning, parrots in this state can prove quite mischievous and may quite uncharacteristically nip when handled.

For parrots new to this it is better to spray them only lightly to start with, and then to gradually increase the amount of water as they become accustomed to it. Plumage will change colour when wet; it generally becomes much darker. Some green parrots, such as amazons take on a brown appearance.

Some parrots take a dislike to sprays. For these birds it is worth offering them a container of water at the same time that you spray them, as some parrots who dislike being sprayed will, when returned to their cages, immediately attempt to start bathing in their water dish.

It is always preferable to bath your parrot earlier in the day, as this allows the plumage to dry prior to the bird roosting for the night.

Pet parrots need bathing at least weekly, the ideal being two or three times per week.

AVIARY PARROTS

Parrots which have access to the elements rarely need to be bathed, as they will take delight in hanging upside-down on the roof of the flight, with their wings out-stretched trying to have contact with as many raindrops as possible. There will be the occasional parrot who will rush into the shelter at the first sign of rain, and these will require spraying as for the pet parrot.

Bathing is frequently a communal activity and once one starts several others will join in, until all the surrounding area has been splashed.

Aviary parrots, like the pet parrot, will often show a preference for bathing either in a container or from a spray. In an aviary situation parrots are less bothered by the temperature variations. It is not unusual for some parrots to bath in water where the ice has just been broken. We have several parrots that do this, and none appear to have suffered any ill-effects by doing so.

Parrots in an outside situation do appear to bath less in winter, and also when breeding.

Some aviary parrots generally bathe themselves by hanging upside-down in the rain, wings outstretched. Pictured: Red-tailed Black Cockatoo.

HYGIENE

Although parrots can generally be described as being hardy, it is important that a good level of hygiene is maintained in order to minimise infection.

Those in cages need to have the cage cleaned thoroughly at least weekly. On a daily basis, it is necessary to replace the newspaper from the bottom of the cage and to clean away droppings that may adhere to the grids that are often used on the bottom of the cages. The water and food dishes need to be cleaned daily, and fresh water and food replaced if these become soiled during the day. It is particularly important to remove any food that is moist in warm weather after a couple of hours, as bacteria can colonise very rapidly in warm, moist conditions.

Perches need to be cleaned and replaced regularly and any parrot toys will also need to be cleaned weekly or more frequently if they become soiled. Disposable toys such as fir-cones can be replaced daily if soiled.

Hygiene measures in the aviary situation are very similar. In warm weather after a few hours, the food that has fallen on the floor ideally needs to be removed daily, although

The bottom of the cage should be cleaned regularly.

most parrots won't pick up uneaten food from the floor.

In the aviary, it is useful to ensure that in areas where birds roost there is an easy means of removing the resulting droppings. This can be accomplished by placing paving slabs on an earth floor that can be scrubbed. If some sand is sprinkled on the paving slab, this makes it much easier to clean away. Similarly, on floors made of concrete, a sprinkling of sand in areas of fouling will make the cleaning much easier.

There are purpose-made disinfectants for aviary use, and it is personal preference if you choose to use one of these. If you have a range of aviaries, a pressure washer can save time. However, it is important to ensure that there is a gully or drain to wash the water down.

In suspended cages, there is still a need to remove the adhering droppings and food. Those which have fallen through will also need cleaning away at regular intervals, as leaving them will encourage flies, rats and mice.

RODENT CONTROL

It is important, particularly in an aviary situation, to put in some control measures as soon as there is any sign of rodent activity. Rodents will cause parrots stress, and can lead to a cessation of breeding activity, and other stress-control behaviours such as feather-plucking.

Rats and mice will quickly colonise in an aviary situation, where they often have unlimited access to food, water and warmth. They urinate frequently, which opens the door to disease. Rats will also physically attack parrots and eat both eggs and chicks. If the parrot has even a small bite, the resulting bacterial infection will frequently cause death.

Most aviculturists put in their own measures to rid themselves of rodents, but it is also possible to employ a rodent controller, either on a once-only basis or on a contract where they take on regular responsibility for the task.

There are four main controlling agents for rodents.

1. Poisons
2. Traps
3. Ultrasonic devices
4. Prevention.

By far the best method of controlling rodents is to prevent their entry. This is best achieved when the aviary is being constructed, and involves concrete floors and mesh which is small enough to prevent rodent access. For the larger parrot, the usual size of mesh available at the correct gauge is 1 inch x 1 inch (2.5cm). Unfortunately, this will not prevent the access of mice, though it will prevent rats.

POISONS

These are widely available from hardware stores and should be placed in runs. These are the pathways where the rodent normally travels. The poison must be placed in such a way that it is not accessible to the birds or domestic animals such as dogs and cats. If there are holes present, it is a simple process to place the poison directly into the hole and cover this with a tile or brick. In outside areas, the tubular down-pipes of guttering systems can be helpful for placing the poison inside.

If you live in a rural situation it is likely that you will need to place poison or traps each year from September, or when the weather becomes cooler. It is important to use gloves when handling poisons. Many of the poisons do not work immediately, but rely on the rodent taking a small amount daily. The amount the rodent eats can be assisted by the removal of uneaten foods particularly before dark, when the rodents' activity is likely to be at its greatest.

TRAPS

These come in two basic designs. One captures the rodent without killing it, and the other kills it. The humane traps that don't kill are available in designs that will allow for the capture of several rodents. It is important if you release the rodents to do so a few miles from home, as studies have indicated that they will return to an area. It is also important that they are released in an area where they won't become a nuisance to others. If these traps are not checked at least daily, the rodents will suffer a cruel death where they will literally starve from lack of food and water.

In conventional traps, any dead rodents need to be removed regularly and the trap reset. Most traps work best if placed against a wall, as it is natural for rodents to skirt areas rather than walk across open spaces. Occasionally rodents will be caught in traps but not killed. In these situations it is important that they are dispatched as quickly as possible to avoid suffering.

Some rodents appear to get wise to particular traps and locations. It is then necessary to be inventive in changing the location, the bait and, if necessary, the trap itself. There are several different designs on the market. Bait that we have used successfully in traps includes chocolate, cheese, peanuts, hulled sunflower, butter, bread, carrot and apple. Whichever bait is used – and the type used may vary with the type of trap used – it is important that the rodent has problems getting the bait, otherwise you may have a situation where the bait is removed and the trap remains set.

ULTRASONIC DEVICES

These are relatively new on the market, only being available for the last few years. They work by emitting a sound which is outside the range of certain animal forms, including humans, but is unpleasant to others, in this case, rodents. They do need to be used with care, as rodents may include pet rabbits and guinea pigs. Most are for use inside buildings, where the sound can bounce off the available walls. Some have a small control that allows the frequency of the sound to be changed, as rodents appear to become desensitised to certain frequencies. These devices usually have another control that allows you to hear the frequency transmitted. They normally run on electricity.

The sound emitted is, in theory, meant to be so unpleasant to rodents that they choose to go and take up residence elsewhere, and we have used one machine with partial success.

Interestingly, a machine has now been developed for use outside to deter cats. It may prove very useful, as a cat on top of an aviary is a particular nuisance.

SIGNS OF RODENT INFESTATION

- Evidence of droppings. These may be on surrounding surfaces, or even in food and water dishes. Rats have much larger droppings than mice, about the size of guinea-pig droppings.
- Gnawing of woodwork, outside the area where parrots can gnaw.
- Smell. Mice in particular have quite a distinctive sweet smell. For the smell to be apparent there is usually quite a large infestation.
- A rise in the amount of food which the parrots are eating.
- A general unease in the parrots which can result in behavioural disorders, such as feather-plucking, or cessation of breeding activity.
- Chewed newspaper in areas where the parrots are unlikely to put it or have access to it. Sometimes paper is brought into the aviary area.
- Wounds on the parrot, particularly on the legs and feet, for which no cause can be found.
- Disappearance of eggs and young.
- Parents of young parrots may have wounds on their faces and head where they have attempted to ward off the rodents.
- Some parrots will have no hesitation in killing small rodents, such as mice, in which case you will find their sometimes quite mangled bodies in the bottom of enclosures.
- Discovery of a cache of food items; sometimes this can be very large.

Blue-throated Macaws: check your aviary parrots regularly. Wounds around the legs and feet may indicate the presence of rats.

If you do have signs of rodent infestation it is important that you check the aviary area for possible places where the rodents may have taken up residence. Sometimes the 'homes' can be much nearer than you believe possible. Unused nest boxes are favourite places for either nests or stores of food. It is important to clean all areas using a broad-spectrum disinfectant. You should use rubber gloves when doing this to prevent possible infection from urine.

The control of rodent infestation can appear quite daunting and can prove extremely anxiety-provoking – in some owners to the degree that they feel it necessary to stop keeping parrots altogether. It is perhaps most sensible to accept that keeping any form of livestock can have the potential of encouraging vermin. The control of vermin, although at times challenging, is relatively easy and quite manageable if dealt with in the longer term.

THE PSYCHOLOGICAL/SOCIAL WELL-BEING OF YOUR PARROT

Parrots are intelligent, inquisitive, and affectionate beings who normally coexist either with a single partner, who they are quite devoted to, or with a flock outside of their reproductive period. Because of this they can become quite emotionally traumatised by being deprived of affection, security and variety.

The distress that they exhibit can, in some parrots, be quite overt, as is commonly seen in newly imported parrots where their fear and distress is demonstrated by alarm calls, growling, and attempts to hide. They may also descend into sheer panic, which involves them throwing themselves around the cage or aviary, and in the process causing traumatic injuries. In some ways this overt distress, which is so upsetting to humans, can be easier to manage because it is easily

Lovebirds: parrots are generally sociable creatures. If deprived of attention or contact, there can be serious consequences.

identifiable. Perhaps more difficult is the tame parrot who is so stressed by their environment that they quietly mutilate themselves or exhibit stereotypical behaviour traits which appear to result in them losing contact with reality.

There are examples of quite extreme behaviours. Most common perhaps, are those parrots that start to feather-pluck, are very noisy, or start stereotypical actions, such as clicking the bars of the cage. Enrichment programmes are, as the name suggests, ways of adding a richness to the parrot's existence, and this alone may be enough to stop the adverse behaviour.

Parrots need affection, if not from another parrot, then from a loving owner. Parrots that are pets in cages need to have time spent with them. Most, as they get older, appear to enjoy a routine when they can be let out of their cages at similar times each day. More ideal is for the parrot to be stand-trained, but it should not be expected that this will take the place of affection. Most parrots that are tame enjoy a time when they are given attention totally to the exclusion of all else. In our household, this is often when watching television, which is cheating slightly, but the parrots don't appear to mind.

During this time of 'mutual affection,' the parrot will naturally expect to have their feathers tickled and stroked. Some have particular areas that they find pleasurable, such as being tickled under the wing, whereas other parrots may feel this is a real liberty not to be tolerated. Most prefer their heads being given attention. The parrot in return will want to be as close to you as possible, and they too will want to give attention to your head and, as confidence grows, you may well allow this. In our household, the preening of eyelashes and eyebrows is the expected norm.

Some would argue that this practice is dangerous and the risk of the parrot inflicting injury, especially near the eyes, should be

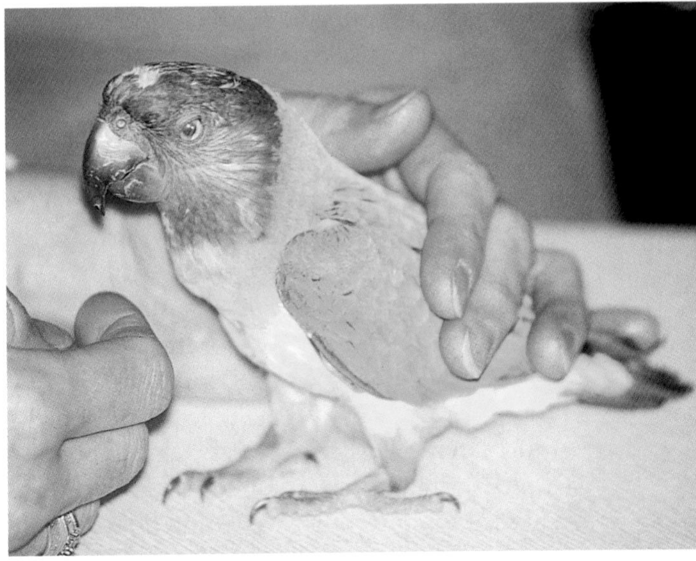

Some parrots enjoy being stroked, though others may not tolerate it. Pictured: Senegal Parrot.

avoided at all cost. Parrot owners have to make their own choice. The affection that a parrot bestows upon their chosen has really to be experienced to be appreciated. Parrots also need to feel secure in their surroundings; they are naturally very responsive to changes in their environment. In the wild, not being responsive could result in their capture by a predator; this 'move away quickly' trait is therefore essential.

STRESSFUL SITUATIONS

If parrots are kept in situations that give them cause for anxiety, they are likely to suffer greatly because it is not possible for them to be able to fly from a perceived danger. In a caged situation this is particularly acute, as the range of movement is so restricted. However, even in an aviary situation where the ability to move away is greater, stress can still be caused. We have a Red-bellied Macaw that will feather-pluck when there is a particularly bad thunderstorm, and we also have a Blue-fronted Amazon who will pluck her chest and legs bare if mice have managed to find their way into the aviary.

As previously stated, cages need to be sited in a position where the parrot is free from draughts, ideally near a corner, and away from temperature extremes. Sunlight shining directly into the cage can be quite uncomfortable for parrots if they cannot get away from it. It is important to ensure that the parrot feels safe – and parrots will have individual ideas of what they consider anxiety-provoking or not. For instance, some parrots will have absolutely no worries at all about a cat being near the cage, whereas others may feel very uncomfortable about it. Similarly, in aviaries, some birds become stressed by things that we would not consider to be overly worrying.

VITAL STIMULATION

Coupled with this need for security is the balance required of not allowing your parrot to become bored. As stated, parrots are highly intelligent and inquisitive beings which have need for change, even though on occasions this change gives a temporary increase in anxiety. In the cage situation, parrots will appreciate a regular change of toys. It is a good idea to have several toys of varying designs so that they can be changed at regular intervals.

As mentioned previously in Chapter Five, it is also beneficial to have disposable toys, those that are expected to be destroyed and thrown away. Included within this are items such as fir-cones, toilet roll tubes and discarded small cardboard boxes. Some woods such as elder are quite soft, and many parrots will gain immense pleasure from quickly gnawing this wood into small slivers. Perches should be changed regularly and be of varying thickness. This will give the parrot's feet good exercise and the spring of the smaller twigs adds a further dimension.

Different foods such as nuts in their shells and, for a change, whole small apples also add interest for the parrot. Some successful enrichment programmes have included food activities, where morsels of food are hidden in and around items in the cage. This means that the parrot has to actively seek out the food to eat.

NEED FOR COMPANY

In an aviary situation loneliness tends not to be as acute as in cages, but it does still exist. Most aviary parrots are in a pair, therefore, it is likely that the affection is taken care of. Of course, if the pair are not compatible, then affection has not been addressed. An easy and quick way of checking this is to look for unopened feather sheaths around the head: normally parrots who are compatible, or at least friendly, will preen their partner's head-feathers, thus removing these. Some parrots, including the large Macaws will regularly preen one another and even mate, but will produce infertile eggs. However, if their partners are swapped, they then breed successfully, thus demonstrating that they were not compatible even though they appeared to be and may have been together as a pair for several years.

Most aviary birds live in pairs. Pictured: Red-topped Amazons.

Some macaw breeds enjoy preening their partners. Pictured: Illiger's Macaw.

If parrots are not obviously compatible, and a reasonable time has elapsed for them to get to know one another, it is preferable to try a different partner. Sometimes the results of this can be very surprising. Parrots who do not really get on find it particularly stressful being in an enclosed space together; this is particularly true for the subservient member of the pair who may be frightened of the dominant partner.

Some compatible pairs of parrots can find changes to their aviary, which we would consider pleasing and healthy, quite anxiety-provoking. An example to illustrate this was when we introduced some fresh perches, with green vegetation attached, to an established pair of parrots. They went off their food, spent as little time as possible in the shelter part of their accommodation where the greenery was, and were quite anxious-looking in their appearance, regularly uttering alarm calls and not appearing to rest.

This situation was resolved totally by the removal of the greenery. Within 30 minutes the pair was acting quite normally. The changes to their environment had been too great for them to cope with. They eventually did accept fresh perches with greenery, but this was accomplished in small steps by gradually increasing the amount of vegetation. On reflection, their behaviour was not extreme. They were captive-bred in very stark but hygienic conditions, and it was probably unlikely that they had been allowed to have anything to do with vegetation, their early socialisation being in an artificially lit, temperature-controlled building where there were several suspended aviaries.

Parrots in aviary situations still have the need to explore and chew. This is quite natural, and good husbandry requires that we should make a decision regarding what is acceptable for parrots to have and what is not. We made the decision that we would not allow them to have the aviary framework, but the nest boxes, perches and other disposable items were theirs to chew and explore.

SAFEGUARDING YOUR PARROT'S FUTURE – WILLS AND TRUST FUNDS

Annette De Saulles

Unlike pet cats or dogs, parrots can be a lifetime's commitment. Cockatiels can live to about 25 years of age, African Greys to 50 and the large macaws and cockatoos can reach 100 years of age or even more. Yet how many of us consider the bird's life-span when we take it on?

It is important to make the right provision for your parrot in the event that it outlives you. Simply stating in your will that you wish your daughter or neighbour to take on the bird after your death may not be appropriate. Your beloved pet may seem to another person as no more than a nuisance, to be sold on through a local advertisement or pet shop.

FINDING THE RIGHT PERSON

You need to ensure that your daughter/neighbour/friend really wants to look after your parrot. Ask yourself the following questions:

- Do they understand the bird's needs?
- Do they know about the level of care and attention it is used to?
- Could they afford possible vet's fees?
- Would they make suitable provision for the bird if their own circumstances subsequently changed?
- Does the bird know the prospective new keeper – and, importantly, like him or her?

Finding the right person to take on your parrot is, therefore, the most important first step. You can then include a suitable clause in your will expressing your wishes and possibly including a bequest to the new carer for their trouble.

With a life-span of around 25 years, the Cockatiel is one of the more short-lived breeds.

Establishing a trust fund and nominating a suitable trustee will safeguard your parrot's future. Pictured: Green-winged Macaw.

TRUST FUND

An alternative to the above is to establish a trust fund to secure your parrot's future welfare. Money cannot be left directly to your parrot, so the trust would be administered by a carefully chosen trustee, who would ensure that money or property left by you for the benefit of your parrot would be used specifically as requested by you, to continue for the lifetime of your bird. Rather than just leaving a one-time lump sum, funds can be made available over time on a regular basis to ensure ongoing care and provision.

As before, it is essential that the trustee is willing to take on this task, and also that a secondary trustee is held in reserve, in case this becomes necessary through the original trustee's death or inability to continue with his or her duties.

Another point to consider – to protect the parrot against a breach of trust – would be to appoint joint trustees, who will keep an eye on each other, what's happening to the money and, of course, the parrot's welfare.

The important thing when setting up a trust, once a reliable trustee has been found, is to be very clear and precise in your instructions as to how your bird is to be cared for and how funds are to be used. Monetary compensation for the trustee is usual and this should help ensure a continuing compliance with the arrangement.

Some parrot keepers prepare in advance a detailed account of their bird's lifestyle and routine, its past history, food/toy likes and dislikes, vocabulary, etc. This is one way of ensuring the new keeper will understand your bird's preferences and provide the routine and diet it is familiar and happy with.

To avoid any unforeseen problems, it is always a good idea to seek legal advice when considering the future of your parrot. The law will vary in some countries (and between States in the USA). A solicitor will be able to advise on the best form of wording on the will or trust document to ensure that your express wishes are understood and carried out for as long as your bird lives.

THE SICK PARROT

Anyone who keeps either one parrot or several may eventually have a sick bird. This will either be as a result of trauma, perhaps caused by fighting with a fellow parrot or being attacked by a cat, or as a result of a disease process resulting from an infection or failure of an internal organ.

Regularly check your parrot – even if he is healthy. Pictured: Rosa Bourkes in peak condition.

The appearance of an ill parrot may vary depending upon the cause. The owner of the parrot will have the best knowledge of the routines that give the parrot its own individuality. Because of this, the owner may intuitively recognise that something is not quite right, even though it may take further exploration to find out exactly what is wrong. The smallest signs may be as simple as a pet parrot that is quieter than usual or, in a communal aviary setting, a parrot that is perching in a different place.

It is quite natural for birds to attempt to hide any signs of weakness or illness, as, in their natural habitat, their predators will be astute at picking out any signs which will give them a better chance of an easy meal. For this reason many parrots will appear normal even when they are in reality quite sick.

Because of this, often the parrot is really very ill by the time the owner notices. It is common for the parrot to be found on the floor of the cage or aviary, the feathers fluffed up and the eyes shutting. Sometimes the breathing is laboured and noisy, and the tail may bob with each breath (tail pumping). If the parrot is found exhibiting all or some of these signs, it is important that it is taken to a vet, preferably an avian vet or, if you are not near one, to a general veterinary surgeon.

Before taking the parrot to the vet, it is useful to look out for other signs that may assist the diagnosis, such as abnormal droppings. If this is the case, take a sample with you. There may be signs of blood loss, vomiting or regurgitation.

A parrot in this poor physical condition needs to be treated as gently as possible, causing the least amount of stress. It is useful to get everything ready before physically moving the parrot.

VISITING THE VET

1. Phone the vet to arrange when you will take the parrot.
2. Have the carrying box ready with fresh newspaper in the bottom. If the parrot is unsteady, put in a towel for it to grip.
3. Remove perches from the carrying box.
4. Have the car ready for the journey.
5. Make sure you take relevant information for the vet – age, previous medical conditions, any known allergies etc.

With everything ready it is then time to pick up the parrot. In an aviary situation, if the parrot can still move, it is often simpler to use a net to catch the parrot quickly. But it is preferable to approach the parrot from behind using a towel to restrain it, and grasping it behind the jaws to prevent it biting, with the second hand holding the feet and tail.

It is important not to grasp the parrot's middle as parrots rely heavily on their abdominal muscles when breathing. If you restrict these muscles, you are further reducing the parrot's respiration, which can in turn lead to suffocation.

If the parrot is unsteady, put the towel in the travelling box with it, as this will give the parrot something to hold on to. Ideally, someone will accompany you to the vet, so that there is someone to hold the box on their lap to prevent it from slipping around.

Sometimes it will not be possible for the vet to make a diagnosis then and there, as further tests may be necessary. However, the vet is likely to prescribe care and treatment for the presenting symptoms, in order to alleviate suffering and prolong life. If it is not possible to see the vet immediately – by far the most preferable option – you will need to take action to assist the parrot.

NEEDS OF A PARROT PATIENT

1. Warmth.
2. Removal from others – either other parrots, or noisy areas of the home.
3. Tempting items of food.
4. Use of probiotic and electrolyte solution.

PRIORITIES FOR A SICK BIRD

Warmth ideally needs to be given up to 30 degrees centigrade (86F). We use infra-red dull emitters (with a ceramic element). These do not give light, but give a concentrated heat to a certain area. This means that it is possible for the parrot to move away from the heat source if it becomes uncomfortable.

Heat is extremely important when caring for shocked or ill birds and must never be underestimated. At times the application of heat has quite dramatic positive results. We would firmly recommend all parrot keepers to keep a heat lamp – the above-mentioned one will last for many years for emergencies.

The ill parrot needs to be removed from others. A parrot that is sick may have infections which can be passed to other parrots, and an ill parrot will be stressed, resulting in the immune system being compromised. In effect this means that it will be more prone to catching infections from others.

If the parrot is a home pet, it is preferable to move the parrot to an area of low activity. The reduction in stimulus will allow the parrot to rest. In this state your parrot will not appreciate such things as loud music or the use of vacuum cleaners, so it is important to make other members of the household aware of the needs of the sick parrot.

If you have an enclosed shelter in an aviary, it is possible to set up the heat in a restricted area. This will prove much less stressful for your parrot than bringing it into the house. There is still a need, in this type of

Lutino Cockatiel: try to tempt your parrot with something appetising if he refuses to eat.

set-up, to allow sufficient room for the parrot to move away from the heat source should it wish to.

Parrots that are quite sick will often eat even just prior to dying. So the fact that your parrot is eating should not lull you into a false sense of security, or into believing that the bird is not seriously ill. However, the reverse is also true, and for this reason you should make attempts to tempt the parrot to keep eating regularly.

Most owners are well aware of what the parrot's favourite items of food are. If the food is soft and moist, it will need replacing regularly as, with the heat, bacteria will colonise the food rapidly. If the parrot will not eat, it will need urgent veterinary care.

The vet may decide that the parrot requires tube feeding. This necessitates passing a tube into the crop. A food solution or drugs can then be passed through the tube into the crop. It is not advisable to undertake this procedure without being shown the correct method, because of the serious complications that can arise from this.

Specialist bird care companies supply quick-energy electrolyte solutions. These are high in calories and salts. They will quickly give the parrot extra calories and at the same time replace any valuable salts which may have been lost due to the illness.

Illness can upset the natural balance of the gut flora, and for this reason probiotics have been found to be extremely beneficial for the ill and stressed bird. Probiotics are preparations that contain gut-friendly bacteria known as lactic acid bacteria.

Illness and stress can quickly cause the multiplication of harmful gut bacteria. The regular use of probiotics during periods of illness and stress will help to ensure that the gut is not over-colonised by harmful bacteria that would further jeopardise the health of the parrot.

It must be emphasised that the parrot will require veterinary attention as soon as possible, especially if no improvement is noted.

AVIAN VETERINARY SURGEONS

These are vets who have specialist knowledge and expertise in treating birds. In addition to this, their practice will hold specialist equipment, drugs and diets for bird use. For these reasons, it is particularly useful if you can locate the nearest practice that specialises in this way.

It is unfortunately often the case that your nearest may be several miles away – lists of avian vets are regularly published in parrot magazines. Even though the avian vet of your choice may be several miles away, it is still worth seeing them for a consultation, as many will then agree to your general vet phoning for advice should the need arise in an emergency. Many avian vets give talks and presentations at local bird clubs and societies, and in this way you can make a decision as to which would best suit your needs.

Avian vets are specialist practitioners who have frequently undertaken extra training and have had to purchase specialist equipment for their practice. The treatment and care that they prescribe is consequently often expensive, and for this reason it is advisable to insure your parrot. This is relatively inexpensive if you only have a few birds and it will give you the security of being able to have necessary treatment without the worry of a vet bill that may be particularly large.

GIVING MEDICATIONS

At some point in your parrot's life, there will come a time when it will require medicines. These are likely to be in one of the following forms: oral medicines, injections, and topical applications.

ORAL MEDICATION

It is much easier to medicate a parrot that is tame. If hand-reared, they will often take food from a spoon, even though they may not have done this for several years. It can then be quite a simple matter to camouflage a crushed tablet or add a solution to some favourite items of food.

The same can be achieved with parrots in an outdoor aviary, which again will often accept medication that has been hidden in a favourite item. It is important, however, that no other parrots have access to the medicated

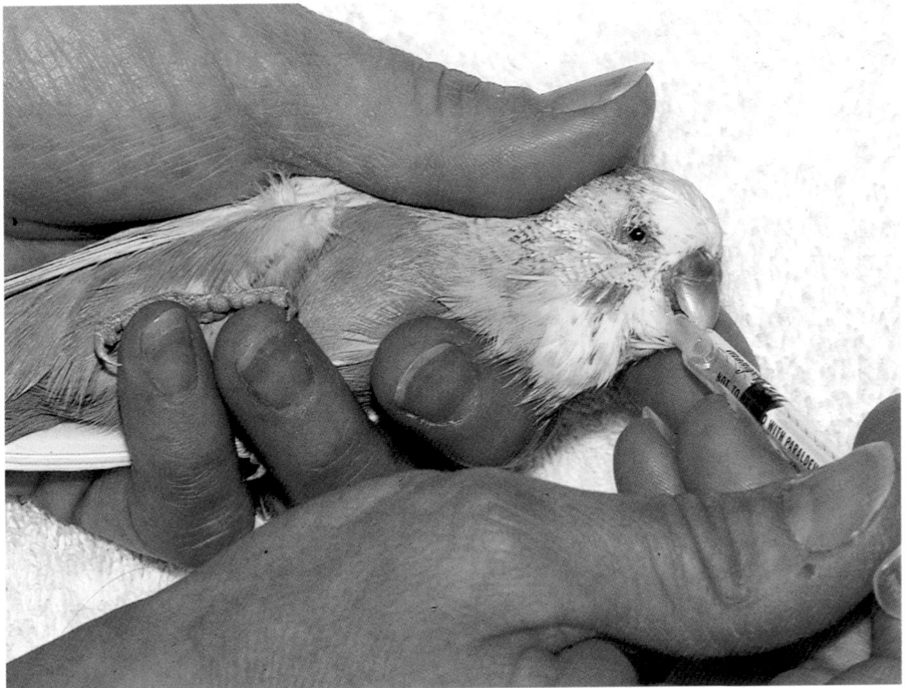

Budgerigar: if your parrot will not accept 'doctored' food, medication will have to be given orally via a syringe.

food. It is therefore simpler to separate a pair of parrots as a temporary measure.

Giving medicines in this way is always preferable, as it does not cause anxiety to what may already be quite a debilitated bird.

If your parrot will not accept 'doctored' food, more invasive techniques may be required. It is possible to crush tablets and mix them into a liquid or to ask for a syrup form of the medication from the vet. It is then possible for one person to restrain the parrot and a second person to slowly drip the solution into the beak, usually with the aid of a syringe. This needs to be undertaken very slowly, as it is important that the parrot does not choke on the solution.

Some parrots can be extremely resistive to this, to the point where very little of the medication is being successfully administered. If this is the case, it is wise to discuss the situation with your vet who may advise a different route of administration.

USING A CROP TUBE

The vet may suggest the use of a crop tube to give medication or food. If you have not carried out this procedure yourself, ask the vet to show you how to do it. Crop tubes can be rubber or stainless steel. Some of the metal crop tubes have a crimp on the end to help prevent the tube from accidentally entering the trachea (airway) instead of the crop.

It is preferable for two people to undertake this procedure, the first to restrain the parrot in a towel (see Nail Clipping) and the second person to pass the tube.

Before approaching the parrot with the tube, it is important to check that the tube does not contain any food or medicines that could obstruct the airway while the procedure is being carried out.

If the person holding the parrot's beak exerts slight pressure on the jaws, this will open the bird's beak. You can allow the bird to bite a metal tube. The tube needs to be rolled over the tongue to the left side of the bird. The tube is then passed down the throat and into the crop. You should be able to feel the tube in the crop. The syringe containing the food or drug can then be attached to the crop tube.

The plunger on the syringe must be gently and slowly pushed down without overfilling the crop. Then withdraw the tube gently. Once you have become skilled in this technique, it can be a safe and effective way of giving both medication and food.

INJECTIONS

Giving medication by injection has some advantages over the oral route. Gut absorption can be variable. As a result drug dosage can be less accurate, and higher concentrations of the drug can be achieved in the blood stream by injecting the drug. In addition, some drugs are destroyed by the gastric juices.

Injections are usually given intramuscularly into the breast muscle. If you have to give a course of injections, it is preferable to vary the site; for example, right side then left side.

- The parrot will need to be restrained in a towel by an assistant.
- Some vets will advise that the area of the injection be swabbed with an alcohol swab.
- The drug should be drawn up ready in the syringe before restraining the parrot.
- Once the needle is in the muscle, pull back the plunger slightly.
- If blood comes into the syringe, you have entered a blood vessel, therefore you will need to withdraw the needle and inject in a different place.
- When the needle is correctly sited, the plunger should be slowly pushed down.
- When the injection has been completed, the needle should be taken out and the area gently massaged.

As you are using an invasive technique, it is important that you wash your hands before and after the procedure. The needle and syringe should be disposed of safely.

TOPICAL APPLICATIONS

This refers to giving medication externally, most commonly to the skin or by means of eye drops. Caution is needed with either, and would not normally be used unless prescribed by a vet.

Eye-drops can be quite a stressful procedure especially for a not-tame bird. If the eye-drops need to be given more than once a day, it is preferable to cage the parrot, as this reduces the stress of being caught. There is a need to put either the ointment or the drops directly into the eye, which may necessitate restraining the parrot.

Direct application of ointments on to the skin is usually avoided if possible, as they clog up the feathers. This will prevent the feathers from functioning effectively in temperature control; consequently, in cold weather there is a very real danger of the parrot suffering from hypothermia and dying.

If the parrot has a localised wound, ointment or an aerosol spray may be prescribed for the injured area. In this instance, only treat the specific area and use the smallest of amounts.

An aviary parrot should be brought into a cage if regular treatment is needed.

7 BEHAVIOUR AND TRAINING

To understand parrots, and therefore to train them with compassion, we need to see the world through their eyes. And train them we must, if we are to share our homes with them. An untrained bird is going to damage property, people, and most importantly, itself. Also, its quality of life will be affected: an unruly bird will be allowed less and less 'out' time if it is annoying to its keeper, which results in a very sad situation.

Behavioural problems occur in unhappy, stressed, and spoilt birds, and the causes of these problems can usually be traced back to some event in the bird's past. In order to address these problems and avoid any undesirable behaviour, we can look at how parrots naturally behave and modify that behaviour accordingly.

Parrots reared by their parents are fully dependent on them until they fledge, and for some time after that. The voice, appearance and behaviour of a young bird all differ from that of adults. Most youngsters will beg for food by uttering a staccato or whining call, while squatting, fluffed-up and flicking their wings. In the hand-reared humanised bird, this behaviour will be directed towards its human 'parents'.

The parrot parents will feed, preen and sit close to the infant to reassure it. As surrogate parents, you must fulfil the same role. A newly weaned, hand-reared bird will need

Blue and Gold Macaw: your parrot should learn to enjoy his own company occasionally, so he does not crave constant attention from you.

Opposite page: Military Macaw.

Above: once he is familiar with the step-up, your parrot can be taught to perch on a number of items. Pictured: Cockatiel.

Right: your parrot should not be allowed to sit on your head or shoulders until he has accepted you are top of the pecking order. Pictured: African Grey.

plenty of reassurance that it is safe and secure with you. However, just as with the parrot parents, there will be long periods of time when you will not be with the baby. This is the first and most valuable lesson the youngster will learn. Spoiling the young parrot with your constant attention will inevitably result in a cawing, whining and self-destructive parrot in later months when you simply don't have the luxury of being able to give it your full attention.

To prevent this situation from arising, the first lesson is to put the parrot in its cage with toys and food for a few hours each day – even if you can spare every hour of the day to be with it. There may come a time when you can't – and many parrots outlive their original owners – so this prepares the baby for any eventuality it may encounter in later life. If the young parrot cries, screams or clamours for your attention during this training period, simply ignore it. The baby will soon learn to entertain itself with the toys and food provided.

PECKING ORDER

Another aspect of a young parrot's life is learning their place in the pecking order. When raised amongst their own kind, other birds will threaten them by fluffing up their feathers and spreading their wings in order to look bigger, while approaching them menacingly. They may even lunge at the youngster with open beaks. To teach your youngster the same lesson, you can assert your dominance over the young parrot by ensuring that you are physically above it at all times. This means the baby should not be

allowed to sit on your head or shoulder, but should be taught a step-up routine to sit on your hand on command.

This behaviour should be encouraged every time the parrot is brought out of its cage; if it is not allowed to climb out of the cage, it will eventually learn to look forward to the proffered hand which brings it out.

STEP-UP

Step-up is taught most easily outside the cage to begin with. Ideally, place the bird on a 'T' bar stand, facing you at chest height. Then offer your hand to the bird at the height of its chest, while giving the command "step-up".

Some birds will automatically step on to your hand but if yours does not, push the hand, with a flat downward-facing palm against the bird's chest. You may have to push firmly enough to unbalance the bird if you do not get any initial reaction. Once he has done what is required, verbally praise and stroke him. Then repeat the exercise several more times before leaving the bird to relax, perhaps with its favourite tidbit.

It is very important to reinforce this exercise continually through the companion bird's life with you. Apart from asserting your dominance over the parrot by teaching it 'step-up,' once it is obedient to this command it is much easier to retrieve it from any potentially dangerous situation, or from where it is not allowed to go – from the top of doors and curtains, for example!

This behaviour can also be extended into teaching the bird to fly to you, by placing the parrot on the T-stand and stepping back a few feet from it. Then offer the hand and give the command, praising him copiously when he does what is required. The distance between you and the bird can gradually be extended until he is flying some distance to you. An extra reward in the form of his favourite food treat will not go amiss at this stage.

Teach your parrot to step from one wooden

Once he is familiar w
ready to step on to yo

When he has mastered the 'step-up' you can work on him flying to your hand. Pictured: Yellow-fronted Amazon.

Should you be unfortunate enough to lose your parrot through an open window or door, you have a much better chance of retrieving him from the dangers of the outside world if you have taught him this as routine and he is confident in flying to you.

It is surprising the number of escaped parrots who simply haven't the confidence to ly down from a tall tree they have landed in, ven though they are desperate to come to ou. This is similar to a newly-fledged parrot's ehaviour on leaving the nest and launching to the great unknown: youngsters will often for a long period in the tree where they t land and wait for their parents to come hem. It is often hours, or even days, re they re-launch themselves.

and-reared babies who never learn to fly, who have their wings clipped at an early may never gain the confidence to fly in life, even though they have grown back formed wings. This is an important to consider before clipping a ster's wings.

HOUSE TRAINING

The next important training stage in a companion parrot will be house-training. Again, if your parrot does not make a mess around the house, he is more likely to enjoy extra 'out' time with you. To encourage this desirable behaviour, we can again look at how parrots behave in the wild.

Due to the nature of their diet, and the fact that flying birds need to be as light as possible, parrots will defecate quite frequently. The largest droppings will occur when they wake after sleeping through the night. Parrots will often expel their night's store on waking, or on flying from their roosting tree. As such, you can expect your parrot to 'go' soon after you remove him from his cage in the morning.

The best approach is to put him directly on the T-stand with newspaper underneath it, and wait for him to perform. Then lavish him with praise, and perhaps play with him for a while, before returning him to the stand after 20 or so minutes, when he will probably

defecate again. Always praise him for doing what is required in the right place, but do not admonish him for any mistakes.

He will soon learn where is the desired place to do his toilet, and will start to fly to his stand on his own when necessary. Some birds even learn to go on command – although this shouldn't be abused by making him strain unnecessarily. It is wise to continually reinforce this good behaviour with lavish praise whenever you are aware of it happening.

You can often tell when a parrot is about to defecate as he will fluff up the feathers around the vent, raise the tail and possibly even lean forward slightly. If you see these signs try to replace him on the T-stand quickly, and praise him when he defecates there.

SHOWERING

To keep their feathers in good condition, many parrots will raise them in the rain and thoroughly soak them, before preening each individual feather thoroughly. If rain is not forthcoming, puddles and lake edges will be utilised, with the parrot wading in and splashing about in the water to wet itself.

As the housebound parrot is unable to access these luxuries, he should be trained to allow you to mist him with a plant sprayer. If this is done gently while talking to him, he will soon come to welcome it. Some birds even enjoy showering with their keepers. If you do this, beware of having the water too hot or getting soap on the parrot.

Ideally, shower the parrot in the morning so that it is completely dry before it goes to bed in the evening. The frequency of showers

After completing basic training, there is no end to what you can teach your parrot – whether it is playing dead on your head (top left), flying through hoops (bottom left), or kissing on command (right).

Blue and Gold Macaw.

Illiger's Macaw.

Green-winged Macaw.

A Blue and Gold Macaw severely plucked around the shoulders and wings.

The Moluccan Cockatoo on the left has a severely plucked chest.

really depends on how often the bird 'requests' it – every day is not too often for a light shower, and at least once a week is desirable in today's modern centrally-heated homes. The parrot should be allowed to dry naturally – drying with a hairdryer will make the feathers brittle and encourage the parrot to bite at them.

Feather-chewing and plucking is virtually unknown in the wild, and so is a vice brought on by captivity. As well as regular bathing, encouraging the captive parrot to play with toys and to chew twigs, fir cones and logs will go a long way towards preventing boredom and frustration, which are the primary causes of feather mutilation. In the wild, a parrot is surrounded by a veritable plethora of chew-things and they make full use of them.

NAILS

Another useful training tip for young birds is to encourage them to offer a foot to enable you to groom their nails. Parrots at liberty will wear their nails on a variety of surfaces, but the pet bird will need to have the tips trimmed or filed, if only for the comfort of the person handling it. This can be achieved from an early age by grasping the parrot's foot and gently filing the tip of the nail, again talking and praising quietly while doing so. A simple command such as "foot please", whilst grasping the foot, will encourage him to offer it on command.

Training your parrot to offer a foot will make claw-trimming a much easier procedure. Pictured: Yellow-fronted Amazon.

By making this process a regular occurrence, you will avoid the stressful situation of having to physically restrain the parrot in order to trim its nails. This is a simple process, but one which is well worth teaching.

BITING

As touched on previously, parrots have a complex communication system. Aggressive interaction in the wild is largely avoided by giving warnings and adopting threat postures. Territorial disputes are settled with a minimum of violence, and parrots soon come to recognise their superiors and then avoid confrontations with them.

We, as humans, sometimes do not understand this body language and as a result we may get bitten. Very rarely will parrots attack humans without provocation, so we need to understand which situations are potentially dangerous, and avoid them.

A pet parrot will think of its cage as its territory and will repel any intrusion into it. This is one of the reasons why it is best to have a T-stand on which to place the bird away from its cage. Some cages have an opening top with a perch on it, and are unsuitable for some because parrots will want to keep everyone away from their territory.

As such, we must respect the fact that the cage is a feeding and sleeping area for the bird, and if he is doing either of these things we should leave him in peace. Similarly, if we surprise the parrot by touching his head, back or tail unexpectedly we can expect to be bitten. A little talking and patience will go a long way towards winning the parrot's trust and, when he is ready, he will invite you to stroke him and handle him by coming towards you and raising the feathers on his head tantalisingly.

Strangers very often come in two categories – those that avoid parrots like the plague, and those who rush in, poking and prodding, and then complain that their fingers have been bitten. A little advance warning and advice on restraint in the first instance will often prevent upset to both parrot and guest.

DEALING WITH BITING

If all the preventative measures don't work, or you have a pet which has been spoiled, there are various measures you can take to prevent biting becoming a regular occurrence from your pet. Trying to avoid the situation where you are invading the parrot's territory is paramount. Then if the 'step-up' is not yet established, you must work to teach the parrot this behaviour.

If he is difficult to remove from the cage, throwing a towel over him and removing him manually to a neutral territory may be the only answer. When he is placed on the T-stand, a length of wood may be used as a substitute for the hand to teach the 'step-up' to an aggressive parrot. Then, if the parrot bites, your are not tempted to snatch away – an action which will reinforce the biting behaviour.

When you are pressing the wood against the parrot's chest, he will probably bite at it and try to push it away. Simply continue with the pressure until he steps up, and then repeat the exercise several times. Eventually, he will step on to the wood without biting it, and then gradually the hand can be introduced to him with less risk of being bitten.

When his bite doesn't create a reaction, the parrot will have no stimulus to continue biting and he will cease doing so in that situation. Similarly, if the parrot bites when you are trying to stroke his head, a twig can be used to gently tickle his nape and when, after several experiences of this, he realises that it is pleasurable, the twig can be replaced with a finger. It is all a question of gaining the parrot's confidence while not reinforcing the biting behaviour by snatching away or crying out.

When using articles such as a length of wood or a twig, you must be careful not to frighten the bird with them – you may need to leave the object near the bird, or even in its cage for a while, to give him time to familiarise himself with it (and probably chew it) before you attempt to use it as a tool.

Eye contact is also very important in discouraging biting. A hard stare directly into the eye of a misbehaving parrot will disarm him and make him aware that this is undesirable behaviour. Following this up by placing him in his cage for 10 minutes can also serve to reinforce your expression of disapproval.

Importantly, one must recognise when the parrot is biting from malice, which is very rare, or acting out of mischief, or – most importantly – from fright. A parrot which attacks you – in other words, flies at you and bites you on landing – is probably protecting his territory and may need to be moved to neutral territory to have his behaviour adjusted to an acceptable level, or possibly be introduced to a breeding aviary situation. Mischievous behaviour will be well controlled by applying the behaviour modifications already described, whereas a frightened parrot, which bites and strikes out in fear, must be handled with much positive reassurance and time spent gaining his trust.

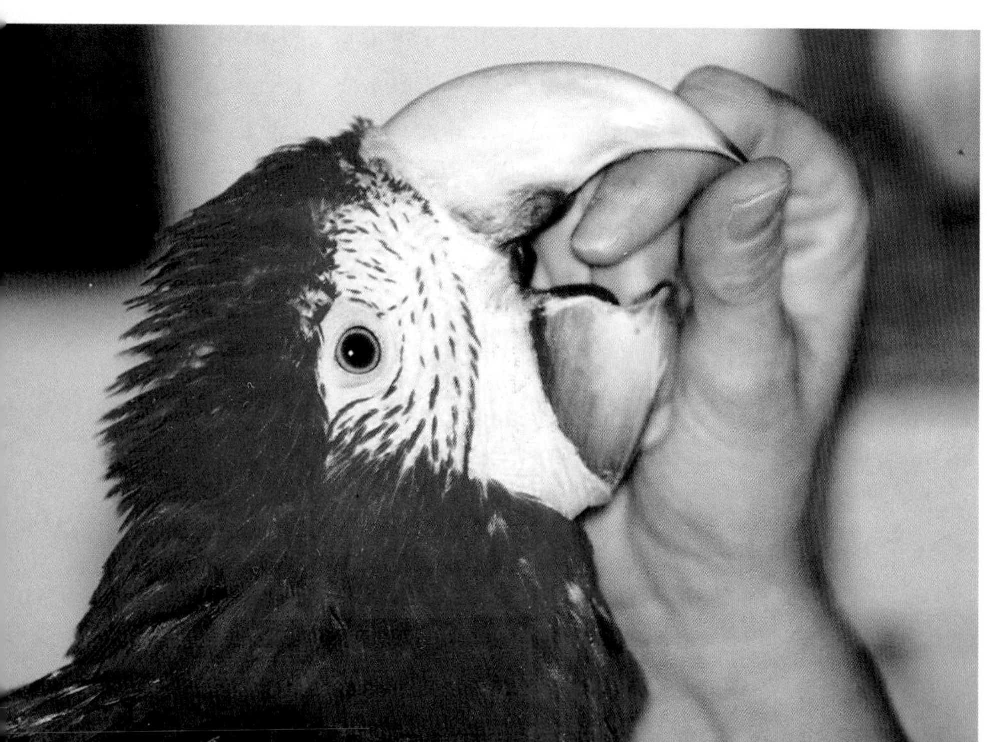

Green-winged Macaw: handling a bird from a young enough age should stop him growing into a biter.

African Grey: feeding the correct diet may help to prevent behavioural problems.

EATING

Wild parrots range from the omnivorous majority to some which are highly specialised feeders. Beak size and shape gives some indication of the preferred diet of many species. The seed-eaters such as budgerigars, cockatiels and lovebirds have relatively small and neat beaks for cracking seeds, and a muscular tongue to aid in manoeuvring them.

Enormous mandibles adorn the heads of the large macaws and Palm Cockatoos. These magnificent birds make short work of some of the toughest nuts in the world such as brazils and macadamia nuts, whereas the elongated upper mandibles of Long-billed Corellas and Slender-billed Conures indicate that these species dig for roots and grubs.

The lories use their longish bills and papillae-covered tongues to retrieve pollen and nectar from flowers.

The Kea from New Zealand has a long, downward-curving upper mandible for, amongst other things, tearing meat from carrion and even from live prey such as the young of other birds. Some parrots, such as the Galahs and little corellas of Australia, are hugely successful due to of their adaptability and omnivorous habits, which enable them to exploit any given situation. Others, such as the Lear's Macaws, are so highly specialised that their tiny population could be devastated if their main food source, the fruit of the licuri palm, is unavailable to them.

NATURAL FEEDING BEHAVIOUR

Most wild parrots will awake at first light and greet the dawn with a series of calls. They will then fly to the nearest feeding area with a muted contact call to enable them to stick together. They feed continuously for a few hours until their crops are full, following which they will rest quietly and digest their food until late afternoon. Then, after another bout of feeding, they will fly off noisily as a flock to the roosting tree and once again settle down for the night.

This natural behaviour gives us an insight into how to make a captive parrot's life as comfortable and enjoyable as possible. This natural cycle also makes them fit well into a working household as a pet, with a high level of activity first thing in the morning and a good meal, then time to rest and digest while the carer is at work, before another session of activity in the evening. These are also the times when you will observe the highest noise levels, but this is natural and is to be expected from a healthy parrot. So, as part of its training, a parrot will come to expect regular meals and, if it is a pet, it will also expect exercise and stimulation at least twice a day.

Wild parrots often have to work hard to get food – extracting nuts from their shells, teasing the tough, pithy outer layer off some fruits to enjoy the flesh inside, or as in the case of the Black Cockatoos, debarking wood to get at the grubs underneath. Giving parrots such food in captivity will go a long way towards preventing boredom and the development of some of the vices already mentioned. Corn on the cob, sunflower heads, pinecones, and nuts in their shells are great favourites with most psittacines. The provision of fresh twigs, cardboard tubes and boxes will also guarantee entertainment whilst you are busy.

COMMUNICATION

As well as communicating with their voices, parrots will also interact visually. As described when discussing behaviour, parrots will threaten one another, and people, in a variety of ways including puffing up their feathers and spreading their wings to make themselves look bigger. They will also erect the feathers on their heads and lean forward to encourage a mate/friend/human to scratch and preen their head, the only place they cannot get to themselves with the beak. This leads to mutual preening, with beak-to-vent preening commonly occurring in breeding pairs.

A rapid nodding of the head indicates the desire of an adult bird to feed his mate by regurgitation – and often a pet will do this to his or her owner, which should be taken as a somewhat messy compliment. However, to discourage this behaviour, simply keep the bird away from your mouth and face, and walk away if you see the head nodding beginning – and also ignore any amorous gestures towards you.

Parrots also have very expressive eyes. They will look directly at one another, turn their heads to focus better and lower their gaze if threatened. Excited or angry parrots will also dilate their pupils, and in those species with

Parrots communicate in a number of ways. This Umbrella Cockatoo's erect head feathers shows it is excited or alarmed.

light-coloured irises, the eyes will flash with amazing brightness. When enjoying contact with others of their own kind, or the human substitute, the eyes will often half-close in pleasure.

TEACHING TO TALK

Mention parrots to almost anybody and they will initially think about their talking ability. The different species have a wide range of voices including the melodious whistles and songs of African species like the Greys and Cape parrots, and the unusual Vasa parrots. Many of the conures and small macaws have repetitive shrieks, while the large macaws and some of the cockatoos have the capacity to be almost ear-splitting!

However, parrot language is complex and many will maintain vocal contact, whilst feeding or flying, with a series of low mumblings, mutterings and calls. A sentinel bird, which is often poised on a high perch whilst the rest of the flock are feeding, will utter a loud sharp call if danger is spotted, instantly alerting the flock. Why parrots copy and repeat other sounds they hear has not yet been discovered and, despite clearly having the ability to do so, they have not shown signs of doing this in the wild.

From an early age, parrots in the company of humans will repeat words that they hear, with many babies saying "hello" before they are fully feathered. Sadly, many people want a parrot just to hear it repeat words, and are therefore disappointed, because often they will not oblige. The most sought-after talkers are the African Greys and Yellow-naped and Double Yellow-headed Amazons, but even with these normally prolific talkers, some never utter a single word. Parrots should be viewed as individuals and if they talk as well, then that is a bonus.

The brain of a parrot is complex and they have much more understanding than one would imagine. If you talk with them as you would with a child they soon connect words with actions. Often parrots will say "hello" unprompted on your arrival and "bye-bye" on your departure, because those are the words they hear from you. We have macaws that say "thank you" when given food or a tidbit, and even one who looks in his food bowl in the morning and on viewing the contents says "Mmm... lovely"!

When one of our pets wants to come out of her cage she excitedly repeats "step-up, step-up", the command she associates with being allowed out. Our birds also call us by name, rather then mindlessly repeating their own names as some bored birds do. Again, this is achieved by our interaction with them as cognitive beings rather than as automatons repeatedly uttering the same words.

Great work has been done by Dr Irene Pepperberg in America with the African Grey 'Alex'. Having worked with her for a number of years, Alex recognises and repeats the names of various subjects shown to him, including their colours and shapes. He will

The African Grey is one of the most popular talking breeds. This one is concentrating on learning to talk by watching and listening to his handler.

also ask for particular foodstuffs such as a nut, banana or apple, and if given the wrong food will say, for instance, "no nut." Alex and many other individual parrots show us that we still have much to learn about the intelligence of these animals, and how by interacting with and stimulating these wonderful beings we can tap into a whole new world.

READING FACES

Rather like children, parrots will study the facial expressions of the person speaking to them, and take much more interest in this than in listening to inanimate objects 'speaking', such as radios and tape recorders. Even the pictures on a television don't seem to capture a parrot's attention in the way face-to-face communication does.

If you want to 'teach' a parrot to speak, then ideally you should enunciate the word you want him to say, clearly and with his attention on your face whilst you are repeating it. These training sessions should be short and fun for the bird.

The timescale within which you can expect your pet to start to speak his first words will vary from bird to bird, and often when you have just given up on the parrot ever saying a word, he will surprise you by talking quite clearly.

As stated earlier, some birds will never speak at all, but others will start to speak at four or five years of age, and all have the capacity to learn throughout their lives, unlike many other mimics such as the corvids and mynahs.

Parrots are fascinated by faces, and learn to talk not only by listening to their owners, but by watching them too.

HOW TO HANDLE DEMANDING BREEDS – MOLUCCAN COCKATOOS: A CASE STUDY

Barrett Watson

Much maligned by some, revered and adored by others, the Moluccan Cockatoo is greatly misunderstood by many. Unbearably noisy and destructive Moluccans are usually the result of human interference. It is very easy to spoil these intelligent hand-reared babies in those crucial, formative first few months after weaning. A little firm training and some understanding at this stage will prevent bad habits.

Like all breeds of parrot, the Moluccan Cockatoo can be noisy and destructive if neglected.

GROUND RULES

Hand-reared babies can make adorable pets, but it is very important to teach them a few ground rules from an early age. Youngsters should be encouraged to spend time playing with toys on their own, and not be allowed to come to expect constant human attention. If you go to the baby every time he whines or screams, it won't take much time for him to discover just what it takes to get your attention – just like a human baby. Also, Moluccans hand-reared in isolation can become very imprinted on humans, and therefore maladjusted.

I am fortunate in having four breeding-pairs of Moluccans, so I rarely have to rear a chick on its own, as two or more pairs are usually breeding at similar times. Some pairs with two chicks do not give them equal attention, feeding the larger and more vigorous chick to the detriment of the second which they let fade away. I rear these youngsters, and also those chicks from a pair which totally denude their chicks once their pin feathers come through, despite feeding both chicks very well.

My pairs are a mixture of hand-reared, parent-reared and wild-caught birds. It has to be said that the best parents are hand-reared ex-pets. However, nothing is certain in the animal kingdom. This is where good husbandry comes to the fore – knowing your birds and getting an instinctive feel for when things are not going according to plan.

I am as guilty as the next man of noting that a chick is not doing as well as it might but deciding to leave it for just one more day and finding it dead the next day. We learn from our mistakes and so do the parents. However, I believe it is just as easy to become paranoid and whisk away every chick or egg at the first opportunity – to the detriment of future breeding stock. If the parents did not get it right occasionally, Moluccans would have been extinct long ago.

SECLUSION

Despite the extrovert characters of many hand-reared Moluccans, breeding adults are often shy and retiring. To cater for this, I try to house them in secluded quarters. Each pair is kept in an aviary 10 feet (3m) square, with three sides enclosed. The nestbox is hung in the farthest corner from human traffic. I do not have the entrance-hole facing the front, not to make the interior dark, but to prevent startled birds from rushing into the box and damaging eggs or chicks. Making them turn a corner to reach the entrance has the effect of slowing their progress a little.

Three of my pairs spend a great part of the day hiding in the boxes, which led a friend to remark that giving them an aviary was a waste of time, as all they needed was food and water in the nestbox. Of course, this is not true, as when they feel unthreatened they have a wonderful time playing with twigs and perches, feeding, rain-bathing, and just snoozing quietly or watching the world go by.

Moluccans are avid chewers of nestboxes, but I don't think this should be discouraged as it is natural behaviour and often precedes breeding activity. Assuming the base and frame are secure (that is, metal-lined) I think we must resign ourselves to replacing nestboxes at regular intervals. My attempts at completely metal-lining nestboxes did not meet with the birds' approval; they go on strike if they are not allowed to chew, and who can blame them? I wonder if being deprived of this chewing behaviour increases chick-plucking? Normally, the parents would continually splinter the interior of the nesting tree to cover the chicks' faeces.

FEEDING TIME

Like most cockatoos, Moluccans seem to do well on a fairly meagre diet compared with other parrots, eating about half by volume what a macaw would eat. I feed a staple diet of soaked washed pulses (beans), fruit, vegetables, cheese, chicken (bones and meat) a little sunflower and a few nuts – with walnuts and brazils in their shells being a favourite, although they will often take these into the nest and 'incubate' them for months on end!

Hand-reared, well-socialised Moluccans are a joy to own.

INCUBATION

Moluccans normally lay two eggs in a clutch, sometimes just one, and mine have never had three. Both parents normally incubate, but I find that it does vary with my pairs, with some hens doing most, if not all, of the work. One of my pairs even had the endearing habit of sitting side-by-side incubating one egg each.

Moluccans are notoriously difficult to artificially incubate, but I have successfully incubated them from day one in the cheapest and simplest incubator, as well as in a classier one. I have also achieved success with foster parents. Perhaps incubators are often blamed when other factors are involved – that is, poor diet, genetic defects, or bad handling of eggs.

Breeders have a responsibility to keep the magnificent Moluccan breed alive.

ARRIVAL

The newly hatched chicks weigh 18-24 grams (5/8-7/8oz) and are darkish pink with wisps of yellow down. Their arrival in the nest box is usually announced with quite a loud piping noise as they feed. If you hand-rear them, be prepared to be frustrated, as they nearly all seem to reach a stage at a few weeks old when they decide eating is boring and push out the food as quickly as it is put in their mouths. We then cut the number of feeds right down so that they regain a little enthusiasm.

One must be careful not to over-feed babies anyway, as they are prone to fatty liver and kidney syndrome. Remember that at this stage whiny babies can be avoided by the hand-rearer if they are group-fed and not fussed over unduly. Weaning can be a prolonged affair, with chicks picking at food from 10 weeks of age, but still accepting a top-up hand-feed at five months of age. Of course, the parents would still feed them at this age and beyond, so we should follow their example.

AGGRESSION

Meanwhile, back at the nestbox, the babies will fledge at approximately 15 weeks of age, in the form of stunning replicas of their parents. It is at this stage that a watchful eye should be kept on them in case of any aggression from the cock towards the young, although I have luckily not experienced this.

As with all white cockatoos, aggression is a very real possibility, and any screaming or signs of blood on the hen should be investigated immediately. If the hen is cowering on the floor or has bite marks on her legs, beak or wings, the cock should be removed without delay. Reintroducing him should only be done under strict supervision, and only when the hen is fully recovered. Again, vigilance is of utmost importance. All in all, these problems are rare, and compatible pairs should have long, productive lives.

The Moluccan Cockatoo is surely one of the most magnificent birds in existence today. It deserves all our assistance in allowing it to procreate, as well as our understanding if we are fortunate to keep a hand-reared baby as a pet in our home.

8 DIET AND NUTRITION

The importance of diet can never be over-emphasised. It has two major functions. Firstly, a balanced diet is the way in which our parrots receive all the nutrients, vitamins and essential elements which are necessary to allow them to live a healthy and productive life. Secondly, their diet is something that can be enjoyed, and those parrots that regularly receive a variety of different foods become actively excited when being given their food.

There are three main diets available for parrots – the seed diet, the pulse diet and the pelleted diet. Parrot nutrition has made considerable advances in recent years, and it would appear in no small measure to be due to the research undertaken by the manufacturers of pelleted foods. These diets have gained considerable following in the United States. In Europe pelleted diets, whilst gaining some popularity, haven't yet reached the same level of use as in the United States.

SEED DIET

The seed diet is the one that the majority of parrot keepers use. These are usually sold as 'parrot mix' in pet shops. There are several different ones available on the market and they vary quite considerably in quality, those at the lower end being comprised mainly of sunflower seed and peanuts. This mixture, if fed in isolation, is inadequate.

Opposite page: Scarlet Macaw.

Seed diets at the upper end of the market contain a range of different seeds, nuts, and dried fruits. This allows the parrot to have a choice, and also limits the high-fat foods, such as sunflower seeds, which many parrots will eat to the exclusion of other foods if given the opportunity. Parrots who consume high levels of fatty foods over time become obese and lose their lustre. This is because high-fat foods are deficient in some vitamins and trace elements. Fresh fruit and vegetables need to be added daily to the seed diet.

A selection of dried foods suitable for parrots.

PULSE (BEAN) DIET

This is the diet that many would argue is the most natural for parrots. Pulses contain a higher protein level that will often bring parrots into breeding condition. The pulses are normally purchased in a dry state. To prepare, they need to be rinsed in clean cold water and then left to soak for 24 hours. After 12 hours the pulses will need to be rinsed again and the container refilled with clean cold water. After 24 hours they are ready to feed.

Some advocate boiling the pulses, in the belief that this will destroy harmful toxins, and this certainly speeds up the preparation time. If red kidney beans are included in the pulse mix, then there is a need to boil pulses.

PELLETED DIET

These are available from a variety of manufacturers, some being brightly coloured, which would appear to increase their palatability. This is the main drawback to this type of diet – it can prove quite difficult to get parrots to accept them as a chosen food.

The pelleted diet generally contains all the nutritional elements necessary for physical health and can now be fed with fresh fruit and vegetables. This adds to the parrots' mental health and helps to prevent boredom. There have been many instances of parrots who have been reluctant to breed being fed a pelleted diet and then going on to breed very successfully.

In colder weather, aviary birds may need a higher fat diet to keep them warm. Pictured: Lovebirds.

Never feed your parrot junk food, or drink that could be harmful to him. Pictured: African Grey.

INTRODUCING FOODS

Parrots can be very conservative in the foods they will try if they are not given a variety of foodstuffs from weaning, some more noticeably so than others.

Particular culprits who fall into this category have to be African Greys and some cockatoos, although it has to be said that all types of parrots can exhibit this behaviour. These parrots are sometimes referred to as 'sunflower junkies', as the food that is always invariably accepted is sunflower seed. When introducing new foods, there is a need to keep supplying the new variety of food even though the different food item may be rejected for several weeks.

Many parrot keepers vary their diet and give some of each of the main types of diets available. Particular times when this is likely to occur is during the colder winter months when, if parrots are kept outside, they require a higher fat diet to enable them to lay down fat deposits in their bodies, which will help them to keep warm when winter temperatures drop. Those parrot owners who wish to breed their parrots often increase the protein levels in the diet 6-8 weeks before they expect the parrots to breed. This is usually accomplished by giving pulses and cooked meat.

Parrots that are kept as pets in the home don't require such profound changes to their diet, since for indoor parrots it is unlikely that temperature and energy requirements will differ in such a marked and contrasting way. The main priority in this situation is to ensure that the pet parrot receives and eats a variety of foods, particularly fresh fruit and vegetables.

Do not give extras from your table in the form of high-fat foods such as chips, or foods that may prove harmful, such as chocolate. However, most other unsalted foodstuffs can only be beneficial as additions to the diet.

SOCIAL EATING

Pet parrots can exhibit quite difficult behaviour if regularly out of their cage during your meal times. Parrots are naturally sociable and eating is to them highly sociable activity. While many parrot owners may not mind their pet eating with them at the table, problems can occur when the pet is prevented from having certain unhealthy items. Some parrots may then develop strategies to get their own way, which may include threatening behaviour, being noisy or even biting. It is much easier and more comfortable for both parrot and owner if these adverse behaviours are never allowed to develop.

FRESH FRUIT AND VEGETABLES

Parrots will readily accept most fruits and all have their use in season, some also out of season if the fruit can be frozen; examples of this include pomegranate and plums. Some naturally occurring produce can also be fed, or frozen for future use, such as rose-hips, haws and elderberries. Most vegetables will also be accepted and, like fruit, may be more acceptable if fed in a particular way. For example carrots, if not accepted in slices or cubes, will often be accepted grated.

Fresh foods are usually cubed or cut into smaller pieces before being given to parrots. This is because parrots are naturally fairly wasteful, often selecting an item from the food dish, taking a piece from it and then dropping the remainder on the floor. Parrots won't normally eat items from the floor; so the amount of fresh food available should be limited. By cutting their food into smaller chunks less is wasted.

A selection of fresh fruit and vegetables suitable for parrots.

HARMFUL FOODS

The two main foods that are harmful to parrots are avocado, which can prove fatal if eaten even in small amounts, and cabbage, because the oxalic acid content hinders the absorption of calcium.

MIXED OR SEPARATE?

Some parrot keepers give their foods in different dishes, for example putting seed in one dish and fresh foods in another. Others mix the foods together. There are advantages and disadvantages to both these methods.

If foods are fed separately, the parrot keeper can easily see which food is being ignored and which is being eaten and so can feed only foods which will be eaten, thus avoiding waste. With this method it is also easy to judge quite accurately the amounts of feed being taken, which can alert the parrot keeper if a smaller amount of food than usual is being eaten.

The main advantage to mixing foods together is that it encourages parrots to taste and feel the different textures of different foods even if this is only to move some foods to get to favourite items of food. This method of feeding can be particularly useful when encouraging fussy eaters to try different types of food.

Grapes, pomegranates and sweetcorn are usually items of fresh foods that the majority of parrots will find irresistible. It is then quite a simple procedure to mix less favoured food items with these, and with seed. Once this type of feeding has become established, even if the less favoured items are being ignored, it is possible to gradually reduce the favourite items and then usually the less favoured items will start to be consumed.

CHANGING DIETS

When making changes to parrot diets, it is important to make the changes gradually. Some parrots have been known to starve themselves to death when dietary changes have been undertaken without thought and sensitive monitoring. Some of the most difficult parrots in relation to accepting a variety of foods are the African Grey parrots. In the wild, these feed regularly on palm nuts, which have a high fat content. This is fine if they are taking exercise and thus using up the energy produced from the fat. In the domestic situation, those confined to small aviaries or cages for long periods won't use up these

Greys are notoriously fussy eaters, who do not adapt well to sudden diet changes. Pictured: Timneh Grey.

Some parrot breeds obtain nectar from flowering plants by using their long tongues. Pictured: Rajah Lory.

excess calories, which then results in them becoming obese. So it is very important for them to accept and enjoy less high fat foods.

When giving fresh food, it is important to remember that this will spoil in a relatively short space of time if the weather is hot. Not only is the food less appealing in this state, it can also prove dangerous.

In warm weather, fresh foods are quickly colonised by bacteria and fungi which, if eaten by the parrot, can prove harmful or even fatal. For this reason it is important to remove fresh foods after a few hours in hot weather. In cooler weather the fresh foods will stay palatable for longer periods.

WATER

For similar reasons water dishes need to be cleaned daily and fresh water added. For some parrots this will need to be more often, as some appear to delight in putting items of food in their water, and others will pass their droppings into their water. It is important to clean the water dish and give fresh water if this occurs. If the parrot is regularly passing droppings into their water, there will be a need to relocate the water or to move the perch.

Because parrots are so individual in their tastes, some fruits and vegetables may never be accepted, but these should be in the minority, as parrots that have always been given a wide variety of fresh foods will accept all manner of foods.

SPECIALIST DIETS

The vast majority of parrots eat similar types of foods. The notable exceptions to this are the lories and lorikeets and some parrots which, although not in this family, are closely enough related that they require some nectar in their diet, for example the hanging parrots and swift parakeets. These are often referred to as brush-tongued parrots, on account of the papillae which are present at the end of their tongues, and which are used to brush up the pollen from flowering plants.

The diet used for this group of birds used to be expensive and time-consuming to make, and it must be said that some lory and lorikeet keepers do still mix their own, getting various ingredients from health food shops and then mixing a fresh amount of the 'nectar' daily. However, there are now several propriety nectar solutions available for this group of birds, which simply need mixing with water. It is still necessary to add fruit to the diet. This is particularly important for this group of parrots, not only for their physical wellbeing but also for their psychological health.

This group of parrots is particularly intelligent, inquisitive and playful, and really do make use of every bit of stimulus put their way, and this includes their diet.

Because of the liquid state of the diet, it is important to monitor the temperature where they are fed. In hot weather, the solution, being sweet, will quickly spoil and will need replacing, and in the winter it is important that the solution doesn't freeze. If this is happening, it is important that it is replenished at regular intervals.

Food dishes will need to be washed in hot soapy water, because of the stickiness of the solution, as will the area in which the food is eaten.

Lories and lorikeets require nectar in their diet. Pictured: the popular Dusky Lory.

9 BREEDING PARROTS

Anyone, who one day decides they are going to breed parrots, may swiftly become hugely disappointed. Sadly, they do not always comply with our desire to breed them. If they did, then parrots would no longer command the prices that they do, or be the challenge that they are.

However, there is much that we can do to encourage this natural behaviour. Looking at parrots in nature, we see that they have a choice of mates from their fellow/flock members. If we can replicate this choice in captivity then we stand a better chance of finding a pair that is compatible.

Ideally, several young unrelated parrots of the same species and opposite sexes can be reared together and allowed to form a bond with one another. This will be a loose connection at first, but will gradually develop into something more. Your job, as the keeper, is to be able to identify each individual and observe the behaviour between birds.

Identification of similar birds can be achieved by ringing with various split rings, for example on the left leg of one bird, the right leg on another, a ring on each leg with the third and perhaps no rings on the fourth. Food dye can be used to mark light-coloured birds, or the face patch of macaws and Greys.

MATCHING INDIVIDUALS

Once the identification of each individual is established, it is then prudent to make notes of the behaviour of the pairs. Who sits next to whom, particularly when roosting at night, any preening or feeding of partners, if consistent, will give a good indication of well-matched pairs, and from your notes you will see a pattern emerging.

Equally any aggression that is observed can be noted, and great care taken not to confine an aggressive male with the female object of his attention where she cannot escape. This is particularly important in some of the white cockatoos, amazons, and Australian parakeets, but no pairing is immune to this potential danger. Once again, we can look at the parrots' behaviour in the wild to see that, if a female does not welcome an amorous male's advances, she simply avoids him, something she cannot do in the close confines of captivity.

Sometimes, even in mixed-sex groups of parrots, homosexual pairings will occur. These can be very strongly bonded indeed, leading the keeper to wonder if his sexing of the birds is accurate. As a first step, it may be wise to re-sex any birds bought in as a particular sex, or check your records to ensure you are correct in your knowledge of a particular bird's sex. Unfortunately, many purchased as 'proven pairs' (birds that have produced fertile eggs) of parrots turn out to be two cocks, when the trusting buyer

Opposite page: Pennant's Rosella.

eventually has them sexed after fruitless years of waiting.

SEXING PARROTS

Sadly some sellers lie about the birds they are selling, and it may save a lot of wasted time to always check for yourself. With modern methods of sexing parrots, all you may need to do is pluck three or four breast feathers from your bird and send them to a DNA-testing laboratory (your aviary vet will have details). A result is available in approximately a week. They achieve this by breaking down the strands of DNA and counting the sex chromosomes for an accurate answer to the sex of the bird. Alternatively, a toenail can be cut too short in order to extract a few drops of blood, which will be processed in the same way to get a result. With this method, even an unfeathered chick can be sexed.

Thirdly, surgical sexing is a procedure where by a laparoscope is inserted into the side of an anaesthetised parrot to examine its gonads and thereby assess its sex. Apart from the obvious dangers in anaesthetising the bird, there is a small chance of infection, or even of damage to the internal organs from the laparoscope. Also, mistakes can be made by this method, as the gonads of immature birds of both sexes may look similar. However, this invasion may also be useful in assessing the condition of the bird's other internal organs, and could even give information on the parrot's potential breeding performance, or lack of it.

The last and least trustworthy method of sexing parrots is the guessing game. Monomorphic species, when grouped together may give clues as to their sex by size, head-shape, or behaviour, but there are always going to be the exceptions that prove the rule. It can be a very costly procedure, both financially and time-wise, keeping two birds of the same sex together indefinitely under the mistaken impression that they are a true pair.

There are, of course, some parrots who are sexually dimorphic, the eclectus being the most obvious and extreme example of this, with the hen being red and purple and the cocks mainly green. Cape Parrot hens have orange foreheads, which the cocks lack, and some of the white cockatoos show black eyes in cocks and light brown-red in hens; but in both of these species, immatures do not show these differences, and there are black-eyed cockatoo hens.

It can be difficult to sex a parrot unless scientific measures are used. However, some breeds' colouring is a giveaway. The male Eclectus chick can be identified when his green feathers start to sprout. The female's red feathers give it away.

COMPATIBILITY

Now that the sex of your bird has been established, we return to the very important issue of compatibility. If you cannot flock several youngsters in the manner described earlier, then great care must be taken when bringing two birds together. A successful method is to cage a potential pair in separate cages next to each other. Leave a gap between the two cages so that the birds cannot inflict damage on each other. Over a period of days, observe their behaviour, particularly where they sit when at rest: if they sit near the bars of the cage as close to each other as they can, then this looks hopeful. Flashing eyes, fanning tails and excited shrieks may accompany amazon reactions upon seeing each other; but an attack may also ensue in this highly charged atmosphere – hence the need to keep the birds separate until compatibility is assured

When you feel that headway is being made, the cages can be inched closer together whilst you are present, and again you must gauge the reaction the birds have to one another. Gently nibbling one another's beaks and head feathers, and even attempts at feeding each other are very good sign. Lunging at each other with open beaks and wings is the signal to keep them apart, as is sitting at opposite ends of the cages with complete indifference to each other.

It is difficult to decide on the length of time to allow before deciding that this is a pairing that won't work. Suffice it to say that sometimes it is love at first sight, and these pairs tend to be very successful breeders. Sometimes it will take a few weeks for a pair to bond, and if there is not much progress after a couple of months, it might be wise to try a different pairing. This is one of the difficulties in our attempts to breed parrots: they are as fussy as humans in the choice of partners.

It can take some time for a pair to bond. Pictured: pair of Eastern Long-billed Corella.

Overcoming this first hurdle of potential compatibility is a major step forward. However, it must be remembered that even

BREEDING SEASONS

The season in which parrots breed varies with the species, with the majority commencing breeding activities in the spring, although the psittacula parrakeets will nest in February if given the chance. We tend to hang nestboxes or move pairs to breeding aviaries in early March. The amazons are usually the first to lay, and often if you are late in setting them up for breeding you will not be successful. March to July seem to be their most productive months. Very rarely will they lay after this, and most will lay only one or two clutches. Macaws and cockatoos also peak in this period, but will continue to lay as late as October, and even sporadically in the winter months as well.

The African Greys and poicephalus seem to do the reverse, and the majority will lay from October to March as well as in the more 'normal' season. Then some, such as the eclectus and great-billed parrots will lay almost continually, a clutch every six weeks or so if they are not rearing chicks. For the good of their health these highly productive pairs should be 'rested' by flying them in a large flight with other birds, and without the stimulation of nestboxes or logs, for a few months a year. This gives their bodies time to get fit and build up reserves.

compatible pairs that have bred may start to fight in the future, and have to be separated, even if only temporarily. This may be due to a rise in hormone levels of the male at the onset of the breeding season that is not matched by the hen. He then becomes frustrated at her reluctance to mate and attacks his unwilling mate who is unable to flee in the confinement of captivity. Alternatively, it may be misplaced aggression whereby the attacker is stressed by the close proximity of other birds or humans and strikes out at the nearest object – his mate. Seclusion and privacy in the aviary will usually resolve this problem.

Nestboxes come in a range of shapes and sizes.

INTRODUCING THE BIRDS

So, once you have your potentially compatible pair, what is the next step? They should ideally be introduced into an aviary that is neutral territory, either at the same time or, in species with overly aggressive males (cockatoos and amazons), the female could be placed in the aviary first, followed by the male a few days later when she has settled down. This gives her a slight edge. Never try this with female-dominant species such as eclectus, great-bills, ringnecks or Lovebirds.

To minimise disturbances, the aviary should already be set up with a variety of firmly fixed perches, ensuring adequate head and tail clearance, and a nestbox – or variety of nestboxes for potentially fussy occupants. In general, parrots are inquisitive and will investigate most holes. The criteria they are looking for are seclusion, height, darkness to a degree, and safety from predators.

Umbrella Cockatoo: chewing the nestbox opening will encourage the bird to breed.

NESTBOXES

To fulfil this, place the nestbox high up in a quiet corner of the aviary. The entrance hole should be just big enough for the adult bird to squeeze through – most feel more confident if they fill this space when defending the nest against predators. Likewise, some birds feel more secure in a fairly restricted space in the nestbox.

Many incubating adults whittle away at the inside of a nestbox or log to provide a suitable substance for the chicks and to elevate them above the droppings. Provision should be made for this by using thick wood for the sides of the box and by screwing lengths of 4" x 2" (10 x 5cm) at chewing level to the inside of the box. Without these, many parrots, particularly macaws and cockatoos will chew huge holes in undesirable places in the nestbox, including into the floor.

Whilst metal can be used to cover the outside of the box to prevent loss of eggs, all-metal cans and boxes should not be used, as the need to chew will not be satisfied – a frustration which could terminate breeding attempts or encourage egg-eating or plucking of themselves and chicks.

In the wild, parrots will nest in holes in the trunks and boughs of trees, which are what we replicate with upright and horizontal or angled nestboxes. Others, notably Palm Cockatoos, Red-bellied and Blue-throated Macaws, often nest in open-topped dead tree trunks and would appreciate these being replicated in captivity. Some will even prefer to nest at ground level, most notably the Kea.

It is thought that if the hole in the nestbox is made smaller than the birds are able to get through, the birds will chew and enlarge it and, by so doing, their breeding cycle is stimulated. It is usually when trying to encourage the birds to breed in the first instance that such tricks are necessary: once they have bred the first year, they become much less fussy about the choice of nesting site in the effort to reproduce again each new season. But, as always with living creatures, there are exceptions: we have some pairs that lay twice a year, and some that will lay for several seasons, then have a year off.

DIETARY CONSIDERATIONS

It should be borne in mind that breeding is a strain on the resources of the hen in particular, and as such careful attention must be paid to ensuring that she is consuming a balanced diet. In the lead-up to the presumed breeding season, the protein levels of the diet can be increased gradually, as this will bring on the so-called breeding condition, as well as increase the hen's reserves ready for laying.

PREPARING THE NEST

In many parrot species it is the cock bird that inspects and prepares the nest first, with the hen applying the finishing touches. Many a time we have been told the tale of woe that only the cock has been seen entering the nestbox with the hen appearing disinterested. However, this is usually followed some weeks later with the hen not only spending time in the box but laying in it as well.

Much speculation is put forward as to how much disturbance breeding birds can tolerate. In our experience, it is sudden or unusual disturbances that upset birds. If you have the birds situated next to a railway and every day trains thunder past, they will become immune to this disturbance. Similarly, parrots in zoos get used to a constant procession of onlookers, and will breed within a few feet of these, whereas birds in a private collection suddenly faced with an onslaught of visitors may find this worrying enough to abandon or damage eggs or chicks.

Some species and some individuals are more nervous than others and, as such, they will over-react to minor changes in the routine. Stockmanship is all about knowing your charges and treating them accordingly – putting nervous species in secluded areas and bolder ones where the traffic occurs.

We try to accustom our breeding birds to nestbox inspection well before they are due to lay, and therefore they will accept this as part of the routine. Every day at feeding

The nestbox should be positioned in a quiet location in the aviary. Pictured: St. Vincent Amazon (the green morph).

time, we tap twice on the nestbox to warn the residents, then open the inspection door. Even if they are not in the box, the tapping and door-opening noises become regular and accepted occurrences.

REGULAR INSPECTIONS

When there are eggs or chicks in the nest these inspections can save valuable lives. Some hens in captivity will lay more eggs than they can comfortably sit, so the extras can be fostered out or placed in an artificial incubator to give them all a better chance of survival. Upon inspection you may discover dented, cracked or broken eggs, and then you are able to repair slight damage or remove the remaining eggs if you think that they may be damaged also. There are a surprising number of pairs that eat or break eggs.

Most importantly, an eye can be kept on the chicks to ensure that they are being fed well, as, despite an easily accessible, good-quality diet in captivity, many pairs will only feed one or two chicks well, allowing the smaller, weaker chicks to fade. Again, should the keeper see a chick not doing well, if caught early enough it can be given supplemental feeding or hand-rearing.

Usually, given the chance to accustom themselves to this intrusion, pairs will accept it without major disapproval, but care must be taken that you do not get bitten, and more so that the chicks do not get damaged by the parents' misplaced aggression.

The easiest way of doing nest inspections for these difficult pairs is to have the nestbox situated in the outside of the aviary, and to try to entice the adult birds out of it, distracting them with something edible whilst you peek in. For pairs who just won't budge, if we must look in, we use a stiff piece of cardboard to gently move the parents off the eggs or chicks, which enables us to do anything necessary without damage.

INCUBATING EGGS

One can usually tell when a hen first lays by her appearance and behaviour. Sometimes, notably with amazons, the hen becomes swollen around the vent area in the days preceding laying and most hens will spend more time in the box in preparation. Where they will probably leave the box upon hearing your arrival, once they have an egg they will be much more reluctant to leave it, and will appear fluffed-up and slow-moving.

It is unusual for hens to start incubation in earnest upon the arrival of the first egg, usually waiting for the second or third before they start sitting tightly. Good hens will only leave the nest, once incubation has commenced, to defecate and maybe eat and drink a little – the cock will usually feed her.

The anxiety of seeing a hen off her eggs is usually unfounded: the eggs seem to be unaffected if left for up to 20 minutes, in all but the most severe weather. It is usually only the hen that incubates in parrot species, with the exception of some cockatoos and cockatiels, where the cock usually does the daytime shift, with the hen taking over at night, although some pairs will incubate one egg each.

The incubation period is usually around that listed in the table, but can be a little shorter or much longer depending on the surrounding temperature and how tightly the parent bird sits. Similarly the clutch size is an average but clutches can be only one egg or twice the average.

Very often the first clutch of a young pair will be infertile, usually due to the cock's immaturity or inexperience at mating. It may even be a year or two before he starts to fertilise the eggs – although most smaller parrots are capable of fertilising them at two years of age, and even the large macaws have bred at three years.

Inspecting the eggs/chicks can save lives should problems occur. Pictured: Blue and Gold Macaw.

Hyacinthine Macaws: incubating the eggs is usually done by hens, though some parrot breeds share the duties.

INFERTILE EGGS

Similarly, even pairs that have bred before will sometimes have infertile eggs in a clutch and maybe even whole clutches of infertile ones. The amazons are the species who most frequently have infertile eggs, usually due to the hen laying before the cock is in breeding condition. If the eggs are candled after 10 days' incubation and found to be infertile, they can be taken away, which may induce the hen to lay another, hopefully fertile, clutch. However, a note of caution: we had an amazon egg that didn't show any signs of fertility until 12 days in an incubator. We will leave an undamaged, infertile egg in a clutch of fertile ones, as it acts as a support and a hot-water bottle to newly hatched chicks.

PARENTAL CARE

Whether to leave chicks with new parents or take them for hand-rearing is the subject of much debate. Many pairs seem to need

SPECIES	AVERAGE INCUBATION PERIOD (DAYS)	CLUTCH SIZE
Conure	22 - 24	4 – larger species; up to 9 in the smaller species
Senegal	27 - 30	2 - 4
African Grey	28 - 30	3 - 5
Lories/lorikeets	23 - 25	2
Cockatoo	23 (up to 30 in larger species)	2 usually, some more prolific
Macaw	24 - 26	2 - 4
Amazon	25 - 28	3 - 4

practice with a chick or two before they are successful in rearing chicks to fledging.

However, if a pair are never given the chance we will never know if they are good parents or not. A good compromise, if there is more than one fertile egg, is to leave one with the parents and artificially incubate the other – a procedure not without danger itself. Then, at least, all the eggs are not in one basket.

Candling an egg.

If the species in question is rare or very valuable, and if you are fortunate enough to have a more common but similar species with eggs or chicks at the same stage, you could swap one of these to assess the parents' rearing capabilities. It goes without saying that good parents do a much better job of rearing than we do and where possible should be left to get on with it.

As well as being vigilant for any potential problems, our input is to ensure that there is ample food, of sufficient variety, available to the rearing parents. This may mean feeding fresh food twice or three times daily instead of the usual once and, as the chicks get bigger, in surprisingly large quantities.

Some of the favoured rearing foods are wholemeal bread with a little milk, corn-on-the-cob and pears. Most varieties of parrots will take these along with their normal rations with great gusto.

Blue and Green Macaw: there is some controversy as to whether first-time parents should be left to raise their young or whether the handler should intervene to hand-rear.

PLUCKING

Another problem that occurs with the parents rearing young is that of plucking the young. This is most common in lories, but all species have been known to do this. Very often, if the parent is plucked itself, the young will be plucked as well.

As mentioned earlier, provision of plenty to chew in the box will go a long way to preventing this, but sadly, no matter what steps you take, some pairs will continue to pluck the young nevertheless. An early sign of this is where even the downy wisps are removed from the chicks. An eye must be kept on the chicks' toes as well, as the nibbling can go as far as the removal of claws, toes and even wing-tips.

Obviously, if any signs of damage to the extremities are discovered then the chicks should be removed immediately. Half-grown chicks that are plucked are prone to being chilled, as the parents will cease brooding them, so they are candidates for hand-rearing. It is usually the soft baby feathers that are chewed, but if the flights are involved then permanent damage can occur, rendering the bird flightless.

HEALTHY YOUNG

Young chicks in the nest should appear plump and tight-skinned with a shiny appearance to the skin. Any that look thin or wrinkled with a dull appearance need immediate attention. Their legs should be examined and any bends or deformity, as well as legs stuck out at right angles, may be due to a calcium deficiency which will only be rectified if caught early enough. Greys are the most susceptible to this malady. Fungal and bacterial infections may also be the cause of unhealthy-looking chicks, and as such they must be taken and monitored or they will surely die.

It must be remembered that parrots with chicks will be fiercely protective of their space, and amazons and macaws will not hesitate to attack the keeper – cock amazons usually flying straight at the face. Also, if you haven't taken the precaution of having solid partitions between the aviaries, you may find that the pairs spend most of the time trying to fight the pair next door, even if they cannot reach them but can only see them.

FOSTERING

Sometimes you may be fortunate enough to have two or three pairs of the same species breeding at the same time. In this case, if you have a pair who do not rear babies successfully, there is the possibility of fostering eggs or young with others. Pairs that have infertile eggs or just one chick may potentially rear for others. When incubating eggs, pairs will usually accept the swapping of their infertile eggs for fertile ones. It is all right if they are due to hatch a week or ten days before the due date of their own eggs, but eggs are more likely to be abandoned if more than a day or two over the normal incubation period. Of course there are exceptions.

Similarly very few parrots will tolerate a newly-hatched baby being placed among its eggs, although some will. Ideally, put a pipping egg in the nest and the chick's call from inside the egg will alert the parents to its imminent arrival. If you already have pairs with a chick or chicks in the nest, then it is usually a simple procedure to distract the parents as described earlier and slip the baby to be fostered into the nest.

Again, chicks should be of similar ages if they are all to have a chance of survival. Some pairs will even tolerate feeding young chicks for a week and then having these replaced by others to rear for a period. This can go on for a fairly lengthy period, but care must be taken to see that unfeathered chicks are being brooded as well as fed. If you know your pair of parrots and how they behave towards their young, you will learn what liberties you can take with them.

Some parents will rear babies of different species, even if mixed with their own young. Macaws, conures and amazons will mix, as will cockatoos of different species – even cockatiels will rear young cockatoos to a certain point. African Greys have been known to rear many different species. Common sense will tell you how many risks you can take. As usual, vigilance is the keyword here.

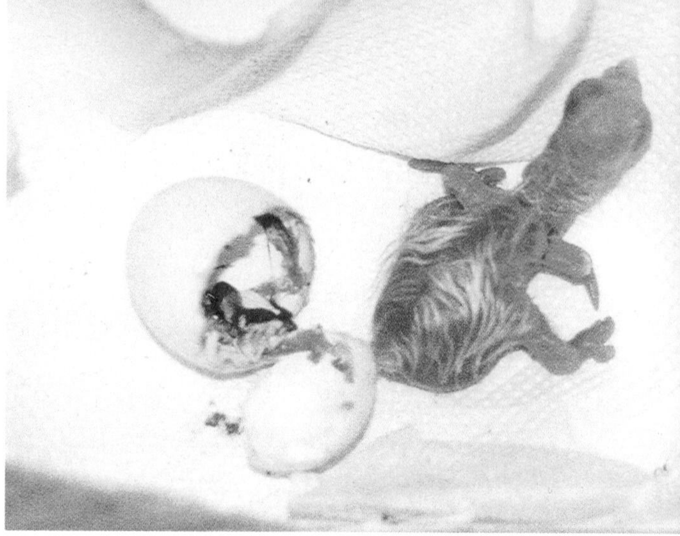

A newly-hatched chick.

The chick has dried out and is ready for its first feed.

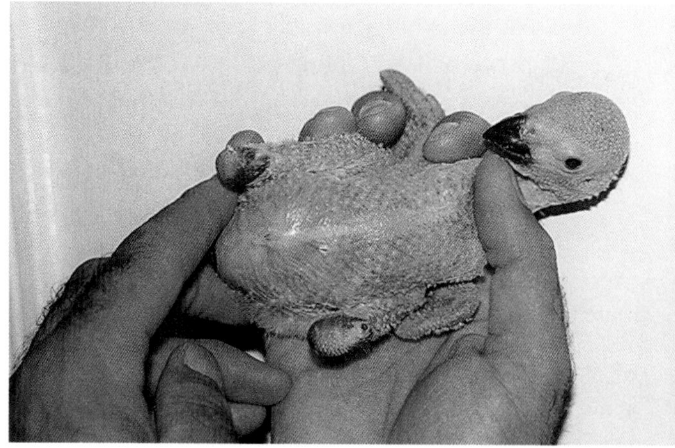

Some parents can pluck or nibble their young. This African Grey chick has had its feet bitten off by its parents.

Growth of a Healthy Chick

1. Three-and-a-half-week-old Moluccan Cockatoos.

2. A chick at four weeks old. Note: the full crop.

3. Six weeks old. At this age, cockatoo youngsters will often splay their legs like this. It should not be considered a deformity unless they cannot sit properly as well.

4. Seven-week-old Moluccan in the pin-feather stage.

5. Just feathering up at about eight weeks.

6. A ten-week-old Moluccan. Note: the feet are not fully coloured grey yet.

SENEGAL PARROTS: A CASE STUDY

by Barrett Watson

My introduction to these delightful little parrots was purely by accident. I would occasionally hear an unusual bird call in the village but could never see where it came from. One day, looking out of the window, I saw a small green and orange bird perched precariously on top of an aviary containing my young macaws. Amazingly, the Senegal showed no fear of its giant cousins, obviously relishing the company and 'kissing' through the wire!

It spent more and more time with my parrots, ignoring the food I put out for it and preferring instead the berries, buds and leaves growing at the time. His favourite haunt was a cotoneaster bush outside the kitchen window, where he would gorge on the berries and then sleep off his meal during the afternoon. As winter turned to spring and then summer, he would come through the open windows at will and sit with a pet Blue and Gold Macaw, or steal the macaw's peanuts.

SEXING SENEGALS

I refer to the Senegal as 'him' as I assumed this bold little creature must be a cock. So I decided he needed company of his own size, and started scanning the ads for a hen. When I saw a proven hen advertised, I thought it must be fate and bought her there and then, over the phone.

She duly arrived and after the initial quarantine period I put the very nervous hen in a flight with the cock. Sadly it was not love at first sight, as they sat at opposite ends of the flight ignoring one another. Undeterred, I left them together, encouraging them to eat a diet of pulses, fruit, vegetables, seed and nuts, along with some of the favoured berries.

Gradually they seemed to grow to like each other; the space between them diminished with the passing weeks. Then in November, about three months after their meeting, I noticed that the cock was spending more time in the nestbox – and swelling in the vent area. My DIY sexing was wrong! She went on to lay a clutch of three. So, I had two proven hens and no cocks. It could be worse. I didn't want to move the poor nervous hen that I had bought to another home, so I thought I would look out for two cocks for them.

However, before I had found any, I noticed that the eggs on which the hen was sitting were looking suspiciously dark – so I candled them. Yes, they were fertile. My guaranteed proven hen was now a guaranteed proven cock.

THE MYSTERY BEGINS

After the normal 27-day incubation period, three tiny, pink chicks hatched with a profusion of white down. Despite the cold of midwinter, the babies were kept warm and well fed by the parents, who showed their disapproval of my intrusions by growling. As well as the normal diet, the parents consumed copious quantities of bread and milk and sweetcorn. When the eldest chick was two weeks old I noticed the hen was out of the nestbox for the first time since they had hatched. I was horrified to find that all three chicks were dead. Their bodies were unmarked and their crops full – but with large pieces of seed in them. Could this have been the cause of their demise?

Clutch of Senegal parrots at one to two weeks old.

SECOND TRAGEDY

The hen laid a second clutch only 28 days later. When they were due to hatch, I decided to cut out the seeds and nuts and only provide them with soft food. Three out of the four eggs hatched, and all was well until the eldest was 12 days old, when again all were found dead. Post-mortem, bacteriology and virology tests all revealed nothing.

The chicks at three to four weeks old.

THIRD TIME LUCKY?

Surprisingly, she went on to lay a third clutch in February and again, three out of three hatched – no problem with fertility. By now I was wondering if she was not brooding them as I thought but just dashing into the nestbox on hearing my approach. So I took the eldest for hand-rearing at 10 days old and the others two days later. They grew slowly until 19-21 days old, when they all died over a 24-hour period, again for no apparent reason. The adult pair decided to have a holiday until October when again they hatched three. I brought the babies in for hand-rearing at 10 days old when they weighed 16, 22 and 26 grams ($^{9}/_{16}$, $^{3}/_{4}$ and $^{15}/_{16}$oz) from a hatch weight of six grams ($^{3}/_{16}$oz).

ENCHANTING

Of course, by now I didn't wonder *if* they would die – just *when*. However, they reached three weeks – eyes open, pin feathers appearing and all was well. I was still feeding every three hours as their tiny crops held no volume of food. At 28 days, they were still thriving. And at 35, 42, 49 and 56 days they were still going strong (and with feathers). By now the babies were very alert and shared a tub with two cockatoos, using them as hot-water-bottles.

I am very happy to report that they fledged into miniature bundles of mischief, enchanting all whose paths they crossed. My guess is that the first is a cock and the other two hens. But with my track record, I could be wrong.

At weanling stage. The chicks are fed on a wire-covered tray which is easy for them to grip on to, and quick to clean.

10 INCUBATING AND HAND-REARING

It has to be said that, on the whole, the parents do a much better job of incubating their eggs and rearing the chicks than we do. There are occasions, though, when things go wrong. Eggs may be repeatedly damaged, or even consumed, and chicks mutilated, plucked or killed. In these circumstances our only option if we are to save the chicks is to incubate the eggs and hand-rear the young. Incubating eggs is an art. Sometimes they will be successful with a minimum of effort and care. At other times, despite your best efforts, the embryos will be lost.

The first important consideration is to breed from healthy stock that is well fed. Eggs from such parents are much more likely to be viable. The chicks that come out are only as good as the food that goes in. The most critical stage of the egg's life is the first 7-10 days, and great care should be taken not to shake or jolt them at this stage as this could kill the developing embryo.

Every breeder of parrots should invest in an incubator as a standby in case of emergency. Even if you don't intend to incubate or hand-rear, you may have to one day. Which sort of incubator to buy is purely a matter of preference. When incubating only a few eggs, it is probably better to invest in a smallish unit, as incubators seem to run much better when filled.

The main thing that eggs require is warmth, humidity and constant turning to stop the embryo from adhering to a certain portion of the shell. Modern incubators tend to have 'forced' air; in other words the air within the incubator is kept moving by a fan

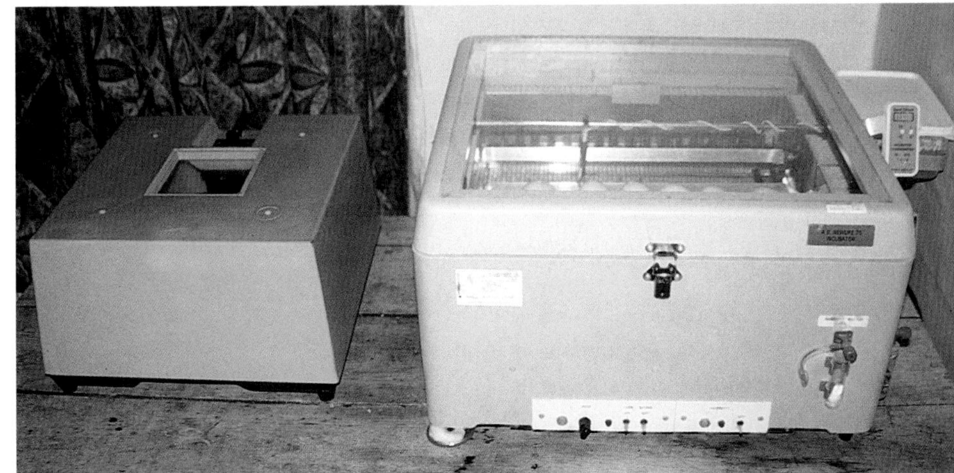

Hatcher and incubator.

Opposite page: Budgerigar.

Eggs in the incubator are started on rollers then moved to tilting trays.

over the heating elements. The turning mechanism can be by means of moving rollers, tilting trays or a moving carpet. The former and latter rotate the eggs through 360 degrees, whilst the tilting trays rock them from side to side.

We have personally used all these with success, with perhaps a preference for the rollers. The humidity can be controlled, whether crudely by having a shallow tray of distilled water within the unit, or by employing a more sophisticated automatic system.

In the long run it is prudent to discuss your requirements with the manufacturers and make your choice with their help.

Handling them carefully, the eggs to be incubated should be gently cleaned with a little warm, previously boiled, water and dipped in a purpose-made bactericidal solution before being very gently dried and placed in the incubator.

The incubator should be set up and running a week or two before you anticipate needing to use it, to ensure that it remains at a constant temperature of 37.5°C (100°F), for most species. You can also check the turning mechanism by placing a plastic egg with an arrow on it on the rollers or carpet to ensure it is being turned. We also turn them from end to end 3-7 times daily.

Attaching a hygrometer to the incubator will give a reading of the humidity, which should average 40%, depending on the weight-loss of the eggs. The egg will ideally lose 15% of its total weight during incubation. Too little lost and the chick will drown, too much and the membranes will dry preventing the chick from hatching. Keep an eye on the air space to decide on the humidity you need.

MENDING CRACKS

Any cracks or small holes in the eggs can be repaired with a light coat of clear nail varnish. Take care not to apply too much as it is not porous like the shell. Also if painted on where the chick will pip and hatch, it may inhibit the chick's escape. In this case, lightly sandpaper the excess off just before the due hatch date.

Sometimes small cracks will not be seen without the aid of a candler – a torch-like instrument with which you can illuminate the egg to spot any imperfections in the shell or the contents of the egg. You can also determine fertility with this.

STAGES OF GROWTH

After five days to a week, upon candling you can see a faint red circle within the yolk of the egg. This is the first stage of growth. This will be followed by a red blob appearing within the circle – the embryo – and then veins radiating out from it.

As the embryo grows, the veins will occupy more and more of the egg until gradually they cover the entire mass with the exception of the air space. This is the gap located at the blunt end of the egg at the end of incubation.

HATCHING

It is into this area that the chick will puncture

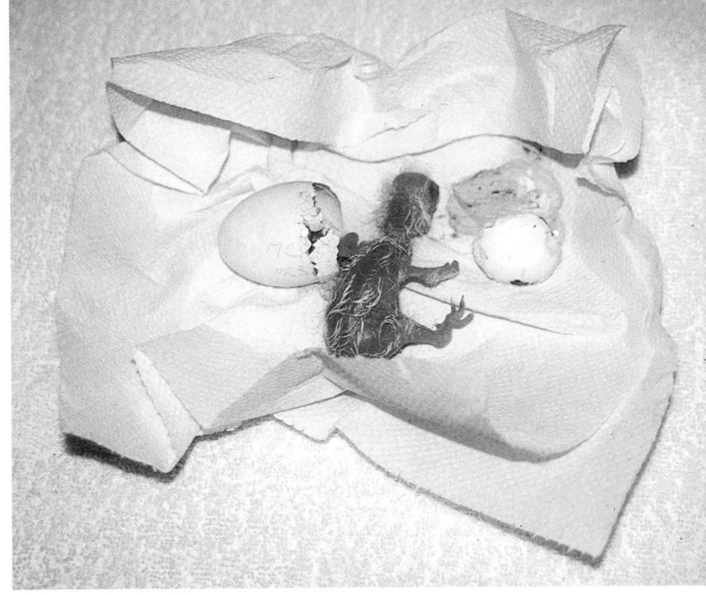

This newly-hatched chick has defecated, and is ready for his first watery feed.

a hole through the membrane and start to breathe as a prelude to hatching. As the carbon dioxide builds up and oxygen diminishes in this space, the chick then punctures the shell in one or two places to allow more air in. This is external pipping. This normally precedes hatching by 24-48 hours, but can be up to 80 hours. During this time, the chick will absorb the remainder of the yolk sac into its abdomen. Once hatching commences it can be as little as 20 minutes or as much as 3 hours before the chick struggles free of the egg.

After external pipping, the egg should be placed into a hatcher – a still-air unit set at 36.5°C (98°F) with a tray of water inside for increased humidity. Chicks can spend up to the first week of their lives in the hatcher.

EARLY CARE OF THE CHICK

After hatching, the chick should be allowed to rest for a couple of hours after having the navel dabbed with an iodine solution and being placed in a small pot, on and surrounded by tissues. In this period it will dry out whilst resting.

When the chick becomes restless and cries, it is the time to offer it a few drops of warm, previously boiled, water with an electrolyte solution added (Avipro from Vetark or similar) on the tip of a teaspoon with the sides bent in. Depending on the species and the strength of the chick, it will either lap up the water or pump on to the spoon.

On no account should any liquid be forced into the chick as this could easily drown it. However, it is important to keep young chicks well hydrated as this facilitates digestion and disease prevention. The newly hatched chick should be offered this solution every two hours for two or three feeds, before adding a little pure fruit puree such as that designed for human babies. Apple, banana, mango, papaya and pear are good ones. If buying ready-processed tins or bottles ensure that it is pure fruit with no sugar or additives. A little sprinkle of powdered food can also be added at this stage. There are now many proprietary brands of parrot-rearing food available such as Kaytee, Prettybird and others, which makes life very much easier.

Alternatively, human baby food can be used – a meat and vegetable combination, such as chicken and vegetables being the best choice. During the first week of life, the mixture should be hot and runny. When mixing up the minute quantities needed for new chicks it is usually difficult to make it too hot as a small amount will cool in the time it takes to mix it. We usually use an eggcup, and pre-warm this and the spoon before making the mixture.

Also at this stage, a pinch of paediatric probiotic (Vetark) should also be added to each feed. This helps to replicate the beneficial flora found in the parents' crops. Some breeders go to the extent of washing the crop of a healthy adult bird and adding a little of the wash to each feed. This seems unnecessary to us with the luxury of probiotics available these days.

As the chick grows, it can be moved from the hatcher to a brooder with a slightly lower temperature. From then on it can be lowered every few days by a degree or two until it is at room temperature, whereupon the chick or chicks can be kept in shaving-filled tubs in the room. We tend to only keep very young chicks on tissue for a few days to ensure that they are passing droppings regularly and easily. After that they are on the much more natural medium of wood shavings.

GROWING NEEDS

With the growth of the chicks, the crop enlarges and so more food can be given at each feed. Therefore the interval between feeds increases. The consistency of the formula can also become thicker gradually until the thickness is only decided by the ease of delivery to the chick. For large chicks or when feeding large numbers, a bulb syringe is very useful. Less messy and time-consuming than spoon-feeding, the formula can be gently dropped into a pumping chick's mouth. Great care must be taken not to force the feed or deliver it to a non-pumping youngster as it may well go into the lungs causing pneumonia and even drowning.

After the first few days of two-hourly feeds, the chicks will soon go three and four hours, until at two weeks of age most chicks will have food in the crop for six hours. From four to six weeks, feeding twice daily will be adequate, and when the chicks start to pick at solid food themselves, a daily offering of formula will suffice. Chicks tend to tell you when they are being fed too often, by refusing or regurgitating food.

The question of whether chicks need feeding during the night is debatable. We have done both – fed at intervals during the night and left tiny chicks from midnight to 6 am with no ill-effects. Unless a chick is particularly tiny or weak, there is not much to be gained from your lack of sleep – in fact if overtired you may miss something or make mistakes you would not normally do. Examination of parent-reared chicks first thing in the morning usually reveals empty crops, so perhaps this is the more natural

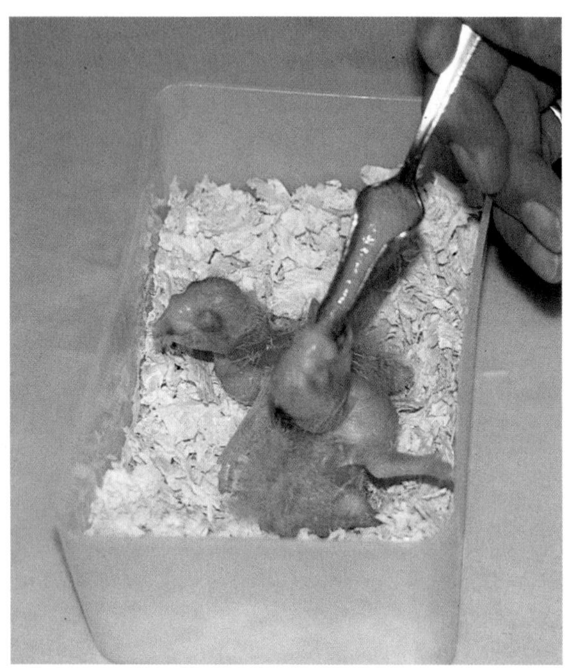

These three-day-old macaw chicks are being fed in a tub to avoid over handling and potential organ damage.

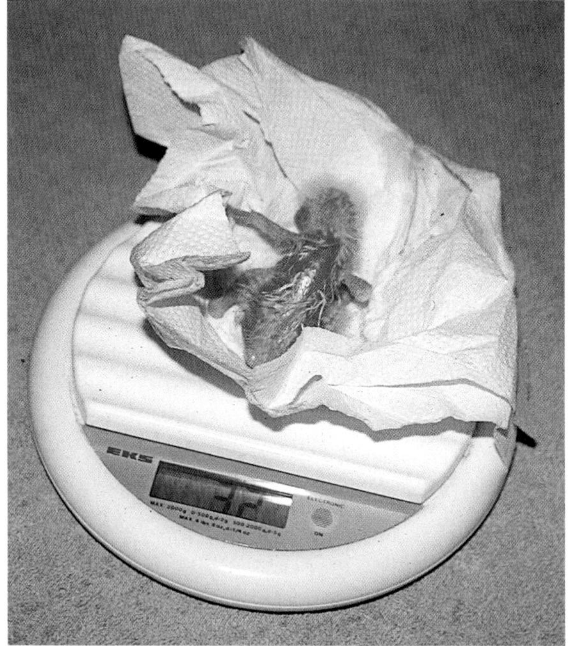

Weighing the chicks regularly and recording the results will help you to assess whether they are growing at a healthy rate.

Red-bellied Macaw at two weeks, looking dehydrated. Note the red skin and thin, pinched look in general.

Red-bellied Macaw at the same age, looking plump and healthy.

way. It is certainly prudent to ensure that a chick's crop is empty of the previous feed before adding more to it. This way you do not get a build-up of static food in the crops.

Any chick that is slow to empty the crop should be viewed suspiciously. It may be getting dehydrated, in which case administrating fluids and electrolytes for a few feeds may do the trick and get the crop moving again. Or it may be a bacterial infection, in which case antibiotics may have to be administered quickly. Thirdly, there may be a fungal infection such as candida that can be treated with Nystatin. A dehydrated baby will appear thin and dry, with a dark red tone to the skin rather than the normal healthy pink.

CHANGING BEHAVIOUR

Chicks do better when reared with others of a similar age. They seem to settle and sleep better when in contact with others. Some, macaws particularly, will sleep in very strange positions such as outstretched on their sides, upside down on their backs, and in other contorted postures. When in small groups, you can tell what temperature the chicks need by their behaviour. Cold youngsters will huddle together, whilst those that are too hot will spread out and even apart.

Some chicks of various species will go through a stage where they appear to be frightened of you and throw themselves on their backs in fear, striking out with their feet and even biting. Red-bellied Macaws and eclectus parrots are notable in this respect. It is usually a passing phase and, as such, if you treat them with patience and speak gently to them, always warning them of your impending arrival, moving slowly and deliberately around them, you will gain their confidence.

Exposing potential pets to a variety of different people will help them gain trust

Do not be alarmed – baby macaws sleep in a lot of funny positions, including upside-down!

and confidence when they go on to a new life in a new home. However, only those who are used to handling parrots should be allowed to do so at this stage lest they should frighten or upset the babies unintentionally.

Alternatively, some youngsters – most notably eclectus parrots – may become aggressive in defence of the 'nest'. The hens particularly will bite the hand that feeds them, and they can bite quite hard, especially near weaning time. Again, with time and patience, this period can be overcome, although eclectus hens tend not to be the most cuddly pets.

DANGER OF HANDFEEDING

Thought should be given to the future of any hand-reared parrots. Some become highly imprinted on the hand-feeder to the detriment of their future wellbeing. Cockatoos, males in particular, may be so imprinted that they are useless as future breeders. Steps taken to avoid over-imprinting are sensible, in case the birds do not remain as pets for their entire lives. With this in mind, if any bird is potentially going to be imprinted, it should just be fed, cleaned up and returned to its 'nest'.

If possible, easily imprinted species should be reared with others of the same species, and even of other species. In this way, the babies will identify with the fact that they are parrots and not people. Some breeders go to the extent of using a glove puppet, simulating the head of a parent bird. It is thought that even a crude fashioning of the shapes, colours and contours of the parent's head will go a long way towards avoiding imprinting. Even those parrots that are destined to be pets will possibly be less noisy and attention-seeking when reared in this manner.

GOOD HYGIENE

Mention should be made of cleaning up babies after they have been fed. Very small babies can be wiped clean with a soft tissue after being fed the watery formula. We use a freshly-washed cotton cloth to clean up older chicks that would otherwise get food adhering to their developing feathers. Don't be afraid to use a little warm water to wash any spilled food off the plumage, followed

With a breed as easily imprinted as the cockatoo, it is worth raising them with other birds, so the chicks grow up realising they are parrots, not humans.

by patting the feathers dry and then leaving nature to finish off the drying process. We have yet to have a chick suffer any ill-effects from this process, and it eliminates any bacterial build-up from dried food around the beak.

Hygiene is an important issue when rearing babies, who have not developed their full immune system, but we believe it should not be carried to extremes. Otherwise you can end up with a young bird unable to cope physiologically when exposed to the 'outside' world. Hands should be washed, preferably in an antibacterial wash, before handling eggs, chicks or their food.

The chicks themselves should be kept clean as described above. Tissue that they are bedded on should be changed at every feed, or shavings once a day. The feeding implements can be soaked in a sterilising solution (used for human infants) in between feeds. Incubators and brooders can have any mess washed off them and then be wiped over with a mild disinfectant whenever necessary.

When not in use, incubators and brooders can be thoroughly cleaned, wiped off with bleach and even fumigated where possible. This can be done by placing the unit in a well-ventilated room, away from livestock, and placing a shallow bowl inside. Into this, a mixture of a splash of formaldehyde and a half-teaspoon of potassium permanganate crystals should be added. This produces a vapour that will kill all organisms and can be left for 24 hours within the unit. Once the dish is removed, the unit should be left open to the air for a couple of days before being used again.

RINGING

We believe that chicks should be close-ringed wherever possible, with the year of birth and a personal coded number for identification purposes stamped on the ring. Aluminium rings are fine for the smaller species, but stainless steel ones are preferable in that they cannot be easily crushed or tampered with. The downside is that they are harder to remove in an emergency – but equally difficult for thieves to remove. A properly fitted, correctly sized ring stays with the parrot for life and is very useful for record keeping. It is surprising how easy it is to forget such simple facts as the year of birth, and from which pair a bird comes.

The age at which a youngster should be ringed is dependent on many factors, such as species, whether parent- or hand-reared, and how rapid the growth rate is. Most of the smaller, quicker-growing species are ready to be ringed from 10-14 days old, while the larger species may be three weeks or more before the foot is large enough to prevent the ring from slipping off. Correctly, the foot shouldn't be so big that you have to force the ring on.

To ring a chick is a simple procedure, made simpler if there are two of you. Ensure that the chick hasn't got a full crop, as handling it like this could force the food out and choke

Red-bellied Macaw at seven weeks old. Note: the closed ring is caked with excreta which must be cleaned before it constricts the blood supply.

it. Then one person can hold the chick securely in cupped hands, extending the leg through the fingers. The second person can then grasp the foot and line up the largest backward facing toe with the two forward facing ones. It is then just a matter of slipping the ring over these three toes and pulling the fourth one through afterwards. If this one is reluctant to come through, a small blunt knitting needle can be used to aid its passage. An eye should then be kept on the ring for a couple of days in case it should slip off and have to be replaced.

If, on the other hand, you have left it a little late to ring the chick, a little Vaseline rubbed on the foot can help to ease it on, but this should be cleaned off well afterwards. As a last resort, a ring one size bigger could be used, but the danger of something getting caught between the ring and the leg is obviously greater. Rings can be ordered from either specialist societies or direct from the manufacturers.

OTHER IDENTIFICATION

Other methods of identification can include tattooing and microchipping, although these can be done at any age. As a theft-deterrent tattoos can be done on the bare skin of macaws', Palm Cockatoos' and African Greys' faces – not attractive but hard for thieves to disguise. Otherwise it can be done somewhere discreet, such as under a wing.

Microchipping is a useful aid in the proof of ownership if stolen parrots are found. Birds on CITES (see chapter Thirteen) have to be microchipped if they are not close-ringed and you wish to apply for exemption certificates to offer them for sale or display. It is quite a simple procedure, rather like a large injection into the breast muscle, where once installed it is very hard to locate and remove, but is picked up on a scanner passed over the bird.

WEANING

When the chicks are virtually fully-feathered and taking an interest in their surroundings, it is the time to start the weaning process. They should be placed in a box cage (one with three sides enclosed for security and draught prevention). The base should be 1/2"x 1/2" or 1"x1" (1.25cm or 2.5cm) welded mesh, depending on the size of the chick. They will sit on this to start with, so they then will not come into contact with their faeces. A low perch, a couple of inches above the mesh, can be fitted. This can be gradually raised as the chicks start perching and become more confident and secure in their grip.

Various food items can be placed on the floor, which the chicks will start to sample and nibble at. A shallow bowl of pulses, corn-on-the-cob, half an apple and a slice of wholemeal bread are all usually treated with interest. The chicks may still need two hand-feeds a day at this stage, but as they begin to ingest more and more food for themselves, this can be reduced to one feed daily. We usually give this in the morning as, somewhat surprisingly, many chicks will sample more food when they already have food in the crop. Otherwise, they may just sit and cry

If stressed, African Greys can revert to begging to be hand-fed even into adulthood.

Weanlings should be introduced to a low perch, which is gradually raised. Pictured: Red-bellied Macaws aged 10-11 weeks.

and wait for a parent to appear and feed them.

As the chicks start to eat more food a greater variety can be offered, such as seeds and nuts, and also one of the complete pelleted diets now available. The more types of food parrots are introduced to at an early age, the greater the likelihood of them being less fussy as they grow older. Once the chicks are perching, the feed bowls can be raised up to perch level to lessen the risk of soiling.

There is no age at which one can say a parrot will be weaned – some refuse hand-feeds after a relatively short period of time, whilst others, particularly the large macaws and cockatoos, will still beg for food at a year old. This is quite natural, as they would stay with their parents in the wild for this period and longer, so they should not be refused food.

Quite remarkable in the weaning process are the lories and lorikeets, which will start to lap warm nectar mixture from an early age – even before they are fully feathered – and once they have mastered this they are virtually self-sustaining. However, they can be a little over-enthusiastic at this stage and cover themselves in this mixture, and so will need careful cleaning after each feed. Mention should be made that, whilst rearing lories, the same basic formula will be used for the young as well as for the adult birds.

Some youngsters of the more sensitive species such as Greys and cockatoos, will revert to begging for a hand-feed when they have been weaned for a while, especially when stressed, such as when moving home. Again this should not be denied them, but should be restricted to once daily, so encouraging them to seek food for themselves. Doing this will do no harm and in fact it will make them feel more secure. Youngsters should always have access to unlimited food – as in fact should adult parrots – just not too much of the same thing, especially sunflower seed.

WHEN THINGS GO WRONG

Sometimes, upon candling eggs, it can be seen that all is not as it should be. The embryo may be malpositioned, in that it just fills a portion of the egg at a stage when it should fill it totally, apart from the air space. In this instance, the egg should be incubated with the unused portion at the bottom, so that gravity encourages it to spread.

Some embryos will also be upside down, with the head at the sharp end of the egg so when it pips there is no air space. Sometimes, because of the malposition, the chick will pip through a vein. Ideally this should be sealed with a styptic pencil or silver nitrate. Then, carefully, with tweezers prise away a little of the shell around the chick's beak to allow it to breathe more easily. Usually the chick will then manage to hatch normally in its own time Otherwise an assisted hatch may be necessary.

Wherever possible, assisting the hatch should be avoided. We tend to intervene too often with hatches, resulting in the death of the chick. This is because we think the chick needs assistance to hatch when in fact it is simply resting and absorbing the remainder of the yolk in readiness to hatch. So, upon our intervention, blood vessels are broken and bacteria enter the abdomen via the unabsorbed yolk sac causing fatal infection.

However, if the chick really is struggling to escape from the egg, due to the membranes being too dry and tough through lack of humidity, or to over-thick shells through calcium deposits (or nail varnish), then we have to intervene. We would very gently remove small pieces of shell, working gradually around the perimeter of the egg space. Moisten the inner membrane with a finger-tip dipped in boiled water and any blood vessels will be exposed. Then, avoiding these, the membrane can be carefully peeled back to reveal the chick's beak and head. This can be done over a period of time, allowing the chick to rest in between.

You may then find the chick will break free of the weakened shell in these rest periods, thereby eliminating the need for further intervention from you. On no account should the chick be pulled from the egg – its struggles will bring it out when it is ready. Once free, the chick should be allowed to rest and then be treated as normal.

As mentioned earlier keeping chicks well hydrated is very important. However, sometimes we can over-stretch the crop due to the liquid nature of the diet, and the chick then gets a condition known as pendulous crop: the food sits below the exit to the stomach. This can lead to sour crop – whereby the food starts to ferment in the crop. The remedy is to feed little and often, massage the crop gently to encourage the food to dissipate, and prop the chick and its crop up with tissues or towels – depending on its size. As a last resort, a crop bra could be used – this is a cotton sling-like affair that supports the crop and is tied up behind the chick's neck to stop the crop from sagging. As the chick grows, if the procedures described above are used, the crop will regain its natural tautness and work normally once more.

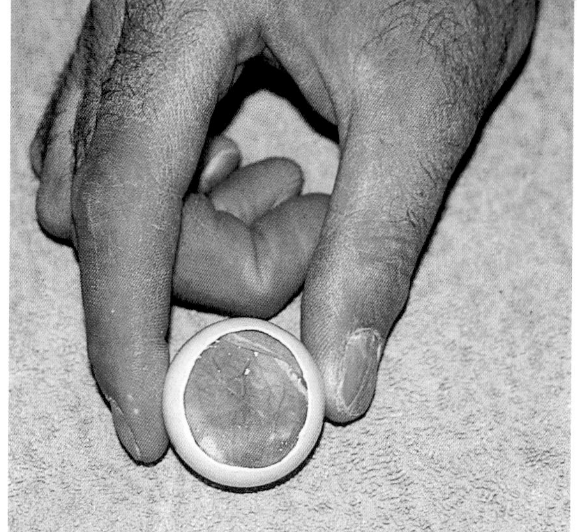

Chick at the point of hatch, having not punctured the membrane. It was successfully assisted.

SKELETAL PROBLEMS

Another relatively common occurrence in chicks is fractures of the legs or wings, or bent limbs due to rickets. These are most commonly seen in Greys and macaws – the former because many pairs of Greys will not eat a varied diet in captivity ending up calcium-deficient, and the latter due to the fast growth-rate of the chicks. Prevention being better than cure, ensure that all pairs are supplemented with calcium. Any chicks displaying signs of rickets – bent limbs or splayed legs – can be given an injection of calcium lactate, topped up with oral supplementation.

Folding fractures in young chicks can be eased straight manually and then taped into position with several layers of gauze, and then bound tightly with Vetrap bandage. Keeping the chick immobile is the difficult part – hanging it in a sling with the legs dangling is probably the most successful. Watch for the toes becoming swollen as this indicates that the binding is too tight. As time goes on the chick can be gradually lowered to become more weight-bearing.

Badly broken limbs may need surgical intervention. Pinning the limbs may be the only way forward. Similarly, fractures in wings can be strapped next to the body, or pinned if too serious. Most chicks' fractures are quick-healing due to the rapid growth of the baby, and are easily supported, as the chick will not destroy the support, unlike an adult parrot.

CROP BURN

Lastly, another occurrence with chicks is crop burn. This is caused by syringing formula that is too hot into the chick's crop where it then burns from within. Spoon-fed chicks will not accept formula that is too hot, spitting it out or throwing themselves backwards away from it. Hot spots in microwaved food are the biggest cause of this condition, so care should be taken to stir the food thoroughly, and ensure that it is the right temperature; a cooking thermometer can be used to stir it.

Burnt crops will appear reddish in the first instance, then blister, scab up and finally a hole will appear and food will trickle out. It is at this stage that the bird should be taken to the vet, who will anaesthetise the baby, cut away the dead portion of the crop, then stitch the crop up internally before sealing the outer skin.

Hand-rearing parrots is largely a matter of common sense and attention to detail and, with luck, should go smoothly and result in a healthy, happy, well-adjusted bird.

Development of a Cropburn

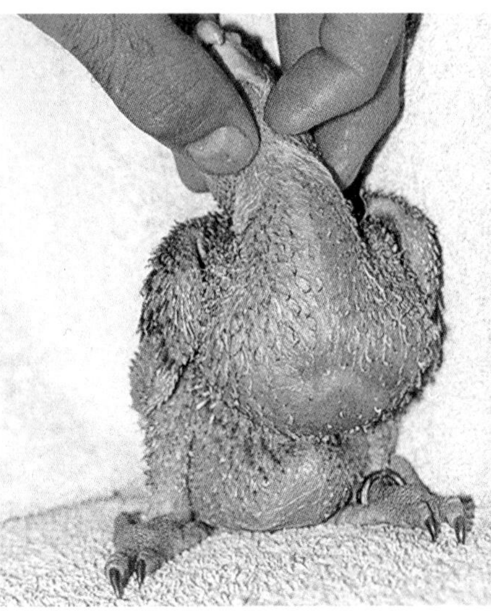

Double Yellow-headed Amazon chick with blistering due to crop burn.

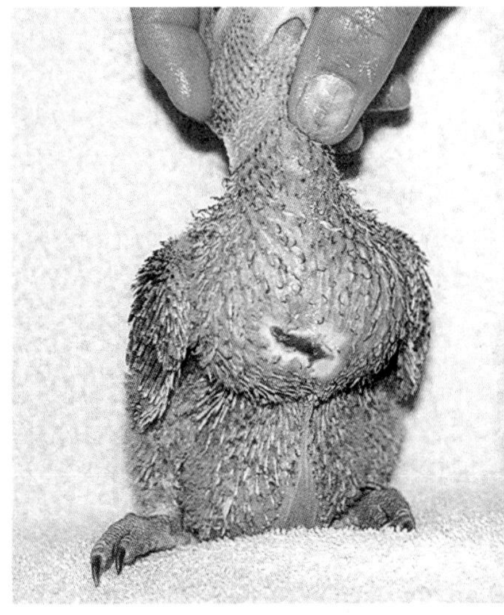

The same chick one week later with scab forming.

Military Macaw, with crop scab ready to be removed. Both chicks made full recoveries after surgery.

THE ENIGMA OF THE RED-BELLIED MACAW

Michael Hurley and Barret Watson

We had been intrigued by this species for some years, attracted by both their colouring and their size. We were also mystified that the Red-bellies should behave so differently from other macaws. Most macaws breed and adapt readily to captivity, so why not these? The ones we had seen appeared highly stressed at being in captivity. All we had read about them gave me the impression that they were difficult to maintain in captivity, dying for no apparent reason, prone to obesity and rarely breeding successfully.

NEW ARRIVALS

We enjoy an avicultural challenge and so decided to purchase a pair of Red-bellied Macaws. Our hope was that with meticulous husbandry, they might breed. The birds arrived by national carrier on the 30th October 1992. We learned from the previous owner that they had been bought from an importer two years before. For most of this time they had been maintained in a suspended cage measuring 4ft x 4ft (1.2m x 1.2m). They had been given a nest box 12in (30.5cm) square and 2ft (61cm) deep. We were told they would not accept having a top to the box. The pair had produced three clutches of eggs, two of which were found to be dead in the shell at varying stages of development. A fourth clutch proved infertile.

The hen had a dropped wing and was unable to fly, but otherwise both birds appeared healthy. We were encouraged by the fact that they had produced fertile eggs, had laid more than one clutch, and had been established in captivity for two years. They had accepted a wide variety of foods, but were also given an unlimited amount of sunflower seeds and pine nuts.

SETTLING IN

The pair were transferred to an aviary with a shelter, in all 8ft x 3ft x 6ft (2.4m x 91.5cm x 1.83m) high. We arranged branches inside to enable the hen to get around without difficulty. Initially they were given a diet of unlimited sunflower seeds with some fresh fruit. At this time they appeared anxious, calling repeatedly in a high-pitched manner when the aviary was approached, but this gradually subsided after the first week. For two weeks they had to be ushered into the shelter at night, but after this they went in themselves.

HOUSING

For maximum security a second aviary was installed along the length of the first one, access being given by a 2ft (61cm) square opening in the wire. This second aviary is larger than the first, being 10ft x 5ft x 6ft (3.05m x 1.5m x 1.83m) high. It is in a very secluded position, the side, back and a third of the roof being enclosed with wood. Nestboxes were installed before the birds were given access. These are upright, approximately 12in (30.5cm) square, and varying in height between 18in (45.5cm) and 36in (91.5cm). They were placed as high as possible in the hope of giving the birds more sense of security. Natural branches of differing thickness were placed around the aviary to allow the hen to roam freely.

Garden containers with conifers and tree mallows were placed around the sides, again with security in mind. The second aviary was treated as the Red-bellies' safe haven. It would be entered only if absolutely essential. The feeding and cleaning-out regime were continued as usual in the first aviary.

SEAL OF APPROVAL

The birds spent the first few days gradually exploring their new extension. They totally destroyed the conifer and half of one of the tree mallows. However, after this they only chewed their perching.

They became very excited with one of the nestboxes. This was the largest of the three, being 36in (91.5cm) in length and located under the sheltered part of the roof. But although very interested and making many attempts at entering the box through the entrance hole, they could not quite bring themselves to enter the box completely. Remembering the previous owner's comments, the top of the nestbox was then removed. Their pleasure at this was a joy to watch and they had both entered the nestbox through the top within 10 minutes. They made delighted chuckling sounds as they went up and down the ladder and looked out at the world through the entrance as though it were a porthole.

They have roosted inside this box ever since. If they feel threatened in any way they go in. Perhaps they feel they can't be seen when they use the nestbox hole to look out – they have never been observed using the entrance hole for going in or out of the box. It became evident that they now only entered the first aviary to feed, spending the rest of their time in the new one.

BEHAVIOUR CHANGE

By the beginning of May there was a definite change in the birds' behaviour. They became very timid, calling in alarm even when fed. They spent long periods in the nestbox and the volume of food consumed reduced by approximately 50%. When seen, they appeared to be in good health, so no action was taken. It was hoped that this change was a prelude to breeding activity. The change was short-lived – after a week their behaviour was back to what it had been before.

The nestbox was checked and found to contain a large amount of excrement. It appeared they had been roosting by clinging to the side of the ladder with the result that the droppings had heavily soiled the floor of the box. This was cleaned out and fresh wood shavings put in.

At the beginning of July their behaviour changed again. They became noisy when the aviary was approached, and they took to chewing their perches and rushing to the nestbox at the slightest disturbance. Once again their food consumption was reduced by about half. This behaviour continued for two weeks after which the hen spent all of her time in the nestbox.

DIET

Having read that this species is prone to obesity, the decision was made to change to a low-fat diet. This was accomplished by a gradual reduction of pine nuts and sunflower seeds and an

The two surviving Red-bellied Macaw chicks at a week old.

increase in fresh fruit and vegetables. Each day they received soaked pulses, sweetcorn, grated carrot and diced apple, together with whatever fruits and vegetables were available. This was mixed with decreasing amounts of sunflower seeds and pine nuts. A vitamin supplement was added daily.

Three months later, they were eating a dessertspoonful of hulled sunflower seeds between them daily, with the addition of about six pine nuts if there were frosts, together with fresh food. It was tempting to cut out the seeds and nuts altogether, but because in the wild they would feed almost exclusively on the fruits of the buriti palm, it was felt this might have been too extreme a measure.

They ate far more than would be expected for birds of their size. And they certainly appeared to enjoy their food, rushing to the dish as soon as it was put in the aviary in the mornings. The hen became increasingly confident and by the end of six months was trying to bite my hand in her eagerness to get to the food.

EGGS LAID

In mid-July the nestbox was checked – with difficulty as the hen refused to move – and an egg was discovered. This was white and more round than is usual for parrot eggs. Reluctantly the decision was made to remove the eggs as soon as they were laid. This was for a number of reasons: the birds' history suggested that their incubation technique was poor; there was a certain amount of disturbance going on as we were preparing to move house; by removing the eggs it was anticipated that the total clutch would be larger, and we were keen to produce steady breeding stock for the future. Six eggs were laid, the last one being the day before the aviary was dismantled. By day three of incubation it was ascertained that all the eggs were fertile.

HAND REARING

The 25-day incubation period was finished in an incubator at 37.5°C (100°F). In this way we could monitor progress and intervene if necessary. The external pip-to-hatch time varied from 24 to 48 hours, and five chicks hatched without assistance. The average weight at hatch was 14g (1/2oz). When dry, the chicks had a profusion of white down, the beak, toes and nails being pink. The first three feeds were of boiled water and Avipro. The chicks were very difficult to feed at first, with no response at all for 36 hours. Only a tiny drop was ingested at each two-hourly feed. Gradually apple and banana baby food was added, with baby food chicken casserole and vegetables.

By the third day, all but one of the chicks were very active and vocal – and eating vigorously. Sadly, the third-hatched chick was weak and lethargic and died at three days without weight gain. At this stage the beaks of the others began to darken and feathers started to appear under the skin by the 14th day. By now their crops had expanded and they were consuming large quantities of food every four hours. At three weeks, ground sunflower and smooth peanut butter were added to the mixture. The chicks were ringed with Parrot Society 'T' rings.

PROBLEMS AND PECULIARITIES

Another difficulty arose at around this time. All the babies became very nervous, squirming and throwing themselves on to their backs if touched or startled. If you have ever tried to feed a chick without touching it, you can imagine how difficult it was. Having consumed some food, they would often lie on their backs afterwards. At five weeks, the pinfeathers on flights, tail and shoulders opened. The feet became dark and the stripe on the culmen was clearly defined. They became calm again, except in the presence of strangers. Another peculiarity of these unique birds was the random formation of teardrops on one or both eyes for no apparent reason. Also unusually, they would stand with one foot on top of the other, feet crossed.

These alert and active babies were placed in a weaning cage at eight weeks of age and on a low perch soon afterwards. Still taking three feeds a day, from about nine weeks they would sample digestive biscuits, sweetcorn, fruit and pulses. The facial skin was still white, unlike the dark yellow of the adults. Their maiden flight was at 10 weeks. Interestingly, the babies tended to cling to the wire sides of the cage, just like their wild-caught counterparts, in preference to perching.

During the rearing of these Red-bellied Macaws, there were two more unusual occurrences. First, the second-hatched became very ill at nine days of age. When we came to give it the first feed of the day, we saw that it was a dark blotchy red, dehydrated and lifeless. Its crop had not emptied from the previous evening's feed. Without much hope for its survival, we dropped some water and Avipro into its beak and massaged its crop gently to try to get things moving. It managed to keep its grip on life and at 11 days it became active again, gaining eight grams (5/16oz) in weight. While the chick still looked dehydrated, a blister-like swelling formed on its neck – so large it had difficulty raising its head. Despite consultations with leading avian veterinarians we found no cause for these strange symptoms. Gradually, over a period of three weeks, the chick regained a normal appearance and soon became a strapping young weanling.

However, the troubles were not yet over. The first-hatched did not make good weight gains and, at 50 days old, it lost half the length of all the growing secondary flight feathers – about one inch (2.5cm). PBFD and polyomavirus tests proved negative and we wondered if this nervous baby could have had a fright when the feathers were growing, the resulting stress-induced weak point causing them to break off. She subsequently grew normal secondaries before weaning.

HOPES FOR THE FUTURE

Despite the setbacks, all the babies were soon boisterous, confident and beautiful healthy youngsters which we hope to integrate into future breeding programmes. We are sure that in the meantime they will be delightful pets. If we are fortunate enough to breed from the pair again, the plan is to replace the eggs with dummy ones and to incubate artificially, but then to return the eggs when they have internally pipped, thus giving the parents the opportunity to raise their young.

A group of Red-bellied Macaw chicks at several stages of growth. Clockwise from right: one week old, five weeks old, ten weeks old and nine weeks old.

11 COMMON HEALTH PROBLEMS AND DISEASES

Parrots are generally very healthy, and will often exist for many years in conditions that are far from ideal. In years gone by, parrots that had this type of existence eventually did fall ill, and a sick bird then becomes a dead bird.

In the present day, there are unfortunately still many parrots that are not given optimum conditions. It is a sad reflection to know that avian vets commonly see parrots that have fallen ill due to poor nutrition. With our increased knowledge and skill in the area of parrot breeding, it is disappointing that most chicks would appear to be hand-reared, with few opportunities for socialisation with their peers. This may result in an increase in emotional disorders.

It must be hoped that eventually parrot keepers' new-found knowledge will be consolidated and translated into more effective practical husbandry techniques, which will prevent these very easily rectified disorders.

Avian medicine has made many advances in recent years. Most parrot keepers will know of an avian vet, and most general veterinary surgeons are willing to consult with the parrot keeper's choice of avian vet. This trend has proved extremely useful, with more parrot disease being correctly diagnosed, which has resulted in improved treatment outcomes.

Young birds are more at risk of illness. Pictured: a young macaw with severe bacterial infection. Note the reddened skin and dehydration.

Opposite page: African Grey.

The popularity of parrot keeping has brought to light some bird diseases which unfortunately appear to be on the increase, and for which there are currently no cures. However, research is being undertaken in various centres around the world and, with increased scientific knowledge, there is every possibility of either a cure or a preventative vaccination. Avian medicine continues to make advances and this looks likely to continue for several years to come.

ASPERGILLOSIS

This is an infectious disease caused by a mould. The fungus that is responsible for the mould is known as Aspergillus fumigatus. A component of this fungus is the green mould sometimes seen on bread, and the mould that sometimes collects on uneaten food at the bottom of the aviary floor. It is important to understand that the spores of this mould are all around us and are transmitted by breathing them in. However, in certain conditions the level of the spores will be much greater, which will increase the chances of birds contracting this disease.

The fungus develops readily in warm moist conditions, often where drying out does not occur and where there is inadequate ventilation. For this reason, bark flooring could increase the likelihood of your parrot developing aspergillosis. It will also flourish in damp aviary dust and stored seed, nuts and grain. Peanuts are frequently blamed for this type of infection.

Parrots that are stressed have a suppressed immune system, as do those with poor nutrition, and those with other illnesses such as Psittacine Beak and Feather Disease. All these conditions are going to increase the risk of this infection.

The symptoms of the disease may vary from bird to bird. Some will have an acute collapse, with difficulty breathing and appearing to be choking. Others have a slower onset, with increased respiratory rate, which may be accompanied by gurgling or clicking sounds. There may also be changes in the voice. Some develop pneumonia. These symptoms may become more severe and eventually may lead to vomiting and partial paralysis of the legs.

It is important that the disease is diagnosed in its early stages, as this will improve the prognosis. The vet can prescribe a range of drugs that may be given in a variety of ways, including by nebulisation – this creates a fine aerosol spray that is breathed in by the bird and delivers the drugs into the respiratory structures. If the parrot is very ill, it may also require tube feeding and other supportive care.

Aspergillosis is not particularly contagious and will tend to affect birds that are in poor condition; good husbandry will significantly decrease the chances of infection.

PSITTACOSIS

This tends to be the disease that the general public associates with parrots. It also comes under the names of ornithosis and chlamydiosis. It doesn't just affect parrots but is found amongst other bird species also. The probable reason why it is so well known is that it is a zoonotic infection. This means that it is an infection which can be transmitted from animals to man. In the case of psittacosis, other birds such as poultry, pigeons and other wild and migratory birds may be affected, and also some other pets such as dogs and cats, plus large herbivores such as cattle and sheep. In one study, it was suggested that up to 45% of cats had evidence of previously having or actively having the infection. It is thought, however, that cats, dogs and humans are unable to transmit this disease to their own kind.

Psittacosis is a highly contagious disease and is caused by an organism called chlamydia psittaci. It is unusual in itself because it is neither a bacterium nor a virus but falls somewhere in-between. There are several different strains of chlamydia psittaci, some causing much more serious conditions than others. Again it would appear that those birds that have a suppressed immune system, caused by stress or another infection, are more likely to contract chlamydia. A major problem in controlling the disease is that some birds will be asymptomatic, that is, they are carriers of the disease and therefore maybe shedding the organism and infecting other birds, but not showing any symptoms themselves.

Quarantine time suggested for this disease is 45 days. Infection is via two routes. The first is via the droppings of the infected bird; this includes droppings that are in a dry state, which may then remain virulent for several months. The second route is through respiratory transmission, from respiratory discharges, feather dust, and ingestion of food and water containing the organism. Unfortunately having the disease once does not prevent re-infection at a later date.

The symptoms of psittacosis will vary dependent upon the infecting strain and on the bird's general health status. The symptoms commonly manifest themselves around respiratory and digestive system involvement. Some parrot species have a tendency to demonstrate particular symptoms. For example, budgerigars and pionus parrots are prone to respiratory problems, and amazons are prone to weight loss and lime-green faeces.

Many symptoms can be indicative of a chlamydia infection and, for this reason, vets will commonly test for the disease. This is not straightforward, as chlamydia psittaci is shed intermittently. This means it is quite possible to have a negative test result when the parrot has the disease. This situation has benefited considerably from antibody test-kits for psittacosis. The vet can give an antibody

The budgerigar is prone to respiratory problems.

level from a reagent kit at the surgery. There is a scale of 1-6, and above 2 is a positive result. The parrot can then be retested every 3-4 weeks, which will further demonstrate antibody levels and response to treatment.

Once diagnosed your vet can prescribe antibiotics for the condition. This may start with injections. The course of treatment for this condition is long, continuing for a minimum of 45 days. Prognosis is variable and is dependent upon the strain of the disease acquired. It is therefore extremely important that there is follow-up after the parrot has made a recovery, because some birds may become carriers. Identification of this status is very important to prevent further spread of the disease. Follow-up investigations are likely at three and six months post-treatment. If your bird has been diagnosed with this disorder, you should seek advice from your vet in relation to your own safety and the safety of your other birds if you have any.

Amazons are susceptible to sinus problems.

PSITTACOSIS IN PARROT-KEEPERS

In humans, the infection normally presents as influenza-type symptoms. The temperature is usually elevated, there may be a dry cough, lethargy, headaches and nausea. Large amounts of mucus are not normally present in the form of a productive cough or a runny nose. If you keep parrots and you are presenting with this set of symptoms, you are well-advised to see your doctor and to advise the doctor of your involvement with parrots. Untreated, psittacosis in humans can develop into pneumonia with serious consequences. Treatment, if started in the early stages, is fast and effective. As with parrots, having the infection once will not give you protection if exposed at a later date.

SINUS PROBLEMS

Some parrots do have problems with their sinuses. Amazon parrots would appear to have a particular predisposition to this. The presenting symptoms are normally a discharge from one or both nostrils. This discharge is usually clear and watery. The reasons for such a discharge can be several, including infection, allergic conditions and environmental irritants such as cigarette smoke, paint fumes and a greater level of dust in the environment, or chronic Vitamin A deficiency.

It is likely that your vet will take a swab, preferably from a sinus flush. This is where the sinus is flushed out. The swab will be sent for culture and sensitivity, as it is important to determine if an infective agent is the cause of the discharge, and what it is, so that the appropriate antibiotic (if bacterial) or anti-fungal agent, is used to treat the bird.

If the cause is thought to be due to an irritant or allergic response, then it is important to remove the parrot from what is thought to be causing the problem. An ioniser and improved ventilation may well assist this. Chronic vitamin A deficiency is unfortunately more common that it should be, and is often seen in African Greys. If this is thought to be the cause, there is a need to ensure that the parrot eats foods that are vitamin A rich. Dark greens, sweetcorn and carrot are good sources. If the parrot isn't good at eating these types of foods, you can supplement the diet with a vitamin preparation which contains the necessary amount of vitamin A. If the condition persists, one can't rule out foreign bodies or tumours. Discharging nostrils or lumps in this area are not normal and it would be unwise to ignore such symptoms.

LEAD POISONING

Not as common as it was, as the amount of lead found in houses has diminished over the years. It is no longer used in paint and children's toys. However, lead does still exist in the pipes of some older homes, and some curtains have lead weights in the bottom. Parrots, being naturally curious and destructive, can ingest particles of lead from either of these sources. The usual symptoms tend to be central nervous system signs, which may result in uncoordinated movement of legs and wings and sometimes partial paralysis of the legs. Loose faeces are another sign in psittacines. Some amazons may have blood in their droppings.

If suspected, it is important that the parrot is taken to the vet, who should be able to confirm the diagnosis by monitoring the blood lead levels. Treatment will involve injections into the muscle, which will be given regularly for 5-7 days.

ZINC POISONING

Whilst it is likely that lead poisoning should be declining, zinc poisoning may be on the increase. It is now common for cheaper cages and aviary wire to be available. These products do not have the same quality standards as those wires that have been hot-dipped and brushed. The cheaper versions have small tags of metal attached, and the wire has not been brushed. This has left a zinc deposit on the wire. If you are using the cheaper wire, it is suggested that it should be thoroughly brushed. The deposit coming off it will be clearly seen. It should then be washed to further remove the deposits.

The symptoms of zinc poisoning are quite variable, as much depends upon how much zinc has been ingested. Macaws, conures and amazons may have a loss of appetite, weight reduction, vomiting and bulky green faeces. African Greys and cockatoos may have liquid droppings and may drink excessively. Feather plucking or picking maybe a problem in both groups. If zinc poisoning is suspected, the vet will take a blood sample to measure the zinc level within the blood, which will confirm the diagnosis. As with lead poisoning, the source of the zinc poisoning must be removed to assist recovery. Treatment from the vet will last for 7-14 days and include drugs which may be given by injection or orally.

AVITAMINOSIS

This condition is caused primarily by the lack of vitamin A in the diet. There are some rare conditions which prevent absorption of vitamin A, but these are quite rare compared to the dietary deficiency. Vitamin A is required for healthy body function. If vitamin A is taken in the diet, the effects will tend to focus on the skin, vision, skeletal development and reproduction. All these body systems are obviously quite important in adult birds, the integrity of the skin particularly so, as the skin is the main barrier to bacteria, viruses and fungi. Vitamin A deficiency can therefore open the pathway to various infections, and this can lead to gradual debilitation of the bird's health.

Skin is made up of epithelial tissue. This tissue also surrounds areas inside the bird's body and can therefore affect the functioning of several body systems. As a result, symptoms can be variable, dependent upon the severity of the vitamin A deficiency and the areas of the body affected.

Common early warning symptoms include frequent minor infections, including fungal infections of the mouth, such as thrush,

Elderly Blue and Gold Macaw with an enlarged nasal passage, due to a past vitamin A deficiency.

gradual reduction of vision, and sneezing. A longer-term effect, which sometimes seen, are bumps around the area of the sinuses, which are between the top of the beak and the eye. These contain cheesy white deposits.

The treatment for this condition primarily involves improving the diet. Seed diets contain insufficient amounts of vitamin A. If you feed your parrots a seed diet alone, it can be expected that they will suffer from this condition. Foods that contain significant amounts of vitamin A include dark vegetables, sweetcorn and carrot. It is important that the improved diet is maintained. This can be further supplemented by a good vitamin supplement that contains vitamin A and D_3. There are several of these manufactured specifically for birds and parrots on the market.

PSITTACINE BEAK AND FEATHER DISEASE (PBFD)

This disease, probably above all others, fills the established parrot owner with fear and dread. At present there is no cure, although there is some promising research being undertaken which may result in effective vaccination. The disease was first thought to affect cockatoos and for this reason is sometimes referred to as Cockatoo rot.

It is now known to be caused by a virus, and this has been named Diminuvirus, which is a descriptive term because of its very small size. PBFD is contagious and does occur in the wild. It is not thought that a carrier state exists, but it is known that baby birds appear to react faster to the virus than mature birds. Progress of the disease can be slow, with some birds succumbing more quickly than others. With good care, which needs to encompass physical, psychological and social care, life expectancy can be extended to a few years.

The symptoms of PBFD fall within two main areas:

(i) Depression of the immune system.
(ii) Beak, feather and skin abnormality.

Some species appear more susceptible to the disease than others do, with neotropical parrots (South American birds) being the least susceptible. The progress of the disease also varies from species to species. For example, Vasa parrots' plumage changes from its normal dark coloration to white. Birds that have a compromised immune system are not able to fight off infection, and therefore suffer from minor infections. Because the cells within the immune system are compromised, they cannot fully fight off what would normally be seen as insignificant infections. What was a minor infection can have serious consequences, even resulting in death.

The second major symptom is the one that most people who know of PBFD think of. That is the effect that the disease has on the feathers, beak and skin. There is often extensive feather loss. This feather loss includes areas where it would be impossible for a parrot to feather-pluck including the face and head. Some parrots' losses of feathers are not replaced. If this happens there is a real danger of the parrot suffering from the cold and having difficulty in temperature control. Some parrots do

Cockatoo suffering from Psittacine Beak and Feather Disease.

Blue and Gold Macaw: a plastic neck collar fitted to prevent the bird from plucking any feathers.

attempt to re-grow the feathers. When this occurs, the feathers are quite abnormal, often appearing twisted, with small haemorrhages within the pinfeather. These feathers are often brittle and will easily break. Some birds do not initially lose all their feathers, but the coloration of the plumage changes.

The beak initially takes on a glossy appearance and it loses its strength, causing parts of the beak to break. The beak and the nails will overgrow. This is particularly noticeable in a beak where one mandible is broken and so doesn't wear against the other mandible. Parrots with this condition often appear depressed in mood, and are no doubt suffering some pain from the feather, nail and beak abnormalities.

Treatment for the condition is limited, and will depend in part what the presenting symptoms are. Infections will need to be treated quickly, as the response to treatment may be poor. Some vets will give drugs to stimulate the immune system, and these are often quite costly. A blood test is available which will confirm the diagnosis. The owner of a parrot suffering from this quite awful disease must consider the options open to him or her, as it would appear unlikely that there will be a cure in the near future. Thankfully, in the more distant future a vaccination is looking hopeful for those who do not already have the disease.

If the parrot is suffering to such an extent that life isn't comfortable, euthanasia needs to be considered. There do appear to be parrots with the disease who have a good quality of life, with their symptoms not being so painful or unmanageable as to warrant euthanasia. These parrots appear to be those that have much attention and love bestowed upon them, perhaps more than the majority of parrot owners could give.

Another major consideration is transmission of the virus to other birds. It is thought that feather dust may play an important role in this, as this could allow transmission of the virus to spread easily via clothes to other parrots. PBFD must be one of the greatest challenges to parrot keepers and one which all parrot owners have a responsibility to control, especially when taking birds to areas where many other birds exist.

LIPOMAS

Lipomas could be described as benign tumours made up of fat cells. Some parrots appear more susceptible to this disorder than others. A variety which appears to suffer from this disorder more than others are Roseate Cockatoos, and for this reason the species shouldn't be given a diet which is high in fat. The disorder is felt to be a problem which results from fat storage, so birds which are obese are more likely to suffer from it. The lipomas often occur in the region of the lower abdomen and cloaca, which affects the parrot's reproductive capacity.

If you notice or feel any sort of lump on your parrot you are well advised to consult with an avian vet. Parrots do suffer from cancers which may be hidden inside the parrot's body or observable from the outside. Early intervention from a vet will affect the outcome of the disease.

NEWCASTLE DISEASE

This is an extremely serious disease affecting a wide variety of birds. Newcastle disease is caused by a virus and can be transmitted via respiratory and oral routes, as well as via faeces. It is highly infectious and has a mortality rate of nearly 100%. Birds confined to small areas will quickly pass on the infection to one another with disastrous consequences.

Interestingly, Slender-billed Conures are said to have suffered greatly from this disease. Slender-billed Conures are very social birds, with large flocks roosting in close proximity to one another at night. Their social existence contributed to their passing on the infection at such a rate that huge flocks were dying as a result of the disease.

As with many viral infections there appear to be waves of infection, which can often be predicted with some accuracy. In Newcastle disease this appears to be every 10-12 years. It is a notifable disease, which means that the Ministry of Agriculture Fisheries and Food require veterinarians to inform them of outbreaks, so that if necessary the transportation of birds can be restricted, to prevent outbreaks from spreading.

In parrots the incubation is generally 3-16 days. However, in an experimental study, an amazon parrot was infected and continued to shed the virus for a year prior to exhibiting symptoms of the disease. The clinical signs can be quite variable. It can be sudden death, or may be a slower onset that can involve respiratory, digestive or central nervous system symptoms. Some birds would appear to have a greater resistance than others. In live birds, the vet will take a swab from the throat or cloaca to confirm diagnosis. It is usual to euthanase any birds that are or could be infected. The most positive steps that the aviculturist can take are to buy only birds that come from a known healthy environment and to ensure the effective quarantine of any new stock.

BUMBLEFOOT (PODODERMATITIS)

This refers to an inflammatory condition of the foot, often but not always referring to the underside of the feet. It is usually caused by inadequate perching arrangements, or previous trauma or infection. This is not an infectious disease in the usual sense of the word. However, an infected wound on the bottom of the foot could infect another parrot in cramped conditions. Any infection causing inflammation needs attention from a vet. Small localised infections can easily become more serious, but in a normal healthy parrot will respond quickly to antibiotics. These will quickly help to relieve the pain and discomfort, and prevent more serious consequences. Parrots naturally climb a great deal, and also use their feet to hold their food. If they do not have access to a range of perch sizes, there can be areas on the foot and hock where excessive wear results in sore areas. Bumblefoot can be prevented by supplying a variety of perches, and allowing the parrot time on the floor to fully utilise the range of movements that their legs and feet are meant to accommodate.

PROVENTRICULAR DILATION SYNDROME

This disease was first described in relation to macaws, and is still referred to as Macaw Wasting Disease in some texts. The disease has been responsible for deaths in various parrot species, not only macaws. It is particularly distressing for the owner, as the disease affects both the digestive system and the nervous system, and in most instances will result in the death of the parrot. The first symptom is usually inability to digest its food, the food being excreted in much the same state as it was in when eaten. This, not surprisingly, is accompanied by weight loss.

Scarlet Macaw: despite its common name, Macaw Wasting Disease is not exclusive to the macaw.

The nervous system symptoms tend to present with a loss of balance and uncoordinated movements. As these two areas of symptoms increase, the parrot may start vomiting, and there may be some paralysis present in the legs.

The condition is thought to be caused by a viral infection and is also thought to be infectious – although not highly contagious. Studies where attempts have been made under controlled conditions to pass on the disease to other parrots have not been conclusive. However, the general advice is still to isolate any bird diagnosed as suffering from the disease. Euthanasia will need consideration as the parrot becomes progressively more ill. There is obviously an ethical consideration where we know that the parrot will die either from starvation, infection due to its poor condition, or from central nervous system damage.

FRACTURES

Fractures are not uncommon in parrot-like birds, the most common sites being the wing or leg. Some parrots, particularly African Greys, appear to have a problem in maintaining normal serum calcium levels, which makes their bones more susceptible to fractures. For this reason, calcium supplements containing vitamin D_3 and phosphorus are often advised.

There are three types of fractures:

1. Simple – there is a break in the bone which doesn't protrude through the skin.
2. Compound – the fracture does protrude through the skin.
3. Greenstick – the bone is not totally broken.

The symptoms that may suggest to you that a limb is fractured include an inability to bear weight, and swelling, and pain. In the case of the wings, they're usually dropped. In some parrots, old fractures which have healed with poor alignment result in the parrot always having a degree of dropped wing. However, the bird may still be able to fly and is not necessarily obviously handicapped by this.

It is essential that you take the bird to the vet as a matter of urgency. The sooner that the vet can stabilise the fracture – that is, prevent movement of the two ends of the broken bone – the less chance there is of damage to the surrounding tissue, nerve and blood vessels. It is preferable to wrap the bird in a towel, as this prevents the parrot from making excessive movements that might further complicate the injury.

BLEEDING

When birds bleed it needs to be taken seriously, as the amount of circulating blood in birds is small. It is important to find out where the blood is coming from. Commonly this is from a damaged pinfeather. As the feathers grow they are encased in a waxy sheath, and as the feather matures it protrudes from the top of the sheath until eventually the parrot will remove the sheath as they preen. In the stages where growth of the pinfeather is taking place, the feather has both a nerve supply and a blood supply. If this is broken, the sheath appears to act as a siphon and blood is lost, sometimes in large quantities. This is sometimes difficult to see immediately, as all the surrounding area may be covered in blood. Where the parrot has flapped its wings, blood may have been splattered onto other areas. When you have located the pinfeather, pull this out with small pliers (the feather shaft needs to be pulled in the direction it grows). The blood loss should then soon stop.

The other area where blood loss is relatively common is from bleeding nails. The application of styptic powder or of flour is often recommended. However, we have found a bar of soap to work most effectively. The nail is pulled against the soap, which then seals the wound.

Bleeding from other areas, such as tissue injuries, will benefit from an application of styptic powder, flour or baking soda. The use of a gauze pad and gentle pressure will assist clot formation and the cessation of bleeding. If this doesn't work, or only works temporarily, it is necessary to take your parrot to the vet urgently as it may be necessary for the blood vessel to be cauterised.

EGG BINDING

This does occur commonly in parrot-like birds, and many have unfortunately died as a consequence. Typically, the parrot is found on the floor of the aviary or the nestbox in a distressed state. The feathers are often fluffed out, and she may be panting with her beak half-open. At times she may appear to be straining. Some parrots will attempt to move when disturbed. The legs may appear weak or even paralysed. A lump, which is the descending egg, can often be observed in the vent area. Sometimes the egg may even be seen starting to protrude as the bird strains to pass it, only for it to disappear again when the muscle contraction relaxes.

It is important that you intervene in these circumstances as quickly as possible. The most important factor would appear to be heat. Ideally this should elevate the temperature of the cage or hospital cage to about 90°F (32°C). This is often enough to resolve the situation. The heat would appear to relax the muscle allowing for an easier passage of the egg. The second consideration is a calcium supplement. Some of these supplements have been developed as super-saturated calcium solutions that are quickly and easily absorbed. Many believe that there is a direct correlation between lack of available calcium and egg binding.

For most hens, these two measures are sufficient. If the hen is still having difficulty, raising the humidity to about 60% is advised, and some would advocate lubricating the cloaca. If the hen is willing to drink, an emergency electrolyte solution could be offered which will give her extra energy. It is important when treating a hen for egg binding to carry out the intervention described, but then to give her peace and quiet, which will allow her to relax and get on with the business.

If no egg has been produced after a few hours, the parrot will need to be seen by the vet as a matter of urgency. This will enable more invasive techniques to be utilised, which could save the parrot's life. It is important when breeding from hen parrots to ensure that they are in good general health and that they consume a healthy diet and are not obese. If you are breeding African Grey parrots, a maintenance calcium supplement should be given, not only for the laying of eggs but also for the developing chicks.

PARASITES

Some parrot-like birds are extremely susceptible to ascarids – worms which live in the intestines. Untreated heavy infestations can result in death. Conures and Australian parakeets are particularly susceptible, and many owners of this type of parrot routinely worm their pets, particularly if they are living in outside aviaries. Diagnosis can be made by taking the droppings to your vet for examination under a microscope to ascertain if worm eggs are present.

Parrots do not always show obvious symptoms of worm infestation; however, the parrot will lose weight and condition and in some instances will pass droppings mixed with blood. This is caused by the worm rupturing the walls of the intestine. It is not just adult birds that suffer, as parents who are regurgitating food for their young will pass the worms on to the chicks. The young appear particularly susceptible to worm infestations and may die before leaving the nest.

There are preparations on the market that will effectively kill the worms. The preparations are bitter-tasting and need either to be put directly into the crop using a crop tube or – another method which we have found to be effective – to be slowly dripped into the beak. But be aware that the parrots don't like the taste! We have never managed to effectively worm parrots by mixing the preparation in their drinking water.

Your vet will advise you of the preparations and the amount to give. These preparations are available from your vet and in the main were intended for agricultural use. The result from the worming can be quite outstanding, with large amounts of worms being passed. It is advised to repeat the process 2-3 weeks later if worms have been passed. We usually give a probiotic for a week after worming, as the worming preparations do appear to disrupt the gut.

Cage birds are unlikely to suffer from worms as they won't normally have access to the worm eggs; however, a parrot which has been brought into the home from an outside aviary may have a worm burden which needs to be treated.

Aviary birds will have more risk of contracting worms. This risk is considerably minimised if the aviary flight is concreted. Earth floors will harbour worm eggs for long periods. It is helpful if the top of the aviary is covered by clear corrugated plastic or glass that will prevent droppings from wild bird populations falling into the aviary.

Conures are prone to heavy worm infestations. Pictured: Blue-throated Conure.

12 PARROT BREEDS

Although all the parrot breeds retain similarities in beak structure, arrangement of the toes and laying white eggs in holes in trees, rocks or even the ground, there the similarities end. Large, small, gregarious or solitary, diurnal or nocturnal, the list is endless. By studying the nuances of differing species we can increase our knowledge and understanding of them. In this chapter, we hope to give you an insight into characteristics and behaviour of the various breeds in order to facilitate your choice and care of them.

THE AFRICAN GREY

Most of the population who know very little about parrots, when hearing that you have a parrot, will commonly ask "Is it a green one or a grey one?" To those who have an interest in parrots this can be understood as meaning that you are likely to have either an Amazon parrot or an African Grey parrot, such is the popularity of these two species.

Of all parrots the African Grey is in all probability the best known of all, and when one considers the various attributes which it possesses, it is not surprising. It is highly intelligent, has an attractive coloration and its mimicry ability is quite outstanding. It is also captive-bred on a regular basis, to the point where it is always easy to obtain a captive-

The African Grey is a very sensitive bird.

Opposite page: Primrose Pearl Cockatiel.

bred youngster. These seem to be invariably hand-reared, thus allowing the prospective owner to have a ready-made tame parrot without the time commitment necessary for hand-taming a young bird.

The downside to all this is that with all the intelligence which the African Grey parrot invariably has, it also has the ability to understand when things are not right in its environment, and if this species of parrot is in conflict it tends to do something about it. The result is what can be termed adverse behaviour – that is behaviour which suggests that the parrot is maladjusted to the degree that results in abnormal behaviour, such as bouts of screaming, feather-plucking or self-mutilation and aggression. Feather-plucking in African Grey parrots is quite common, and it appears to be most common in those that have been hand-reared.

Many African Grey parrots are quite prolific and will breed almost continuously if the 3-5 eggs or young are removed for hand-rearing. It is important that the parents should have some opportunity to rear their young for their own well-being; however, this needs to be undertaken with some caution, as some pairs will physically abuse their young. This would in some instances appear to be in response to stress. The damage that the parents might inflict on their young may in some cases necessitate the young having to be euthanased. We are aware of parents that have bitten the tips off the wings and toes, in one instance actually biting both of the feet off. It would have been impossible for this victim to have ever perched and he would have always required a bed of some sort to rest on. In all probability he would have found it impossible not to have soiled himself; so it was decided to have him euthanased.

In this instance it appeared that the damage had occurred when the youngster was only a few days old as, when the damage was discovered, the stumps were completely healed. As can be imagined, the youngster had been observed a few times but without actually removing it from the nest for a formal examination.

Interestingly many African Greys appear to breed most successfully when restricted to breeding cages of about four feet square, with the nestbox attached to the outside. If this method is adopted it is very important that, when the birds are not breeding, they are accommodated in an aviary with plenty of flying space, and ideally in an outside location where they can have access to the sun and rain. We know of cases where this has not been done, and this has resulted in the eggs becoming progressively smaller and the level of fertility declining. In addition, the young which have successfully hatched have had a high mortality.

DIETARY NEEDS

African Greys have a greater need for calcium than most, if not any other parrots. Owners who do not supplement calcium in the diet will have birds which may get egg-bound, which can result in death, if not recognised and treated, and the young will suffer from greenstick or pathological fractures.

African Greys are prone to becoming what is often called 'sunflower junkies'; this is the term often used for those parrots who will only eat sunflower seeds. If allowed, it is highly likely that your parrots will suffer from Vitamin A deficiency, which will result in small nodules appearing under the skin around the head and beak. You will also have a parrot which won't have the lustre and motivation which a normal African grey should have.

It is easy to understand why this group of parrots have such a high preference for high fat foods, as in the wild they do eat fruits of the African Oil Palm in large quantities. It has been suggested that one of the reasons

The Timneh is a darker version.

for the small amount of feathering around the face is an evolutionary adaptation in relation to keeping the plumage clean when feeding on the highly oily fruit. In the wild their energy requirements are high – large flocks congregate and fly from one feeding location to another. This is in direct contrast to their rather sedentary life in an aviary, where their energy requirements are low. A high-fat diet not utilised for energy will result in obesity and poor health. *Psittacus erithacus erithacus* is the nominate race of the African Greys, *Psittacus erithacus timneh* being the small subspecies. The former is often referred to as a Silver Grey or Congo Grey; this species is an inch larger than the Timneh Grey, the subspecies. Both are characterised by a grey plumage, the Timneh being darker in colour; both have red tails, but again the Timneh's is a darker version. The other main differentiation is the colour of the upper mandible; in the Silver Grey this is black, while in the Timneh it is horn-coloured. Talking and pet potential are said to be the same for both types.

MACAWS

The large macaws on the whole are big, noisy, gregarious and active birds. Among the most intelligent of the parrots, they often learn to talk well, play like puppies and perform simple tasks. Many are very brightly coloured, but are surprisingly difficult to detect when perching amongst foliage and, flying with the sun behind them, they all look dark-coloured.

Hugely popular as pets, thought must be given to their need for space, exercise and constant entertainment. Possessing the most powerful beaks in the parrot world, brazil and macadamia nuts are not much of a challenge to them, and gnawable toys, logs and branches are a must. Perches will need constant replacement, but this behaviour is normal and should not be discouraged.

All the large macaws have powerful voices which carry a long way, but a single pet is rarely as noisy as a number of macaws, who will set each other off in a shouting challenge. They are normally only noisy at first light and late afternoon, although if danger appears a loud warning scream will ensue.

The smaller macaws are mainly green, but still retain the bare cheek patches of the large ones, a distinguishing feature of all macaws. Their behaviour is similar to the large macaws, but their voices can be a little more irritating and repetitive. However, they can be fantastic pets for those who are macaw fans but haven't the space or finances for the larger ones.

Being largely omnivorous, the macaws are easy to cater for – the more variety in the diet the better. All the macaws are long-tailed. Following is a list of the different species and some of their requirements, with Latin names in brackets.

HYACINTHINE MACAW
(*Anodorhynchus hyacinthinus*)
This is the largest of all the parrots, being up to 42 inches (1.07m) from top to tail, although not the heaviest (this honour goes to the kakapo of New Zealand). Uniformly blue-purple, the bright yellow skin around the eyes and beak becomes pale if the bird is 'off colour'. There are more birds of this species in captivity than in the wild, and with an estimated 3-5,000 birds left, great concern is felt for their continued survival. Measures are being taken to encourage breeding success in the wild as well as in captivity.

The lack of nesting sites is one major reason for their decline, and provision of these is partially successful, although they can be taken over by such undesirables as aggressive bees. Notoriously slow breeders, wild pairs may only successfully fledge a youngster every three to four years. With a clutch size of one or two, and rarely three, a single chick only would normally survive without human intervention to save the smaller weaker sibling.

The Hyacinthine Macaw is the largest of the parrot species.

Those lucky enough to breed these magnificent birds often have enormous trouble in hand-rearing the chick, losses occurring at all stages of the rearing period. Wherever possible, parent-rearing should be encouraged, or the young should be fostered to reliable breeders.

Although they make wonderful affectionate pets and many are kept as such, particularly in the USA, every Hyacinth should be given the opportunity to breed. A flight for these birds should be spacious enough to accommodate their size, as they will not fly in cramped conditions. Mesh of less than 10g will be snipped through easily by their powerful beaks. The diet of these birds is usually supplemented by a large quantity of nuts in the shell, particularly brazils, as the wild birds feed almost exclusively on palm drupes.

LEAR'S MACAW (*Anodorhynchus leari*)
This smaller cousin of the Hyacinth Macaw is severely endangered in the wild, and as such is only represented by a handful of specimens in captivity, a situation which is highly unlikely to change.

BUFFON'S MACAW (*Ara ambigua*)
Another giant, also known as the Great Green Macaw, the Buffon's is another macaw threatened by extinction. Fairly well represented in captivity, it has never been kept or bred in huge numbers, due no doubt to its less striking coloration and high price. Fairly sedentary for a macaw, it nonetheless has its own beauty, being a yellowish shade of green, with a red velvety band on the forehead and cheeks that flush crimson. The subtlety of its coloration needs to be admired in a good light to be appreciated. Not

commonly kept as pets, due to their rarity, Buffon's are however gentle giants. Three eggs form the normal clutch and, given the opportunity, they make good parents, raising two or three offspring quite happily. Captive-bred birds are capable of breeding from four or five years of age, similar to the Hyacinth.

MILITARY MACAW (*Ara militaris*)
Smaller, darker green cousins of the Buffon's, these smart macaws are the opposite as far as energy levels go. Always playing or up to mischief, their popularity has waned since the initial enthusiasm in the late 1980s. Usually willing and prolific breeders, the clutch numbers up to four eggs, although in our experience three chicks is the maximum that they will rear successfully. Like most large macaws, they will be quite vigorous in defence of the nest, flushing deep red with excitement and anger.

There are two distinct subspecies of this macaw, *Militaris militaris*, the one most commonly seen, and the Mexican Military Macaw (*Militaris mexicana*), a larger bird with extensive brownish throat markings. If you can look beyond the brighter colours of some of the other macaws to appreciate the subtler hues of bronze, sky-blue and russet, and you want a pet packed with personality, the Military is a superb choice. They are often used to perform parrot shows at zoos and bird parks because of their trainability.

GREEN-WINGED MACAW
(*Ara chloroptera*)
This macaw can, along with the Buffon's, nearly attain the size of the Hyacinth in some specimens. It is a superb bird, with an enormous beak which is sometimes a little off-putting to potential pet owners. It is, however, one of the top ranking pet macaws of all, for as well as its beauty it is gentle and intelligent. Newcomers to parrot keeping are often mystified as to why it is so named, with only a little green on its wing. This is probably to distinguish it from the Scarlet Macaw, which has a similar proportion of yellow on its wings. The red coloration of a Green-wing is a deep rich red as opposed to the rather brighter, more orange red of a Scarlet Macaw.

Although they are the owners of hugely powerful voices, luckily they only tend to use them if threatened rather than shouting for joy as so many others do. The normal clutch is three or four eggs, and most pairs make exceptional parents, to both their own and foster chicks. We have bred from four-year-old captive-bred parents, but they are one of the most reluctant species to start breeding, with imported birds in particular taking much time to settle down and breed. However, once they commence breeding, they are usually reliable and regular breeders. A superb macaw with much to recommend it.

The Green-winged Macaw has a magnificent beak.

The colourful appearance of the Scarlet Macaw has led to its downfall in the wild.

SCARLET MACAW (*Ara macao*)

If you like vivid colours, you would have to go a long way to beat the beauty of a Scarlet. With the overall red colour complemented by wing stripes of yellow, green and blue, this is a very striking bird indeed. Sadly, this very beauty has probably led to its shrinking wild population, as it was captured to meet demand. It is however a very prolific breeder in captivity.

There are regional variations in the colouring of this macaw, those from the south of its range displaying more yellow on the wings, with the green portion enlarging the more north you go. The feather quality of this macaw is softer and looser than that of the other large macaws, some birds presenting a rather dishevelled appearance, due to this very softness.

The Scarlet is perhaps one of the most difficult of the large macaws to pair up compatibly, with unprecedented attacks occurring if forced to spend time in close confinement with another bird and unhappy with the situation. This is a definite candidate for flock-pairing when young. The temperament of hand-reared young as pets is less reliable than that of some of the others in this family such as the Blue and Gold and Green-wing Macaws, many becoming nippy and aggressive as they approach maturity. However, there are, of course, exceptions.

As mentioned earlier, Scarlets can be prolific breeding birds with a normal clutch comprising three to four eggs. If eggs or young chicks are removed for hand-rearing, they can be induced to double- or even treble-clutch. As always it is wise for the long-term mental and physical health of the parents for them to be given the chance to rear young each season.

BLUE AND GOLD MACAW (*Ara ararauna*)

The most popular of the large macaws – and rightly so. Apart from their exquisite coloration, these birds can have exceptional temperaments when kept as pets. They talk well, play, and get on with most people if brought up and socialised correctly. As breeder birds, they are often very capable.

We have had and known of many Blue and Golds who have commenced their breeding careers at three years of age and continued to be prolific well into old age. Similar to the aforementioned, three or four eggs is the

NOT JUST ANOTHER GREEN PARROT: THE MILITARY MACAW

Barrett Watson

Inquisitive, coy, cheeky, and bewitching – these are only some of the words that can describe the Military Macaw. Exquisite in their subtle beauty, you could be forgiven for thinking of *Ara Militaris* as just another green parrot, but far from it. In a good natural light you can discover bronze hues, sky-blue, burgundy and old gold, as well as the green, red, black, brown and white of the face. Blushing when excited or angry, this makes them even more expressive.

I have found these highly sociable birds to be dominant but not overtly aggressive to other macaws and large parrots. Neither are they as difficult to pair as other large macaws, often taking prospective partners quite readily.

HAPPY FAMILIES

My young pair spent the first season priar to laying 'playing house'. An upright nestbox, 3ft x 18in (91cm x 45.5cm) square, was investigated, chewed and dug up by the pair, who showed their excitement with dilated pupils, raised nape feathers and much talking. They were not put off their protracted love-making by the interested onlookers – avian and human.

This hen first laid eggs at three years of age. Military clutches normally consist of three eggs, but can vary by two either way. The 26-day incubation period is not strictly adhered to either. I have had healthy chicks hatch at 24 and 28 days, usually after external pipping has been noticed 48 hours previously. The average weight of a newly-hatched chick is 20g ($^{11}/_{16}$oz).

In appearance the babies are similar to other Ara chicks – pink blobs with large heads, bulbous beaks and protruding skin-covered eyes. White wisps of down adorn their backs. My military chicks have always been active and vigorous, making good weight gains after the initial two- or three-day levelling-out period. They reach 1000g (35oz) just before flying, then lose a little to help with getting airborne.

EARLY STARTERS

At three to four weeks of age the chicks get an incredibly thick grey down covering their entire bodies. These babies are extremely active and vocal, constantly muttering to themselves and shrieking when hungry or excited. The red frontal band is the first noticeable sign of colour.

Being so alert, militaries seem to start picking at food for themselves at an early age, sometimes weaning as early as 10 weeks of age, but more usually 12-14. Initially wholemeal bread, digestive biscuits, corn-on-the-cob, apple and carrots seem to attract their attention.

These birds are excellent talkers and hand-reared babies are already saying "Hello" at this stage. They are also boisterous and will get into everything, grumbling and swearing if disciplined in any way. When they get through the terrible teens, they enjoy being stroked, scratched and cuddled.

POPULAR PETS

As a rule, both hand-reared and parent-reared militaries make excellent, protective parents. I am sure that now more militaries are being bred in this country they will enjoy an even greater upsurge in popularity as pets and as beautiful aviary birds.

Pair of Military Macaws defending their nestbox.

The Blue and Gold Macaw is one of the most popular types of parrot.

norm, but we have experienced larger clutches from these, including one occasion when we had a mammoth 12 chicks from one clutch.

Extinct in some parts of their former range, they still inhabit the larger part of South America, along with the Green-wing Macaw. Sadly there are still shipments of wild-caught Blue and Golds (and Green-winged) Macaws being brought into the country. With the numbers being bred in captivity of both these species, there is absolutely no reason whatsoever to import them.

BLUE-THROATED MACAW
(Ara glaucogularis)

This enigmatic macaw has only relatively recently been propagated in any numbers in captivity. Bearing a marked resemblance to the Blue and Gold Macaw, they have been overlooked by many because of this. They are, however, quite different to the Blue and Gold, being a smaller, more slender and more elegant bird. Their social behaviour is much more tightly knit than the loosely formed flocks of the former. They are easily excited and will dilate their pupils and flush scarlet at the slightest provocation. The call of the Blue-throated is an octave higher than the other large macaws mentioned so far in this chapter.

They have only recently been studied in the wild, where their highly precarious situation has now been acknowledged. At present there are thought to be only one hundred or so individuals in a small pocket of Bolivia and, with a low reproductive rate and a shrinking natural habitat, this is a situation that is unlikely to change.

Gradually more are being bred in captivity, but pairs do show a marked reluctance to nest at an early age, and a clutch comprising usually two or maybe three eggs does not boost numbers tremendously. As with all

There are only an estimated 100 Blue-throated Macaws in the wild.

parrots in captivity, parent-rearing wherever possible should be encouraged to avoid any danger of imprinting and creating incapable future parents. This macaw is most definitely for the connoisseur breeder and not one to be considered as a pet unless they start breeding in huge numbers.

RED-FRONTED MACAW
(*Ara rubrogenys*)
This comical beauty is another character with a small wild population needing our help. Distinctly conure-like in voice and appearance, we have experienced a hugely domineering attitude in mixed collections, even towards birds much larger than themselves.

Red-fronted Macaws seem to specialise in fooling the keeper into thinking that they are going to breed, by copulating, chewing and digging out the nestbox, and then fiercely protecting it – without coming up with the goods. This has been noted in several collections, whilst in others, when they have bred, they become extremely prolific. Clutches can average four to five eggs and the same number of chicks can result from these.

Rather like the Blue-throated Macaw, whose range they encompass, they are highly excitable and their small bare facial patches blush extremely easily on these occasions. The few that are kept as pets prove to be talkative and playful, if slightly nippy, and utterly enchanting.

THE SMALL MACAWS

The link between the conures and the large macaws, small macaws are charmingly

A pair of Red-fronted Macaws.

animated characters. For those with a yearning for macaws, but perhaps lacking the space or finances, these could be the answer.

ILLIGER'S MACAW (*Ara maracana*)
Also known as the Blue-winged Macaw, this is the only species of the small macaws on the CITES Appendix I list. With declining numbers in the wild due to habitat degradation, they are, however, highly prolific in captivity, some pairs producing three clutches of up to five babies annually. Due to this high prolificacy, they are one of the endangered parrots that would be acceptable to be kept as pets, perhaps being introduced to a breeding situation at a later stage in their life. Attractively compact birds, they also have a slightly better voice than some of their counterparts, who can be repetitive in their shrieking.

SEVERE MACAW (*Ara severa*)
Some specimens of this macaw are the largest of the small macaws. They, like the Green-winged, appear to have a proportionally larger head and beak for their size than the others in this group. They also have a powerful voice for their size, used to great effect if excited or frightened. Not commonly kept as a pet, they can be a little more aloof than their counterparts. Another similarity with the Green-wing is the reluctance of some pairs to breed. Often the keeper of these macaws will wait for several years before being rewarded with eggs or chicks. Three is the normal clutch size for this species. A challenging interest for the breeder of macaws, this species may well become endangered in the near future, so we should try to propagate it in captivity.

YELLOW-COLLARED MACAW
(*Ara auricollis*)
The cheeky Yellow-collared Macaw has long been the favourite, and most frequently kept, of the small macaws. A fairly willing breeder in captivity its three or four young should be handled with firmness and authority if they are to be homed as pets – otherwise they quickly learn to dominate the household.

RED-BELLIED MACAW (*Ara manilata*)
The much maligned and unpopular Red-bellied Macaw is finally getting the recognition it deserves. Wild-caught specimens are much the most nervous and highly-strung of the species. This, coupled with the fact that they are prone to obesity, has led to stress-related deaths, compounding their unpopularity. However, both these problems can be overcome by giving them a secluded position for the aviary, and plenty of room – as all these active birds should have.

If you provide these conditions, and a secure nestbox, you may encourage them to breed. We have found that some pairs prefer an upright open-topped nestbox, whilst others will lay in the more conventional type. Trial and error will prove what suits your pair best. Three or four eggs make up the normal clutch, and the chicks appear a little leaner and lankier than other macaws. Another unusual aspect of this species is that the chicks will go through a stage, at a few weeks of age, of throwing themselves over on their backs if surprised or frightened, and striking out with their feet.

This species retain the dark eyes of youth into adulthood, but youngsters can be identified by the white skin on the cheeks, in common with other Ara macaws. This gradually changes to the beige-yellow of adulthood as the chick matures. Chicks also show a white stripe down the culmen of the beak, which gradually darkens to the black of the adults.

One final peculiarity of this species is the fact that they will cling to the side of the cage or aviary and squirt copious droppings out through the bars in a lory-like fashion.

Red-bellied Macaws do not deserve the reputation they have acquired.

Despite being highly strung when wild-caught, hand-reared babies make the most delightfully confiding pets, being calm, cuddly and speaking well in a gravelly voice.

NOBLE MACAW
(*Ara*, or *Diopsittaca, nobilis cumanensis*)
This small macaw is, sadly, rarely seen in captivity, with only a handful of enthusiasts maintaining it in their collections. In these conditions, it will breed willingly from the age of three years, and may have five eggs in a clutch. An attractive pet, it is distinguished from its close relative, the Hahn's Macaw, by its larger size and by a horn-coloured, not black, upper mandible. Its voice would be a little less repetitive than that of the Hahn's. For those lucky enough to find a hand-reared baby, it would make a delightful pet.

HAHN'S MACAW
(*Ara*, or *Diopsittaca, nobilis nobilis*)
This is the smallest of macaws, and is often a good choice for those who want experience in breeding and rearing macaws. Commonly kept and bred, if you can ignore the annoyingly high-pitched repetitive voice, it will prove to be prolific for you, with upward of six eggs in a clutch. Often kept as a pet, care must be taken to discipline these tiny monsters, otherwise the voice will be constant and the nipping will be plentiful and painful.

COULON'S MACAW (*Ara Couloni*)
Also known as the Blue-headed Macaw, the enigmatic Coulon's have been rarely seen in captivity despite being reportedly common in the wild. An unusual-looking bird with its startlingly white eye and ivory-tipped and lined culmen, it appears to be rather more sedentary than the other small macaws. At the time of writing, there are reports of this macaw being kept and bred in Eastern Europe, where its habits do not seem to differ greatly from those of its cousins.

SPIX'S MACAW (*Cyanopsitta spixii*)
Sadly one of the rarest birds in the world, the Spix Macaw boasts a population of only one

known bird in the wild. This is despite an attempt to release a captive female with it, a known male. She was tracked for a number of weeks only to disappear to an unknown fate. Approximately forty birds reside in captivity but, of these, only two or three pairs are successfully breeding. Every effort is being made to increase the population, both in captivity and in the wild. The lone wild male has paired up with an Illiger's Macaw (*Ara maracana*) and the next step being discussed is to replace the eggs of this pair with fertile eggs from the captive pairs to augment the wild population. The resulting chicks, if successful, would be brought up with the knowledge of food and water sources, and any dangers, by the foster pair.

HYBRID MACAWS

Mention should be made of the fact that most macaws will readily hybridise, usually in the absence of a partner of their own species. Some breeders actively encourage this, finding a ready market for the unusually-coloured offspring. Certain crosses are even given names, such as Catalina (Blue and Gold x Scarlet) We believe that this practice should be discouraged in the interest of retaining genetic purity for future generations, no matter how attractive these crosses are.

A hybrid macaw.

COCKATOOS

This highly successful group of parrots has conquered Australasia, their very adaptability ensuring success in even the most arid regions. They are characterised by the mobile crests – some large and beautifully coloured, others barely noticeable. These are absent in all other parrots, Hawk Headed parrots having a movable ruff, not a crest, and Horned parakeets having immobile plumes. They are popular, amusing and active aviary inhabitants and pets. Mention should be made of the fact that they produce a dandruff-like powder down to cleanse the feathers to which some people may have an allergic reaction.

This fascinating group of parrots will delight everyone who has the good fortune to keep them, whether as pets or in an aviary. Some of the smaller species have been known to breed successfully at only two years of age, and even the larger ones may commence breeding between three and five years. Some pairs of, for example, Moluccan and Umbrella Cockatoos will rarely be seen by the keeper, disappearing into the nestbox at the sound of footsteps. This is quite normal and should not be discouraged as it makes the birds feel secure.

ROSEATE COCKATOO
(*Eolophus roseicapillus*)
One of the most abundant of cockatoos, the Roseate or Galah has reached plague proportions in its native land. Although persecuted by farmers, the Australian Government's export ban means that this is a much sought-after and expensive bird in the rest of the world.

One of the quietest of this noisy group of birds, the Roseate is prone to lipomas (fatty tumours) and as such its diet should be watched for the fat content. Plenty of fruit and vegetables, and small amounts of seed along with plenty of exercise should ensure that these birds stay fit and healthy. Unusual in that they (along with Palm Cockatoos) use sticks and leaves in the construction of nests within a nesting hole, they can also lay large clutches of up to six eggs – and usually rear the thin, lanky youngsters well. Females will assume their reddish-brown eyes at 6 months to a year. For a quiet, amusing pet, as well as a gorgeous aviary bird, you could do much worse than choose the Roseate.

GOFFIN'S COCKATOO (*Cacatua goffini*)
The neat little Goffin's cockatoo is a CITES I listed bird, and probably due to this was highly sought-after. Latterly, however, it was found to be more abundant than was once thought. In captivity they are one of the most difficult species of cockatoo to encourage to breed. Some pairs will spend years destroying everything in the aviary, but ignoring the nestbox. Others will chew up every nestbox before any breeding attempt will be started. However, some breeders find that introducing a new nestbox, perhaps a horizontal one if a vertical nestbox has been unsuccessful, will stimulate the pair into breeding. As with most parrot husbandry practices, trial and error will often find the key. Two eggs normally form the clutch, and hand-reared chicks make delightful pets. The voice of this little cockatoo is normally not too harsh.

BARE-EYED COCKATOO
(*Cacatua sanguinea*)
Like the Roseate, the unusual-looking Bare-

Although abundant in its Australian homeland, the Roseate Cockatoo is much sought-after elsewhere in the world.

eyed Cockatoo reaches plague proportions in its native land, enraging farmers whose crops it destroys. Sadly, warfare then ensues, with huge numbers being shot, trapped or poisoned. Due to the export ban, they are really comparatively rare in captivity, some people also finding the bulbous bare patch around and underneath the eye unattractive. Cheeky and bold, they make very entertaining aviary inhabitants as well as pets. The clutch size is normally two, but three or four eggs have been known.

WESTERN LONG-BILLED COCKATOO or CORELLA (*Cacatua pastinator*)
Intelligence and humour abound in this playful comic. Very rarely kept outside Australia, and infrequently bred when it is. When they do breed, three to five eggs can be expected. As with all the bare-eyed species, these hyperactive birds can work themselves into a rage and attack their mates. For this reason, as well as the fact that they are so active, large aviaries well stocked with playthings should be provided for them.

SLENDER-BILLED COCKATOO or CORELLA (*Cacatua tenuirostris*)
These birds are slightly slimmer in build and, as the name suggests, with a longer and more slender bill than their cousins have. These cockatoos are adorned with a slash of scarlet feathers across the chest. Previously abundant, this species now has a frail population in some areas, and care should be taken to ensure its continued survival.

We have found these charming birds to be fairly quiet aviary specimens, although odd cocks can be extremely raucous. With a beak adapted for digging for roots and bulbs, provision should be made for the birds to do this – although if on a natural earth floor, a regular worming routine should be adhered to. The clutch averages three eggs and, where possible, youngsters should go into a breeding programme until captive numbers are built up.

The Slender-billed Cockatoo beak is shaped to unearth roots and bulbs for feeding.

RED-VENTED COCKATOO (*Cacatua haematuropygia*)
This unusual island cockatoo is in serious decline due to deforestation on the islands it inhabits, plus a high susceptibility to Psittacine Beak and Feather Disease. This may possibly also be exacerbated by inbreeding, due to the small number being bred. In captivity, imprinted males may be absolutely murderous, so every effort should be made to parent-rear any youngsters bred from the two or three eggs laid. Alternatively, foster or puppet-rearing may alleviate this problem,

A parrot for the specialist breeder, only hand-reared males should be considered as pets, as there is a great shortage of females, who have reddish eyes as opposed to the black of the males.

DUCORP'S COCKATOO (*Cacatua ducorpsii*)
This pretty cockatoo with its triangular crest is a relative newcomer to the avicultural scene, due to a consignment being released from the Solomon Islands after many years of

not being traded. It has formed a great following and many pairs have settled down to breed. The female usually has a lighter-coloured eye. Two to three eggs are the norm, and with a voice that is not too loud or harsh, they do make delightful pets, as well as interesting aviary specimens.

UMBRELLA COCKATOO (*Cacatua alba*)
Another whiter-than-white cockatoo, the Umbrella was long neglected by the aviculturist when it was freely available and now, having suffered a decline in numbers, it is much sought after. It has the largest crest, a white crown of feathers, for all the world like a Red Indian's head-dress. It is also one of the more prolific of the cockatoos, an established pair laying in almost all months

His large crest has given the Umbrella Cockatoo his name.

of the year. The clutch normally consists of two eggs, but sometimes the smallest chick will be allowed to fade away if left with the parents, so regular nest inspections are essential.

Hand-reared Umbrellas are usually very gentle and loving, but care must be taken to rear them with discipline and a certain amount of independence. This will ensure that they do not become too demanding or noisy. Well-known for their capacity to generate a great deal of noise, this does seem to vary from bird to bird or pair to pair. This is another of the white cockatoos where the female has a reddish eye.

MOLUCCAN COCKATOO
(*Cacatua moluccensis*)
This pink beauty has long been a favourite of bird keepers the world over. Seriously depleted in its deforested island habitat, many more are in captivity than in the wild. Because the Moluccan is much sought after as a pet, most of the young are hand-reared for the pet trade. As such, imprinted males may have temper tantrums and attack the female if she is unreceptive to his advances. These cock birds are usually recognisable as being noisy, excitable and hyperactive. This is not to say that all hand-reared cocks are killers; we have bred from many who have proven to be good fathers. We do, however, strive to allow the parents to rear chicks for further breeding.

Moluccans, like Umbrellas, are tremendous chewers and should be provided with plenty of material to perform this natural need upon. Nestboxes for both these species should have the bottom and at least half the sides metal-lined, or you may find that you are losing eggs or chicks halfway through incubation or rearing from the holes chewed. Regular inspections through the rearing phase will alert the keeper to an underfed chick or, as is fairly common with this

Leadbeater's or Major Mitchell's Cockatoo.

species, plucking of the chicks, growing feathers. We have found that the biggest culprits in this respect are the birds which are themselves plucked. Two eggs are the norm for this species, and a large upright nestbox is ideal for these birds as they spend much time in it.

Moluccan Cockatoos have a reputation for being extremely noisy, and, whilst they certainly have the capacity of high volume, it is mainly spoilt hand-reared birds and the hyperactive males mentioned earlier who are the guilty parties. We have six pairs in a fairly confined area, and they are probably the least noisy of the many species adjacent to them. Hand-reared babies can be very demanding if their every whim is catered for, so a strict regime of discipline and training should be adhered to from the start.

BLUE-EYED COCKATOO
(*Cacatua ophthalmica*)
The Blue-eyed Cockatoo from the islands of New Guinea is extremely rare in aviculture. Chester Zoo in the UK and a few facilities in the USA are the only known breeding centres of this stunning bird. Hopefully, with co-operation and the exchange of unrelated young, the Blue-eyed will become more readily available to ensure a future for it in aviculture.

LEADBEATER'S or MAJOR MITCHELL'S COCKATOO (*Cacatua Leadbeateri*)
The much sought-after Leadbeater's cockatoo is suffering a decline in its native Australia. Predation of eggs, young and sitting hens by Goannas (large lizards) is thought to be a large part of the problem, and a scheme of tinning trees has been successful. This involves sheathing the trunks of the Leadbeater's nesting trees with tin, to create an area where the Goannas and snakes cannot climb to reach the nest. Despite the fact that this species breeds fairly readily in captivity, the demand for it ensures that pairs still command a high price.

Averaging three in a clutch, a fairly deep nestbox is usually favoured. The voice of the Leadbeater's is fairly harsh but not too loud. Not hugely popular as pets, they are probably less intelligent and playful than some of their counterparts.

LESSER SULPHUR-CRESTED COCKATOO (*Cacatua sulphurea sulphurea*)
Mention cockatoos to anyone, and they will probably envisage a white parrot with a yellow crest. The smallest of these birds that fit that description is the Lesser Sulphur-crested Cockatoo. This delightful little bird was once thought of as highly abundant, but now, due to overtrapping in the wild and a large number of females being killed by their mates, it is facing a serious decline.

Every effort should be made to watch for any sign of aggression from the cock bird, and his removal from the hen should be instantaneous if he starts to bully her. He can then be reintroduced when he has calmed down, and you are able to spend time observing his behaviour. Big flights, clipping his wing, a nestbox with escape routes and a closed circuit television can all help to prevent tragedy.

Two eggs form most clutches, with many pairs proving to be excellent parents. However, do not be complacent: long-established cocks with no sign of aggression have been known to turn on the hen without warning. Keepers of Lessers as pets have found them to be playful intelligent birds, with a voice that belies their small stature.

CITRON-CRESTED COCKATOO
(*Cacatua citrinocristata*)
A close cousin of the Lesser, also from the Indonesian islands, is the Citron-crested – a little slimmer and finer than the Lesser, and with an orange crest. Much of the information written about the Lesser applies to the Citron, except the Citron's situation is even more precarious. Both of these species are sexable by eye colour – cocks having black eyes and hens brown.

GREATER SULPHUR-CRESTED COCKATOO (*Cacatua galerita galerita*)
The large and vocal Greater is another cockatoo which has reached pest proportions in Australia. Despite the slaughter of many of these birds, it is a cheap and commonly kept house pet in Australia. One of the most intelligent and playful of the cockatoos, it appears in many of the performing parrot shows at zoos and bird parks.

Again much sought-after outside its homeland, this bird is truly destructive and will chew through all but the strongest of meshes. A very strong voice adds to the impressive display of this gorgeous bird. It strikes us that, morally, it is better to keep as a pet a bird that is common in the wild, so with all the attractive qualities of this bird, perhaps it will be your choice. Two or three eggs form the clutch and the eye colour may not vary much between sexes.

Sulphur-crested Cockatoos are popular pets in their native Australia.

TRITON COCKATOO
(*Cacatua galerita triton*)
Slightly smaller and more slender than the Greater, the Triton hails from New Guinea. The skin around the eyes is bluish, rather than white as in the Greater. It can rival its cousin in vocal capacity; and hand-reared young, if not spoilt, and trained correctly make fantastic pets.

The preceding cockatoos, including the pink ones, are collectively known as the white cockatoos. In these species both male and female will incubate. Following are the so-called black cockatoos.

PALM COCKATOO (*Probosciger aterrimus*)
The spectacular Palm Cockatoo is a highly prized and expensive avicultural subject, despite still being reasonably common in parts of its range. Its unusually large beak and macaw-like bare cheek-patches look out of proportion to its tiny feet and legs. There is also a great variation in size between the sexes and subspecies.

These shy birds appreciate some seclusion in part of the aviary and will lay the single egg in an open-topped log. Twigs will be constantly added to the nest, probably as a provision against flooding if there is a downpour. Another unusual aspect of these birds is the fact that the cock bird will sometimes fashion a stick into a drumming tool and beat it with his foot against a hollow log as a proclamation of territory and as a sexual display. Only the female incubates. Wherever possible, the parents should be left to rear the single chick, as success with hand-rearing is usually proportionally very small. Fungal infections and crop stasis at all stages of rearing are quite common problems encountered by those who try to rear it. This cockatoo is too infrequently bred to be considered as a pet.

The shy Palm Cockatoo is a bird for the experienced parrot keeper.

RED-TAILED BLACK COCKATOO
(*Calyptorhynchus magnificus*)
As the Latin name suggests, this cockatoo is really quite magnificent. With long wings and tail, and a fluttering flight, the Red-tail resembles a huge butterfly in flight. Commonly seen in Australia, this bird is a rare and wondrous sight around the rest of the world.

Remarkably gentle and curious, breeding success has even been achieved with apparently imprinted birds. One or two eggs are incubated, solely by the female. Sexual dimorphism is quite apparent in this species, males having dark beaks and a solid red tail band, the females having a grey horn-coloured beak with a barred tail and yellow spotting on the head.

YELLOW-TAILED BLACK COCKATOOS
(*Calyptorhynchus funereus*)
The Yellow-tail, whilst relatively common in the wild, is kept in captivity even more rarely than the Red-tail. Their details are similar, with the sexual dimorphism being compounded by pink eye skin in males, and grey in females.

WHITE-TAILED BLACK COCKATOOS
(*Calyptorhynchus baudinii*)
The third member of this group – again an enigma outside Australia, where a few aviculturalists keep and breed it.

GLOSSY COCKATOO
(*Calyptorhynchus lathami*)
Very few people outside Australia will have seen this smaller cousin of the previous three cockatoos. If the export ban is lifted for captive-bred members of these four species, we are sure they will have a huge following. This is sadly unlikely at the present time.

GANG GANG COCKATOO
(*Callocephalon fimbriatum*)
The Gang Gang is a most delightful member of the black cockatoos, and the flimsy crest is probably the least mobile of the entire family. Readily sexed by the male's red head, as opposed to the grey of the female, even nestling cocks will show a few red feathers.

Another cockatoo that is rarely seen outside Australia, the lucky few who keep them have had a high incidence of self-plucking to contend with. This can be prevented by housing them in spacious well-planted aviaries, replenishing chewed branches regularly, and giving pine-cones, corn-on-the-cob and chewable toys to the occupants.

The two eggs laid are incubated solely by the female.

ECLECTUS PARROTS
(*Eclectus roratus*)

Another extraordinary group of Australasian parrots, are the Eclectus. No other parrot shows such extreme forms of sexual dimorphism, the males being mainly a bright luminous green and the females red and purple. They also have an unusual hair-like quality to the feathers, not seen in any other psittacine. The Eclectus also has a very long intestinal system, suggesting a highly leguminous diet, which should be replicated in captivity for optimal health. They also seem to have a high requirement for vitamin A.

This is a female-dominated species, and early-age pairing is advised for the greatest hope of success, or the male may be too intimidated to court the female. They can be prolific layers, often having several clutches (of two eggs) in succession. Unfortunately, many hens lay a high proportion of infertile eggs, having warded off the male's advances. The chicks are very dark-skinned and eventually grow a black down, making them look most crow-like. Interestingly some pairs seem to produce same-sex clutches, and others one of each, although this is not a rule.

Although there are seven subspecies of Eclectus, purebred specimens of the most commonly kept, the Red-sided or Vosmaeri, are sadly becoming rarer. This is mainly because all Eclectus cocks are fairly similar, apart from differences in size, and therefore may be unknowingly paired to the wrong subspecies.

The hen of the Red-sided subspecies has very clear demarcation lines between the red and purple of its breast and no yellow on the tail. It also boasts a blue orbital ring.

The Vosmaeri subspecies tends to be larger, and the hen's red and purple tend to blend into one another with a rather jagged line. The undertail coverts and tip of the tail are bright yellow. There is no blue on the orbital ring if it is purebred.

Two jewels which are rarely seen in aviculture are the subspecies *Eclectus roratus cornelia* and *Eclectus roratus riedeli*, in which the female is entirely red. Every effort should be made to breed only from purebred stock to ensure we have well-defined variability of the subspecies in the future.

Eclectus meet with a varied response when viewed as potential pets. Because of their slightly antisocial behaviour towards one another (you will only rarely see a pair of Eclectus cuddled together, a common sight in macaws and cockatoos for instance), they are regarded as standoffish and aloof. Some hens can also be quite aggressive.

PIONUS PARROTS

This delightful family of Mexican and South American parrots are often overlooked in favour of some of the most commonly kept species. There is, however, much to recommend them, being beautiful, quiet and in many cases ready breeders. A particularity of the species is the fact that they will wheeze quite worryingly when stressed or alarmed. They are predisposed to the fungal infection aspergillosis and so should not be exposed to damp or mouldy conditions which may exacerbate the problem.

The pionus species are often willing to nest in their second year, although three-year-old birds are more likely to succeed. The large clutch averages four eggs, with many pairs proving to be good and reliable parents, useful for fostering amazons and macaws as well. For those with limited space and funds, Pionus can make charming pets, not unlike amazons but mostly less nippy than their cousins, although usually not as good mimics. Your dominance must be asserted over pubescent males if they are not going to get ideas above their station – but this is true of most species. A feature of all pionus is that they all carry red undertail coverts. A brief description of the subspecies follows.

The eclectus group is sexually dimorphic: the males are bright green; the females are red and purple. Pictured: Red-sided Eclectus hen.

The Blue-headed Pionus is a popular bird.

BLUE-HEADED PIONUS
(*Pionus menstruus*)
Probably the most commonly kept as an aviary bird and a pet, the Blue-headed, as its name suggests, has a blue head and part of the breast, otherwise it is mainly green.

MAXIMILIAN'S PIONUS (*Pionus maximiliani*) or SCALY-HEADED PIONUS
This mainly green parrot has a vinous area on its upper breast and throat. The alternative name of Scaly-headed applies to the rather reptilian appearance of the head feathers, which are triangular in appearance with the white down showing through. It is probably the least expensive of the pionus.

CORAL-BILLED or SORDID PIONUS
(*Pionus sordidus*)
Similar in appearance to the Maximilian, but with a bright reddish-orange beak, as opposed to the Maximilian's blackish and yellow beak. This species is rarely seen in aviculture and therefore rarely bred, although its requirements are similar to the other pionus.

WHITE-CAPPED PIONUS (*Pionus senilis*)
One of the smaller pionus, at 9 inches (23cm) long, is the White-capped. Sporting a livery of greyish-green, the startling white forecrown and pink eye-skin make it a most attractive little bird.

DUSKY PIONUS (*Pionus fuscus*)
Another small gem, the Dusky is a greyish-brown with suffused shades of red and blue over the body. A great favourite with pionus keepers.

BRONZE-WINGED PIONUS
(*Pionus chalcopterus*)
To our eyes, the nervy Bronze-winged is the most beautiful of the pionus. With a yellow beak and pink eye skin, this bird has a myriad of bronze, blue, pink, green, red and white amongst its colours. There seem to be an excess of females in this species, an unusual occurrence among parrots.

PLUM-CROWNED PIONUS
(*Pionus tumultuosus tumultuosus*)
Rarely seen and bred in captivity, the Plum-crowned has a plum-coloured wash to the head on an otherwise green body. The bill is yellow.

MASSENA'S or WHITE-HEADED PIONUS (*Pionus tumultuosus seniloides*)
This pionus is similar in appearance to the previously described Plum-crowned, with a greyish wash to the breast, and a scattering of

white feathers on the head, including red on the lores. Again it is very rarely kept and bred in captivity.

THE CAIQUE FAMILY

This highly popular group of parrots hails from South America, where they are still fairly abundant in several areas. They form loose flocks of 30-50 birds outside the breeding season. Once breeding commences, they are fiercely protective of the nesting area. Canopy dwellers, the caiques tend to forage, play and nest in the tops of tall trees. Sexually mature at two years of age, the clutch varies from two to four eggs, and the incubation period is normally 26 days. Fledging occurs at ten to twelve weeks. Caiques are normally vigilant parents and do a great job in rearing the young to independence.

Often known as the clowns of the parrot world, caiques are frequently lory-like in their behaviour. Bouncing, hopping, wing flashing and flicking all form part of the everyday behaviour of these extroverts. The beautiful red sides also flash like beacons. The voice of caiques is shrill and fairly loud for a small bird – 9 inches in length – but not altogether unmusical.

Captive birds should be housed in spacious aviaries – a minimum of 10' x 4' x 6' (3.05m x 1.2m x 1.8m) – well furnished with a variety of perches, swings, ropes and toys, all of which will be well utilised by these active birds. Charming and entertaining pets, the caiques must be brought up with loving authority if they are not to become troublesome in later life. As always, a most important point is not to allow the birds to perch anywhere on your body other than the hand. This way you will retain control over a potentially dominant species. Not the greatest of talkers, the caiques will nonetheless repeat a few words in their own voice.

The Black-headed Caique is the most common bird in its family.

BLACK-HEADED CAIQUE
(*Pionites melanocephala*)

Distributed from Southern Colombia, Brazil, Northern Peru and Eastern Ecuador, the Black-headed is the most commonly kept of the caiques. It has, as the name suggests, a black cap continuing from the jet black beak, and this is followed by an orange streak around the neck and cheeks, the white chest which typifies all caiques, orange pantaloons and undertail covers, green wings and blackish flights and tail.

PALLID CAIQUE
(*Pionites melanocephala pallida*)

Similar to the above species, but with yellow replacing the orange areas, the Pallid enjoys a similar but smaller area of distribution to the Black-headed.

WHITE-BELLIED CAIQUE
(*Pionites leucogaster*)
This beautiful bird has a horn-coloured beak, orange cap and yellow cheeks and green thighs. The wings and tail are green. From Northern Brazil, this bird is much more rarely seen in captivity, and commands a greater price than the two preceding species.

YELLOW-TAILED CAIQUE
(*Pionites leucogaster xanthumus*)
Similar to the White-bellied, but generally paler than this species, a beautiful addition is the Yellow Tail. This bird is rarely seen in captivity, bred by only a handful of specialists.

YELLOW-THIGHED CAIQUE
(*Pionites leucogaster xanthomeria*)
Similar to the White-bellied again, the Xanthomeria has yellow instead of green pantaloons. The endeavours of specialist breeders will ensure that these super birds don't die out in captivity.

The Yellow-thighed Caique's future is secure thanks to specialist breeders.

BUDGERIGAR (*Melopsittacus undulatus*)

There is no other parrot-like species which has been kept by so many, and no doubt given so much to so many, who would not readily describe themselves as the owners of parrots. Their size and husbandry requirements make them ideal for the average household. Coupled with this is a personality and character which will endear them to most people. For their size, they demonstrate a surprising level of intelligence. They quickly learn to repeat short phrases or sounds and can be taught to do all manner of tricks, which they appear to derive a tremendous amount of satisfaction from.

Historically, John Gould brought the first budgerigars to Britain in 1840. These budgerigars were as they occur in the wild in Australia today, which are a far cry from the domesticated ones which we see. Not only are the domesticated budgerigars available in a wide variety of colour variations, but their shape is also quite different.

The wild budgerigar has a much more streamlined appearance, the coloration being basically green with a yellow face, the wings having a scalloped appearance, and the head having horizontal barring extending from the top of the head to the nape of the neck. The yellow on the face extends to below the beak, a bib of black dots demarcates the yellow of the face from the green on the chest, and there is a small flash of blue at both ends of the bib. Once sexually mature, the hens can be differentiated from the cocks by different-coloured ceres – in the cocks this is bright blue, in the hens reddish-brown.

The domesticated budgerigar has a much stockier appearance, and is available in a huge variety of different colours. Some of these colours are mixed and can be in different intensities of colour. In addition to this, a crested strain has been developed.

In the wild, budgerigars lead a nomadic existence and exist in large flocks, communally feeding, drinking and breeding together. As soon as the flock runs out of water or food they move off to another location. This lack of territorial behaviour has continued in captive-bred birds, and if a budgerigar escapes, either from its cage in the home or from an outside aviary, it is quite likely that it will fly away and will never be seen again.

Surprisingly, some homing strains of budgerigar have been bred. This feat has not been easy and many losses occurred whilst the development of the strain was being produced. Even so, safeguards have to be taken in the form of specialised doorways, and only allowing part of the flock out at a time.

Budgerigars will adapt well to cage life. It is always preferable to purchase a young bird which has only just become independent if required as a pet, as at this age the youngster will tame readily. Although budgerigars are small birds, being only about 7 inches (18cm) in length (much of which is taken up by the tail), it is always preferable to get the largest cage possible. They are very active birds and will utilise their space well, and as with all caged birds there is a need to allow the pet bird out of the cage at least daily to give the opportunity for flying.

In an aviary environment, it is possible to keep and breed budgerigars in a colony situation. This can prove to be quite successful, and an aviary containing an

The budgerigar is the most popular parrot-like species.

assortment of different coloured budgerigars can prove to be most amusing, as they delight in one another's company and always appear to be undertaking some mischievous plot somewhere. Their behaviour is quite acrobatic, and they will really enjoy being fed

Budgies are very social birds and enjoy company.

items of food which will allow them to expand on this natural ability. Clods of grass placed inside empty hanging baskets hung inside an aviary will allow them to indulge in all sorts of acrobatics, as will a bunch of millet sprays.

Budgerigars will breed from a very early age, hens from the age of 6 months, but, for some, their reproductive life is completed by the age of 3 years. Prior to breeding, the cock will often be observed feeding the hen, and breeding will usually commence 10 days from the time that the nestbox is introduced. Nestboxes specifically made for budgerigars are readily available. Some of these are disposable, and are meant to be discarded after the breeding season. The benefit to this is that any infections resulting from bacteria, parasites or fungi will be disposed of with the nestbox at the end of the breeding season.

The usual nesting material is wood shavings, and both birds will spend time shredding this further. The average clutch is 6 eggs; however, this may vary quite considerably. The incubation period is 18 days, with the hen alone brooding the eggs.

Baby budgerigars mature very quickly, which, one could presume, is an adaptive response from their wild origins: because of their nomadic existence, it is important that the reproductive cycle can be completed in the shortest possible amount of time to enable the flock to move off in search of fresh food supplies. The young remain in the nest for about 4 weeks and finish being weaned at 5-6 weeks. If you are breeding budgerigars within a colony, care will need to be taken, to ensure that no bullying or serious fighting is taking place.

Some budgerigar keepers appear to have great success keeping budgerigars in this manner; however, some collectors do not, with much squabbling taking place. This seriously interferes with the breeding results. In this situation it is probably worth separating the birds for breeding.

The budgerigar is closely related to the grass parrakeet, Neophema, and their dietary requirements are similar. They prefer the smaller seeds, with supplementary green food and egg food in the breeding season. It is likely that the budgerigar will continue with its current popularity, the different colour mutations make them a popular exhibition bird, with many clubs supporting the budgerigar fancy.

COCKATIELS (*Nymphicus hollandicus*)

With the exception of the budgerigar, the cockatiel must surely be the parrot-like bird which is the most loved by the majority of the general public. It is also the parrot which is often responsible for sparking off the interest in parrot keeping. The cockatiel really does have so much to commend it. Young

Cockatiels are early sexual maturers.

birds parent-reared can be readily tamed. This is so easy in the cockatiel that we really do not see any benefits from hand-rearing this species. Cockatiels become sexually mature before they are a year old, therefore not requiring the lengthy wait if breeding is the goal.

The cockatiel could be thought of as a domestic species; many are bred annually, the vast majority in an array of different coloured mutations. So many of these mutations have been bred that it is almost impossible to find purebred normal cockatiels.

They are attractive in appearance, having a crest which can be used to demonstrate their mood. Only 12 inches (30.5cm) in length, their flight feathers and tail are long and tapering which gives an overall elegant shape.

The normal cockatiel has an attractive colour-scheme, which is sadly now so overlooked in preference for the colour mutations. This is often referred to as the normal grey, which gives a good indication of the predominant colour. The majority of the cock bird's body is made up of various shades of grey, the front of the head, cheeks and throat are yellow with a large orange ear-patch, and on each wing there is a broad white bar. The hen's body is a similar colour to the cock's, with the exception being a lack of yellow on the head and ear-patches which are less bright. The underside of the tail-feathers are striped with grey and yellow.

BREEDING RITES

Cockatiels are very free breeding. A pair, if allowed, will start to breed before they are a year old. Most authorities advise not allowing this to happen before they reach a year. Because of their free breeding characteristic, it is often necessary to remove the nestbox as many will breed out of the normal breeding season for the Northern hemisphere – which is from April to September.

Although it is usually acknowledged that more productive breeding results can be obtained from a single pair in an aviary, this species is bred quite extensively on a colony system. This appears more effective if a greater number than two pairs are housed together. As with other parrot colony situations, all pairs need to be introduced at the same time. The nestboxes should be the same size and should all be at the same height, which will minimise squabbling. The average clutch size is five eggs, but frequently only three or four are reared. The young leave the nest at about five weeks old, although both parents will continue to feed the young until they become independent about two weeks later.

AUSTRALIAN ORIGINS

Cockatiels originate from Australia and are closely related to the cockatoos, much of their behaviour being characteristic of cockatoo species. Both parents share the incubation, and it is usual for the cock bird to incubate during the day and the hen at night. Some pairs however do not strictly adhere to this, with many diligent parent birds sharing day and night sitting together. Cockatiels, for all their free breeding activities, do still have to be compatible. It cannot be expected that a cock and hen put together will naturally hit it off, and some pairs show a marked dislike for one another. These will be unlikely to breed successfully.

Cockatiels are extremely hardy, but they do appreciate a shelter which allows them to escape from the elements. In an aviary situation, they will require a regular worming program, as they are particularly susceptible to this problem. Cockatiels make excellent pets; taming readily when young, they are usually extremely affectionate and gentle. Their small size makes them ideal for children. They usually learn to talk and whistle, and will imitate other regularly heard noises. Parakeet seed mixes, together with fresh fruit and vegetables make up their diet.

In Australia, large flocks congregate and lead a nomadic existence. Perhaps because of this, if your cockatiel escapes it tends to fly away. It is unusual for them to stay in the vicinity of their home; the only time when they sometimes do so (and it is only sometimes) is if they have young. As already stated, cockatiels come in a wide variety of different colour mutations; below are descriptions of some of the common ones.

LUTINO COCKATIELS

Many still believe that this is the most beautiful of the colour variants. These cockatiels are yellow, the intensity of which is variable. The ear-patch colour remains unchanged; in the males the head is a richer yellow.

PEARL COCKATIELS

Colouring is the same as the normal grey; however, large areas of the wing feathers have yellow barring. The chest and abdomen have a normal colour mottled with cream/yellow. Interestingly, as males become sexually mature they lose the yellow markings, appearing then as a normal grey.

CINNAMON COCKATIELS

In this colour variant, the grey is replaced with a fawn colour.

PIED COCKATIELS

As the name suggests, the Pied Cockatiel has irregular markings of yellow, grey and white, the amount of colour varying from one individual to the next.

WHITE-FACED COCKATIELS

This is a more recent introduction and is quite different from the previous variations inasmuch as the yellows and oranges have

A Pied Cockatiel.

been replaced with white. The grey colouring has a silver-grey appearance.

WHITE COCKATIELS
This colour represents a lutino form of white-face mutation, and is demonstrated by a pure white bird.

Specialist cockatiel societies exist which have various classes, some of which include two or more colour variations.

PARRAKEETS

The term parrakeet is normally associated with the smaller members of the parrot family who have long tails. In reality there is very little distinction. However it is a useful term when one considers the different husbandry requirements of the larger parrots and the smaller parrakeets – but bearing in mind that there will be large variations. Even within parrot families there is variation, for example the macaws, where the Hahn's Macaw is 13 inches (33cm) and the Hyacinthine is 40 inches (101.5cm), and they have beaks to match their sizes, which is an important consideration when considering the materials required for the construction of an aviary.

Although some parrakeets can be quite destructive to aviary woodwork, this tends to be less of a problem than with some of the larger members of the parrot family. If the framework is of wood, the wire mesh must be on the inside. If the wood is on the inside, it is worth covering it with sheet metal or encasing it with wire mesh. Dependent upon the species kept, 16-18 gauge wire will be sufficient.

Smaller parrakeets appear to attract greater attention from cats and birds of prey, which may necessitate some double wiring, both on the roof and the sides of the aviary. There are now devices on the market which are meant to deter cats by emitting sound waves which are unpleasant to cats but out of the hearing range of birds and humans.

Food requirements of parrakeets are similar to those of the larger parrots, with some slight differences, mostly in relation to the addition of small seeds in the diet. There are some good parrakeet mixtures available, which include the smaller seeds. The smaller parrots also often relish millet sprays. It is important to include the range of fruit and vegetables as suggested for the larger parrots' diet.

Parrakeets make more use of the aviaries in terms of flying than many of the larger parrots, who will often climb rather than fly, and for this reason will require aviaries which may seem quite large when compared to the birds' size.

AUSTRALIAN PARRAKEETS
These parrakeets have a large following. They have been bred in aviary situations for several decades, are often very colourful and not too noisy for those who have close neighbours. An important consideration is the need for regular worming programmes as this family suffers more than most from a worm burden. They will often descend to the aviary floor and

The Australian Parrakeet is particularly prone to worm infestation.

forage at ground level for food items. This makes them particularly susceptible to worm infestation, and this cannot be ignored; it is probable that this is the single most common cause of death in this group of birds.

ROSELLAS

Rosellas have much to commend them and have enjoyed popularity for many years. They are extremely colourful, generally free breeding, and hardy. As their numbers have increased, their cost has become cheaper, to the point where they can be purchased for a few pounds. Some attempts have been made to make pets of the Rosella, but this has not generally been successful, as even those which have been hand-reared can become quite aggressive as they mature. They are active, free-flying parrakeets who make good use of the flying space available to them, and to keep them in a cage severely restricts this. Their aviary flight should be a minimum of twelve feet in length, ideally longer.

Rosellas are naturally aggressive to other birds, particularly other rosellas, so it is important to keep one pair per aviary, and to ensure that aviaries which adjoin theirs are double-wired, to prevent the rosellas from inflicting injury on their neighbours. Pairs of rosellas housed next to each other spend so much of their time defending their territory that this can seriously reduce or even prevent breeding success altogether.

Their calls are quite melodious, and their vocalisation increases in the breeding season. Rosellas enjoy bathing and will often bathe daily in all weathers. Rosellas usually take two years to become sexually mature, but will then breed for many years, often until their mid-twenties. The nestboxes which they prefer are often termed 'grandfather' type nestboxes, recommended sizes being three to four feet high and 9 inches square. They will often double-clutch. Rosellas often enjoy green food, and this should ideally be supplied on a daily basis, with particular favourites including dandelion and plantain. As with many parrakeets from Australia, if they escape from the aviary they tend to fly away and not stay in the vicinity.

GOLDEN-MANTLED ROSELLA

(*Platycercus eximus*)

This is, in all probability, the most popular of all the rosellas, at 12 inches (30.5cm) in length. The head and neck are a bright red with white cheek-patches; the mantle of the wings, as the name suggests, are golden yellow. The feathers are broadly edged with black, the red from the head and neck extends halfway down the chest, the remainder of the chest and the abdomen are yellow, and the outer feathers of the wings are bright blues, as are the outer tail feathers. The rump is light green and the middle tail feathers dark green. The hen's colours are more subdued.

This is a very prolific member of the rosella family, the average clutch consisting of six eggs, and they will often rear two clutches per season. The cock assists the hen in rearing the young. It is important to watch the young closely after they have left the nest, as the cock will sometimes be so impatient to rear a second clutch that he will start to be intolerant of the first clutch as soon as they are independent. It is safe practice to remove the young at this stage. The Golden-mantled Rosella will often successfully act as foster parents for other rosellas and even other families of parrakeets. The young assume adult plumage at about twelve months.

MEALY ROSELLA

(*Platycercus adscitus palliceps*)

Not as common as the Golden-mantled Rosella, but has a consistent following; length 12 inches (30.5cm). The coloration of the Mealys is less bright, but is nonetheless very pleasing. The head is white tinged with yellow, the nape of the neck and mantle are yellow with the feathers having a broad black border. The outer wing feathers are blue and black. The chest is blue, the vent area feathers are bright red, the tail feathers are blue and the rump is light green. The Mealy Rosellas are not always free breeding, with some pairs being very reluctant to start. However, once breeding has been established it is likely to continue, with some clutches numbering as many as eight eggs.

STANLEY ROSELLA
(*Platycercus icterotis*)
This is a smaller member of the rosella family, measuring ten inches in length. It is clearly sexually dimorphic, with the male having quite distinctive colouring compared to that of the hens. The male has a red head and chest, with yellow cheek-patches, the back is green with black borders, and the outer wing feathers are blue. The hen has a much duller coloration, the head and chest having some background red, with green feathers interspersed in this. The head is mainly mottled green with the cheeks a pale yellow.

The Stanley Rosella can be quite an enchanting aviary bird, as it has a natural tameness which is demonstrated by a quiet confidence in the keeper. They soon learn to come to the aviary wire for treats and some will learn a few words. Not always a prolific breeder, and tends to be single-brooded.

PENNANT'S ROSELLA (PARRAKEET)
(*Platycercus elegans*)
Many would argue that this is the most handsome of all the rosellas. Its basic colouring consists of deep red and blue, immature birds differing from adults by having a variable amount of green. It can take a good year for the young to assume the adult plumage. The length of the Pennant's is 14 inches (35.5cm). In adults, the body of the bird is deep red with blue cheeks and blue tail, the wings are red and black, the outer wing feathers are blue.

A Pennant's Rosella.

It often lays 6-8 eggs, most are single-brooded. They often appear quite confiding. This species will feather-pluck, often for no apparent reason. Unfortunately they will also feather-pluck their chicks, sometimes to the degree that the young cannot leave the nest. If feather-plucking of the young reaches this level of severity it will be necessary to either foster the young, preferably to other rosellas, or to hand-rear the young. In the wild it has been noted that this rosella will often be seen eating insects and even caterpillars, so it would be worth increasing the protein level of their diet, perhaps by the regular addition of egg food.

BROWN'S ROSELLA
(*Platycercus venustus*)
This rosella is quite different from the other members of the rosella family, and is only rarely available. Because of its rarity, only those with experience of keeping and breeding other members of the rosella family should contemplate keeping the Brown's Rosella. It is

a small rosella measuring 11 inches (28cm). Its head is dark brown, which sometimes has the odd bright red feathers, and there are white cheek-patches. The chest and back is a creamy yellow with a narrow black/brown border. The outer wing feathers are blue, the area of the vent is bright red and the tail feathers are blue.

In behaviour, this rosella also differs from the others, as it continues to want to breed in the winter months. This often has disastrous results for the eggs or young if a cold snap should arise. It is probable that this is one of the reasons that the Brown's is so infrequently seen. Some parrot keepers who specialise in rosellas have been quite successful with this species by using a specially designed nestbox. The secret of their success has been an added enclosed compartment underneath the floor of the nestbox, in which a low-wattage light bulb has been placed. When illuminated, the light bulb gives off sufficient heat to prevent the death of the eggs or young from exposure, should the hen stop brooding.

The other difficulty encountered with this rosella is the difficulty in pairing them up, as some pairs are not compatible, and it is unfortunate that the cock Brown's Rosella will kill the hen very quickly if she is not to his liking. As with all species of parrot who are known to be difficult in this way, the most successful pairings can be achieved by placing the cock and hen together when very young. When compatible, the clutch can consist of four to five young and the parents may be double-brooded.

POLYTELIS PARRAKEETS

Members of this genus are quite different from the rosella family. They are a larger parrakeet, which tend to be quieter in behaviour, spending long periods sitting on the perch. They also tend to be steadier and to tame quickly, soon getting to know the keeper. They have a popular following and sometimes prove to be quite challenging in getting them to breed successfully. The female is the dominant member of the pair. Although they enjoy both green food and fruit, some pairs can be kept quite successfully in planted aviaries, doing very little damage to the planted vegetation. A regular worming programme is essential for this genus.

BARRABAND'S PARRAKEET
(*Polytelis swainsonii*)

A well-known member of the genus, it is 16 inches (40.5cm) in length. The males are particularly handsome: they are basically green with bright yellow above the beak and forehead, which continues to form a wide bib below the beak; a red band on the lower throat separates this from the green. In contrast the females lack the yellow and red bib. Immature birds resemble the female.

Barraband's Parrakeets have been bred successfully using a colony system. Indeed those who seem to have the most success with this species tend to be those who have more than one pair, and it is likely that they stimulate one another to breed. They lay 4-6 eggs and are normally single clutched. It is often two to three years before the young become sexually mature.

PRINCESS OF WALES PARRAKEET
(*Polytelis alexandrae*)

This has to be one of the most elegant of parrots. This is a large parrakeet, measuring 18 inches (45.5cm). Much of this length is taken up with the tail, which is extremely long and tapering. In the male there is a light blue wash to the forehead, the throat is pink, the body is olive green, the outer wing is a lime green. The thighs and lower abdomen are pink. The tail is quite outstanding when flying, as the underside is striped longitudinally with pink and dark green. The hen has a shorter tail and has much more subdued coloration.

Princess of Wales Parrakeets soon get to know their keeper and many will become confident enough to take treats from their owners through the aviary wire.

In the breeding season particularly, the cock can be noisy. They have been bred successfully using a colony system. Some pairs can be quite prolific, the usual clutch consisting of about four eggs.

ROCK PEBBLER PARRAKEET
(*Polytelis anthopeplus*)
This is the largest member of the genus; the length being 16 inches (40.5cm), which is shorter than the Princess of Wales, but the body is larger and more robust. The cock is bright yellow on the head, chest, rump and the outer part of the wings; there is a band of red across the lower part of the wing feathers; the back of the head and mantle are olive green; the tail feathers are dark green and black. The hen is olive green, although this is brighter on the chest, and her tail feathers are margined and tipped with pink on the underside. This is a popular member of the family; they normally lay 4-6 eggs.

GRASS PARRAKEET (*Neophema*)
The Grass Parrakeets are another group of parrakeets originating from Australia. They are small, only measuring 8-10 inches (20.5 - 25.5cm). They are extremely popular with beginners and those who enjoy breeding specialist mutations. In the winter it is wise to keep these in a fully enclosed shelter, as they find damp, cold conditions stressful. As the name suggests, they enjoy feeding from young growing grasses and seeding grasses. If your aviary has a concrete floor, it is useful to grow grass in seed trays. If you grow four or six trays it is usually possible to rotate these; this will give Grass Parrakeets immense pleasure. As with the other Australian parrakeets, a regular worming programme is advisable.

BOURKE'S PARRAKEET
(*Neophema bourkii*)
Extremely popular, this is a very good parrakeet for the beginner. They are particularly inoffensive and can be kept in mixed collections of birds, including small finches. Interestingly, they are often most active at twilight. In an aviary one can see and hear them making short flights to and from the perches.

The Bourke's has no green in its plumage; the upper parts are brown and the lower parts pink, with some blue on the shoulder extending down the wing and in the ventral area. Most of the feathers have a mottled appearance. The females are similar to the cock but are much more subdued. Bourke's Parrakeets are 8 inches (20cm) in length. They will often breed in their second year and normally have a clutch of 4. They are very steady, generally having a natural confidence. Several colour mutations exist.

The Bourke's Parrakeet can be kept in mixed collections.

ELEGANT GRASS PARRAKEET
(*Neophema elegans*)
The name gives a good indication of the appearance and the behaviour of this parrakeet, which is 9 inches (23cm) in length. The first two features which you notice about Elegances are the narrow frontal band of blue above the beak and the blue band which goes down the outside of the wing. The remainder of the Elegant is a rich golden olive, on the abdomen and the underside of the tail; this lightens to yellow. The female is much duller in appearance. Their normal clutch consists of 3-5 eggs and they are frequently double-brooded. Colour mutations exist.

SPLENDID GRASS PARRAKEET
(*Neophema splendida*)
This must surely be one of the most beautiful of all parrakeets. It measures 8½ inches (21.5cm) in length. The face and head are deep blue, as is the outer area of the wing. The chest is bright red to about halfway down the abdomen, where the colour changes to a rich yellow. This extends to the underside of the tail. The back of the head, nape and back are a deep green. The hen is much duller in appearance and lacks the red on the chest. The clutch size is 4-6. They are peaceful birds and have been kept quite successfully in communal aviaries containing finches. The Splendids are available in several colour mutations, some of which appear even more susceptible to damp and cold weather conditions.

RED-RUMPED PARRAKEET
(*Psephotus haematonotus*)
This bird is of the genus Psephotus and is a larger, more robust bird than the Grass Parrakeet. It measures 10½ inches (26.5cm) in length. The Red-rump is well-known for its fostering ability; in all probability no other small parrakeet has been used to foster the young of other species to such an extent. Some of these fostering arrangements appear quite comical – especially so when the children can be considerably larger than the parents. Red-rumps have been used to foster various parrot-like birds including Rosellas, Princess of Wales Parrakeets and even some conures, to name but a few.

In behaviour, the pair can be very territorial, with the male Red-rump particularly pugnacious towards birds in adjoining aviaries. The male is mainly green, with a blue wash on the face and outer part of the wings. The rump, as the name suggests, is bright red, the abdomen is yellow. The hen is much duller, being mainly a grey-green colour. They breed readily, clutch size being 4-6 eggs, and are often double-brooded.

PSITTACULA PARRAKEETS

These are well-known parrakeets, some of which have been known to man for centuries. The Ringneck in particular has proved readily adaptable to captivity. This adaptability has not just been confined to aviary situations, as quite large feral populations exist in several countries which are not included in their normal range.

In the breeding situation, one needs to be aware that it is the hen who is the dominant member of the pair; the cock will be quite nervous of her. It is advisable to introduce them to each other carefully, several months prior to their breeding season. This will allow the cock to gain confidence in the company of the hen. For the newcomer, it can be frustrating ensuring that you have a cock and a hen. This is in part because the cock doesn't show his differences until he is sometimes two years old. Psittacula parrakeets can breed quite successfully on the colony system, although the results are not usually as good as if pairs are kept segregated in their own

The Indian Ringneck is most suited to aviary life.

accommodation. This group of bird will eat a wide range of fruits, those with the larger beaks appearing to have a greater interest in nuts and seeds.

INDIAN RINGNECK
(*Psittacula krameri manillensis*)
Originating from the South of India and Sri Lanka, this elegant parrakeet is now widely available in aviculture and is also suitable as a pet, but is probably happier as an aviary bird. It is a slender bird, 16 inches (40.5cm) in length. The colour is mostly differing shades of green with a strikingly bright green head leading to a black collar. The upper mandible is red and the lower black. The hen is slightly shorter than the cock, and lacks the ring on the neck. Many mutations occur in the wild population so it is not unexpected that the aviculturist has taken this further, with many colour mutations being now available. The Lutino variations are a golden yellow with a red eye, and are fairly common, as are the Blue mutation.

They breed easily and as such are suitable for the novice and experienced breeder alike. Generally they make excellent parents and rear their 4-5 young with no problems. They tend to nest early in the year, which can be a problem if a late cold snap of weather occurs. These birds are hardy but are susceptible to frostbite on their extremities, so it is advisable that they sleep in a shelter, and avoid clinging to freezing aviary wire where their toes are exposed.

AFRICAN RINGNECK
(*Psittacula krameri krameri*)
This parrakeet comes from central and northern Africa. It is smaller than the Indian Ringneck at $14^{1}/_{2}$ inches (37cm) in length. The males are beautifully marked, with a black ring running from the lower black mandible upwards to the back of the head, where it peters out into an effusion of blue and pink feathers. The hen is smaller and lacks the full ring – in some a faint ring of neck feathers can be seen. Whereas the Indian Ringneck has a red upper mandible, the African is more rose-coloured, with a black tip. Mutations are rare.

They breed well, rearing a clutch of 4-5 young. Young birds lack the full coloration of the mature specimens, taking at least three years to develop into breeding birds. Breeding pairs can be quite aggressive towards other birds, and need to be kept in separate aviaries.

PLUM-HEADED PARRAKEET
(*Psittacula cyanocephala*)
A little gem of a parrakeet with its plum-coloured head, bright green body and long slender tail; it is a welcome addition to any aviary. Originating from India and Pakistan

The plum-headed Parrakeet enjoys aviary life with finches and quails.

through to Nepal and Sri Lanka, it lives in the lowlands eating grass seeds and vegetation.

Again there is sexual dimorphism, with the hen being duller and shorter. The clutch size is 4-5 eggs. They can be rather trying to breed, as they can be unpredictable. They tend to favour a large aviary of mixed birds, but it has been noticed that they get on particularly well living with finches and quail in a planted aviary.

MOUSTACHED PARRAKEET

(*Psittacula alexandri*)

The nominate race comes from Java and Bali, but there are eight recognisable genera. They can be found in Northern India, Nepal, Burma, Southern China and parts of Borneo. Interestingly, they are less common now in Java, probably due to the problems these islands face, namely erosion of habitat. Fortunately they are widely kept and bred in aviculture; even though they can be noisy, they make suitable aviary birds. The length is 13 inches (33cm) and as the name implies they appear to have a moustache of black over the cere. The upper mandible is red and the lower is black, matching the black underchin. The females in most of the species have a black upper and lower mandible. The young have black mandibles which change to red as they mature. The body coloration is green with a beautiful pinky rose-coloured chest, fading to a delicate green, progressing down to the slender tail which is slightly shorter than that of some of the other parrakeets.

The clutch size of 3-4 eggs is usually bred with ease in a compatible pair. They like to be fairly quiet and secretive at these times, so make an aviary for them that is in a secluded spot with a warm shelter and they will be happy.

The Alexandrine Parrakeet takes its name from Alexander the Great, who reputedly owned one.

ALEXANDRINE PARRAKEET
(*Psittacula eupatria*)
Sometimes known as the Alexandrine Ringneck or Indian Rock Parrot, this magnificent bird is thought to be the forefather of parrots being kept as pets – being introduced by Alexander the Great, who is reported to have owned one. It is highly intelligent and makes a good talker, hence it makes an excellent pet. At 23 inches (58.5cm) in length, it is the largest of the Asiatic parrakeets and the coloration is stunning. Beak dark red, eyes yellow. Bright green forehead leading to a greyer-green nape – the characteristic black collar surrounds the neck. The chest is a soft green, the wings and back are bright green with red shoulders, and the tail is yellow. The female lacks the collar and is shorter.

The clutch size of 2-4 eggs are generally reared well by the parents, once the pair have settled down and bonded to each other. The aviary needs to be fairly robust, as the strong beak is capable of chewing the framework. They are fairly commonly kept and have proved to be quite hardy. Several mutations exist, including Blue and Lutino. Originating from India, Nepal, Burma, Thailand and Vietnam, they are widely found in the wild and in aviculture.

DERBYAN PARRAKEET
(*Psittacula derbiana*)
Coming from India, Tibet and parts of China, this parrakeet is rarer than the other Asiatics. Unfortunately it doesn't breed readily, although there are pairs who have adapted well to captivity and do breed successfully. Clutch size of 2-4 eggs. Robust aviaries are needed, as they tend to be destructive. Length is 20 inches (51cm); the general colour is a bright green with a lilac blue head and chest. The lower mandible and chin areas are black, and they also have a small black line of feathers reaching from eye to eye. The upper mandible is red through to yellow; once again, the dimorphic hen has an upper mandible of black and a pink headline. A truly beautiful bird which is becoming more available in aviculture. Its exact status in the wild is uncertain but it is felt to be secure.

LONG-TAILED PARRAKEET
(*Psittacula longicauda*)
This squat bird with a long thin tapering tail is commonly found in its native lands. It originates from Malay, Singapore, Borneo and Sumatra through to the Nicobar Islands.

Length is 17 inches (43cm). Again a mainly green bird with an orange face, green crown and black neck. The beak is the same orange/red as the face, giving it a striking appearance. In aviculture it is rare. Mortality rates are high, as these birds are easily stressed and suffer from stress-related problems. Breeding successes to our knowledge are rare. If they do breed, a normal clutch would be 2-5 eggs, with an incubation period of 23-24 days.

QUAKER PARRAKEET
(*Myiopsitta monachus*)
This is another parrakeet which is hardy, willing to breed and attractive and would undoubtedly be kept much more commonly if it wasn't for its voice. This is loud for the size of the bird, and the alarm call is particularly repetitive and far-reaching. However, if no near neighbours are present this makes an ideal bird for both the beginner and the more experienced, as the nesting behaviour and interaction of the flock, if a flock is kept, can keep one captivated.

The Quaker is a communal nester, with a large flock of birds all nesting together. They make the nest by weaving pliable twigs together. There is a short tunnel leading to the nesting chamber. This makes nest inspection almost impossible. The nest cavity itself is not lined, the eggs being laid directly on the twigs. The clutch usually consists of 5-6 eggs. In captivity they will utilise a nestbox, making a nest of twigs inside this. Conversely, if a wire platform with a few twigs is placed in the aviary they will soon be stimulated to build the nest and breed.

At one time it was common practice when young were in the nest to make a hole in the aviary so the parents could leave the aviary and forage for food. One has to admit, to see them flying at liberty is extremely interesting. However, one needs to bear in mind that allowing a non-endemic species its freedom is illegal. Quakers now have feral populations in several areas including Europe and the USA, which is far from their normal origins in South America.

They will eat a wide variety of food items. Their beak is strong, and they will quickly chew at available wood in the aviary, so any wire mesh less than 16g will soon have holes in it. Quakers can make good pets and will soon learn to utter odd words and phrases. Their appearance is attractive, the top of their head is grey, cheeks and throat are white, the chest is barred with white and fawn, the lower abdomen is cream yellow. The nape and back is green, the outer wing feathers are black. Length is 11 inches (28cm). Colour mutations of blue and yellow are available.

PEACH-FACED LOVEBIRDS
(*Agapornis roseicollis*)

These are ideal for the beginners, both as single pets or pairs for breeding. As single pets they can be quite enchanting, although it has to be said that the cocks when sexually mature appear more even-tempered than the hens. They will often adore their owner, never being happier than when snuggled up close. For this reason many people keep them as pairs, which does release the owner from all the adoration. A word of caution is required here: Lovebirds can be quite murderous, literally, if their partner is not to their liking. There are many stories of owners finding the mutilated bodies of Lovebirds in the bottom of cages. In the confines of a cage it is not possible for the submissive one of the pair (often the cock) to escape. Lovebirds which are happily paired are quite enchanting, and will quickly get into the routine of captivity in a cage. It is of course important that they are allowed out for regular exercise. Some have even successfully flown them at liberty.

Lovebirds always enjoy the smaller seeds,

such as millet, canary and small sunflower, and will readily accept fruit and vegetables when used to it. Peach-faced Lovebirds find immense pleasure in willow branches and twigs, as they chew and strip the bark off endlessly. They also use the strips of willow to make their nest. The hen inserts pieces into her rump feathers and flies to the nest with this. The nestbox is often the size of a cockatiel box. This does seem large for the size of the birds, but this enables the nest to be built inside. Peach-faced Lovebirds will successfully nest in either a cage or an aviary. In the aviary situation, the nestbox needs to be left in place all year round as these are used to roost in. This does on occasions cause problems, as some Lovebirds will breed continuously, if the nestbox is left in place. The usual clutch size is 4-6 eggs. The hen is the dominant partner. They can be kept and bred in a colony.

In appearance the Peach-faced Lovebird is particularly attractive: the front of the head and throat are a rose-peach colour, the rump and upper tail feathers are blue, the body is green – the sexes are indistinguishable. It is

Lutino Peach-faced Lovebirds: pairings are not always successful.

Conures are renowned for being mischief-makers. Pictured: Sun Conure.

important to note that Peach-faced Lovebirds, if outside, will require regular worming. They are 6 inches (15cm) in length and originate from South Africa. A great number of colour mutations exist.

There are several other members of the Lovebird family: the Fischer's (*Agapornis fischeri*) and the Masked (*Agapornis personata*) are regularly available. Their husbandry is similar to that of the Peach-faced variety. Other rarer Lovebirds include the Abyssinian (*Agapornis taranta*), Madagascar (*Agapornis cana*) and the Red-faced (*Agapornis pullaria*). These have much more specialist needs and are not recommended for the novice.

CONURES

The conures form a large group all originating from Central and South America. They vary in size from the Greater Patagonian Conure at 21 inches (53.5cm) to the Painted Conure at 9 inches (23cm). They are characterised by having a long tail and a slender appearance, which gives an indication of their close relationship to the macaws. Some conures' behaviour is very macaw-like. They come in a variety of colours and are generally very trainable, which gives an indication of their intelligence.

Conures are characters, and will often prove to be quite mischievous, and, if not trained, some can be very strong-willed. Many are very playful and will, especially when young, spend long periods playing on the floor together. Conures on the whole are extremely sociable. They appear to gain tremendous satisfaction from others, whether this is from interacting with other birds or by interacting with their owners. Another advantage is that they will often be willing to interrelate with more than just one person or to more than just one bird. This makes them an ideal family bird where children maybe clambering for attention from the pet bird. Most conures are very affectionate and enjoy physical contact.

As an aviary subject, they still have much to commend them. Most will breed willingly if basic breeding principles are followed. In addition, because of their highly sociable nature they function happily within a mixed flock situation. However, care needs to be taken if mixing small conures with larger parrot species, to ensure that no bullying by either party is taking place. A drawback to this type of accommodation for conures is the need for some conures to roost in their nestbox at night. This is a variable need, with some pairs being more attached to their box than others. Unfortunately nestboxes within a communal system can lead to territorial disputes, so will require very careful management and observation.

Most are very hardy and will accept a wide variety of different food items. The main disadvantage to the larger conures is that they can be noisy; their alarm calls in particular can be quite penetrating and repetitive, to the point where this may cause annoyance to neighbours. If a hand-reared conure is purchased this is not so much of a problem: as long as they have been exposed to a variety of different situations when young they will not be alarmed as regularly and will therefore not be as noisy.

The larger conures can also be quite destructive and won't hesitate in demolishing a wooden framework, if the aviary has been constructed in such a way as to make it available to them. If given plenty of space and a regular supply of fresh perches/branches this is much less of a problem. Conures, because of their intelligence and because of their active nature, will need to be occupied. If not given the attention that they quite justifiably deserve, they may develop behavioural problems in the form of feather-plucking, screaming or stereotypical behaviour. These problems can, with patience and thought, be put right in the majority of cases. However, it is much better to prevent the problem in the first place.

There has been confusion, inasmuch as some aviculturists refer to conures as parakeets rather than conures. This is probably because there are several different genera within the conures:

- Pyrrhura – which are the smallest of the conures
- Aratingas – these are larger and similar to macaws
- Cyanoliseus – which represent the Patagonian conures
- Enicognathus – represented by Slender Bills and Austral conures
- *Guaruba Guaruba* or *Aratinga guaruba* – Queen of Bavaria's Conure
- Ognorhynchus icterotis – Yellow-eared Conure
- Nandayus nenday – Nanday Conure.

In addition to the main groups, several conures possess subspecies. Because of the broadness of the group as a whole it is perhaps not surprising that such confusion exists.

PYRRHURA CONURES

There are 16 species within this group, about half of which are generally available. The pyrrhura conures are quiet and highly inquisitive, to the point where even parent-reared birds will become confiding because they need to know what's going on. Many will appreciate some of the smaller seeds and millet sprays in their diet. Because of their small size a 6' (1.8m) flight is acceptable to them, both recreationally and for breeding.

In the last two to three years there has appeared to be a surge of interest in these small conures. This has meant that many of the pyrrhuras, which had until this time been extremely rare in captivity, were suddenly available. To start with, these commanded very high prices and their popularity appeared to get even greater. However, as more aviculturists bred these rarer species, and many proved to be free-breeding, the market ended up with a greater number than was needed and they consequently fell in popularity.

The present situation is that some of the rarer species are available at very low prices. It is unfortunate that many aviculturists have made the decision to sell their pyrrhuras and to replace them with parrot species with a greater value. It must be hoped that the few pyrrhura specialists will be a sufficient number to prevent some of these delightful species being lost to aviculture.

MAROON-BELLIED CONURE (*Pyrrhura frontalis*) and the GREEN-CHEEKED CONURE (*Pyrrhura molinae*)

Together these are the most frequently available of the group. Up until recently these were classified as quite different species; however, chromosomal analysis indicate that they are not separate species. These can make ideal pets, being quite tame and confiding.

Although endangered in the wild, the Blue-throated Conure's numbers are growing in captivity.

Because of their size, 10 inches (25.5cm), they can make good pets for children. As aviary subjects they can be prolific, frequently double-clutching and having as many as 6 young per nest.

CRIMSON-BELLIED CONURE
(*Pyrrhura perlata perlata*)
Quite an avicultural rarity until recent years, it is still quite rare in aviculture outside specialist Pyrrhura breeders. The main characteristic of this small conure (10 inches or 25.5cm) is, as the name suggests, a bright crimson belly. This is not apparent until the young have reached about 6 months. Once a pair has commenced breeding this is likely to re-occur each breeding season. Clutch size usually consists of 4-6.

PAINTED CONURE (*Pyrrhura picta*)
Almost unknown until the mid-1970s, this bird is now often available. Its articulate markings around the neck, where dark feathers are bordered with white, gives it a most attractive appearance. It is free-breeding, with some clutches being as large as 7-8.

BLACK-CAPPED CONURE
(*Pyrrhura rupicola*)
Another of the small conures which hasn't been available until recent years. It remains fairly rare, although is often available from specialist Pyrrhura breeders. It has proved itself to be fairly free-breeding, with some clutches being greater than 7.

BLUE-THROATED CONURE
(*Pyrrhura cruentata*)
Almost unknown until a few years ago, these birds are now available at a quarter of what their value was a few years previously. They are highly endangered in the wild, with vast areas of their habitat being destroyed. They are highly attractive, very playful and mischievous. As pets they can be quite nippy and strong-willed. There appear to be more cocks than hens available, and it is these hand-reared cocks which are at times made available to the pet market.

It is unfortunate that many Blue-throats are hand-reared. As a group they appear to benefit considerably from being reared and socialised by their parents. They are not easy to breed, with many instances of egg-eating and physical abuse of chicks by the parents. They are not easy to hand-rear, but fortunately can be very successfully reared by other members of the pyrrhura group. The females are more dominant and heavier than the males. Some aviculturists have bred them successfully in trios comprising 2 cocks to 1 hen.

ARATINGA CONURES

These are larger and stockier than the previous group. The number of species within this genus falls between 15 and 21, and the number of subspecies to over 50. Although it has already been stated that conures originate from central and south America, as the vast majority in fact do, some Aratinga conures also originate from some of the Caribbean Islands.

All have loud voices and can to a varying degree be destructive to available woodwork. Because of these two vices they have never reached the popularity that they deserve. Generally they can be free-breeding and are most amusing to watch, as they are intelligent, playful and highly sociable. As a group they are not as frequently available as the Pyrrhura conures and there doesn't appear to be as much available data in relation to their breeding activity. The reason for this would appear to be the lack of demand and interest within the specific species. This may be due to economic considerations. The Aratinga conures have never demanded the high prices paid for some other psittacines.

The Aratingas are fairly adaptable as far as their diets are concerned. We have found that the larger the conure the more likely they are to have a preference for a seed and nut diet. Most will accept some of the smaller seeds such as millet, buckwheat and canary. The majority make very good parents and once their parenting skills have become established can be used to foster eggs and chicks of other species.

They can prove to have excellent pet potential, both in environments where the household can be quite noisy and disruptive, when the Aratinga's extrovert personality will come to the fore, and in environments which are more quiet and sedate, when the affectionate and sociable side of their nature will surface. Most will imitate various household sounds, such as the telephone, and will also learn simple phrases. Another interesting fact is that they also tend to be highly territorial; we know of numerous occasions when both pets and aviary birds have escaped but they have always stayed in the vicinity even when at liberty for a week or more until caught.

Although the Aratingas are a large group, Rosemary Low (1988) has suggested that they can be subdivided into three main categories: (i) The Yellow conures; (ii) Green conures with red markings on the head; (iii) Green conures with contrasting colours such as blue or orange on the head. The Aratinga conures have much to offer, and it is to be hoped that there will be sufficient interest to prevent them from dying out in aviculture. Fortunately the majority are not endangered in the wild and some are described as pest species.

SUN CONURE (*Aratinga solstitialis*)
One of the most popular of the conures, it has much to commend it. It is quite beautiful, frequently available and most are free-breeding. At 12 inches (30.5cm), it can be housed in modest accommodation. Pet Sun Conures are affectionate and will often learn to say short phrases. The main disadvantage is the voice, which is loud and harsh. Clutch size is usually 3.

JENDAYA CONURE (*Aratinga jandaya*)
Very similar to the Sun Conure but

differentiated by having a green back. Immature birds have some green feathers on their heads, and they take on a brighter appearance as they mature. They can prove to be exceptionally prolific. If the young are removed for hand-rearing, the parents will often re-clutch several times. It is important that the parents do have the opportunity to rear at least some of their young, both to develop their parenting skills and to ensure their own psychological well-being. Hand-reared Jendaya Conures are extremely affectionate. They can be extremely destructive to wooden structures.

WAGLER'S CONURE (*Aratinga wagleri*)
An extremely handsome conure, 14 inches in length, and of a stocky appearance. The area of red on the head enlarges as they mature and the white orbital ring becomes more striking. A group of these conures playing together can be quite captivating. Unfortunately they are only available infrequently. Hand-reared they make wonderful pets, being both intelligent and affectionate. Some individuals can be quite noisy. Bred infrequently, probably because of lack of interest and the limited numbers kept, clutch size is 3-4. Breeding will often only start after several years. These conures have bred successfully when kept on a colony system, and they are extremely sociable.

FINSCH'S CONURE (*Aratinga finschi*)
In appearance this is similar to the Wagler's Conure; however, it has a slimmer build and the area of red on the head is less. The availability of this conure is greater, as is its breeding success. Clutch size is 3-4.

RED-THROATED CONURE
(*Aratinga rubritorquis*)
This is an unusual conure and is characterised, as the name suggests, by a red area on the throat. It is 12 inches (30.5cm) in length. It is rare in aviculture and is seldom available. Red-throats are often slow to start breeding, and their clutch size is 3-4. They can be aggressive, particularly when coming into breeding condition. In the wild they are described as being of a shy disposition and nomadic. This may give a suggestion as to how hand-reared birds may behave.

MITRED CONURE (*Aratinga mitrata*)
This is probably the best known of this particular group, and may also be the most 'off-putting' of the group. They are good-looking, 15 inches (38cm) in length, and having a bold appearance, the area of red on the head becoming greater as they mature. Hand-reared, they are intelligent and affectionate and can be easily trained. However, they can be extremely noisy and destructive. Wild-caught specimens are shy and will frequently utter their alarm call. Bred infrequently, as few are kept, the Mitred Conure couldn't be described as prolific. The usual clutch size is 3; they are single-brooded even if chicks are removed for hand-rearing. If you are not bothered by the noise, and are creative enough with disposable toys (such as the use of fir cones), they can make quite wonderful pets.

RED-MASKED CONURE
(*Aratinga erythrogenys*)
Sometimes also called the Cherry-headed Conure – and this aptly describes them – they are 13 inches (33cm) in length. The bright red on the head, in some specimens, can extend to the whole of the head. There has been a suggestion that Red-masked Conures with a larger than usual area of red on their heads may represent an undescribed subspecies; chromosomal studies will presumably prove or disprove this suggestion at some stage. Because of their attractive coloration this conure has greater popularity and consequently tends to be more available. Once they have commenced breeding, it appears to

continue with regularity; their normal clutch consists of 3-4 eggs. This conure doesn't appear to chew as much as other members of this group. Some aviculturists have kept this conure at liberty.

WHITE-EYED CONURE
(*Aratinga leucophthalmus*)
What this conure lacks in coloration it makes up in personality. Immature specimens are all green, and as they mature they develop red flecking on the face and neck. They are 12.5 inches (32cm) in length. They are not terribly destructive to woodwork, but can be noisy; however, when breeding, ours are very quiet. As hand-reared pets they are excellent and seem to excel in lively, noisy, active households, where they frequently attempt to dominate all other pets. They can be surprisingly good mimics and have the potential to be well trained. White-eyed Conures are very sociable and seem to crave attention whether it is from a human or from another bird, which doesn't necessarily have to be another White-eyed Conure. They are quite territorial and are good candidates for free-flying. Their normal clutch consists of 3-4; they are often double-brooded and free-breeding.

BLUE-CROWNED CONURE
(*Aratinga acuticaudata*)
Sometimes also known as the Sharp-tailed Conure, it is 14 inches (35.5cm) in length and has a slender appearance. This conure is often available and has proved to be free-breeding. Many are sold as hand-reared pets and have shown themselves to be affectionate and intelligent. A Blue-crowned conure has recently featured in a film, and it is reported that the reason the producers chose this particular species over other parrots was because of their aptitude for being trained. They can however be noisy, especially when exposed to new experiences. Their normal clutch consists of 3 eggs.

The Peach-fronted Conure.

PEACH-FRONTED CONURE
(*Aratinga aurea*)
Also known as the Golden-crowned Conure they are characterised, as the name suggests, by a peach-coloured area just above their beak. They are 10 inches (25.5cm) in length. Although they couldn't be described as common, they do have a dedicated following and can usually be found. They are not too noisy and hand-reared young make delightful pets. They are often double-clutched and are fairly free-breeding, their normal clutch consisting of 4 eggs.

ORANGE-FRONTED CONURE
(*Aratinga canicularis*)
Also known as the Half Moon or Petz Conure, these were once extremely popular in the USA, where their pet potential properties were fully realised. These delightful conures proved to be talented mimics and affectionate pets. Now they are seldom available. This may in part be due to

the fact that in the wild they nest in arboreal termite mounds, and in captivity they appear to have a marked dislike of conventional nestboxes. It is often only after several years that breeding is achieved in a nestbox. More breeding success has been achieved if a rotten log has been used, which then allows the conures to burrow a nest cavity for themselves. Their normal clutch consists of 3-5 eggs. Some individuals can be noisy, but they are not particularly heavy chewers of aviary wood work.

DUSKY-HEADED CONURE
(*Aratinga weddellii*)
Also known as Weddell's Conure, this conure is attractive but in a very quiet sort of way. The head coloration is particularly attractive if caught in the sun. This bird is 11 inches (28cm) in length. It is unfortunate that this conure is not often seen, breeding success being limited. However, some aviculturists report that it is possible for them to triple-clutch. Normal clutch consists of 3-5 eggs.

BROWN-THROATED CONURE
(*Aratinga pertinax*)
Also known as the St Thomas Conure, at one time this bird was quite common in aviculture, but is now not often seen. This conure has 14 subspecies, all of which vary slightly in their coloration. Less active than most Aratingas, they are not particularly noisy. Bred very infrequently – which is probably more to do with their scarcity than with being particularly difficult. Their length is 10 inches (25.5cm) and their normal clutch consists of 4-5 eggs.

NANDAY CONURE (*Nandayus nenday*)
A common and frequently available conure which has attractive coloration. Its popularity appears to have been consistent for several years, although it could be described as noisy. Hand-reared specimens are quieter, and they make attractive and intelligent pets. As aviary birds they are active and playful, and can be successfully maintained and bred on a colony system. They also appear quite happy when flocked with other parrot-like species. These are another conure which seem much happier when they are with someone or with other birds, which they appear to derive much satisfaction from. Their usual clutch consists of 3-6 eggs.

LESSER PATAGONIAN CONURE
(*Cyanoliseus patagonus patagonus*)
A large handsome conure measuring 18 inches (45.5cm) in length, sometimes also known as the Burrowing Parrot. This is because they naturally burrow into the sides of cliffs. The passage-ways which they dig

The Patagonian Conure is also known as the Burrowing Parrot.

may zigzag for up to 10 feet (3.05m) before the nesting chamber is constructed. As they are colony breeders, and the conures nest close to one another, the passageways may create a network. Clutch size is usually 3-5. They are naturally extremely sociable, and this is mirrored in captivity. Many are kept in a colony system where they may breed successfully; however, in most of these instances it is only the dominant pair which breed. If only two pairs are kept, then both pairs may breed. Hand-reared young make delightful pets, and they are never happier than if they are cuddled up to their owner.

Several colonies are also kept at liberty, where they are released in the mornings for the day and then locked up in the evenings when they return to the aviary to roost. They look quite spectacular in flight, their streamlined bodies appearing to cut through the skies with such ease. Their silhouette in flight is quite hawk-like and this will cause anxiety to other birds in aviaries. Their normal clutch size is 3-5. They are commonly available. The main disadvantage to Patagonian conures is their noise. It is unfortunate that even when they are uttering their normal non-alarm sounds it is very loud. Although Lesser Patagonian conures are still imported regularly, enough are being captive-bred to make it relatively easy to obtain them. Captive-bred birds are much quieter.

GREATER PATAGONIAN CONURE

(*Cyanoliseus patagonus byroni*)

This is very similar to the Lesser Patagonian Conure, the main differences being that it is larger, at 21 inches (53.5cm), and that the area of white feathers on the upper chest is greater and appears more unbroken. This bird is extremely rare in captivity with very few birds being maintained. Clutch size is small at 2-4 eggs.

QUEEN OF BAVARIA'S CONURE

(*Guaruba guaruba or Aratinga guaruba*)

This is also known as the Golden Conure. Queen of Bavaria's Conures were previously categorised with the Aratinga conures but now there is a move towards putting them in a group of their own, and we would support this. Of all parrots this is one of the most spectacular, as their golden plumage has a certain richness to it which is different to any other. They are 15 inches (38cm) in length and although they have a somewhat slender appearance, their beak is heavy to the point of being 'un-conure-like'. They are rare both in captivity and in the wild and are classified as being highly endangered, much of their natural habitat having been destroyed. Because of this rarity it is wrong to even consider them for their pet potential.

As aviary subjects they are quite captivating. It is not only their coloration which attracts the observer but also their almost incessant playfulness, as they seem to take great joy in life and in their surroundings. A well-bonded pair is seldom separated and they appear to delight in one another's company. Immature birds frequently have some green feathers particularly on their backs, which gradually disappear as they mature. Breeding is not normally attempted until they are at least three years old, the clutch usually consisting of three. They can be noisy and their strong bill can quickly reduce wood to sawdust.

Queen of Bavaria's Conures are seldom available and should only be considered by the experienced parrot breeder. They are extremely expensive, to the point where it puts them out of the price range of most poeple. A further drawback is that they have a much greater tendency than most to feather-pluck. This can happen overnight, with the trigger for this sometimes never being discovered. Their dietary needs are similar to other conures, although they do appear to have a greater need for higher fat foods.

SLENDER-BILLED CONURES
(*Enicognathus Leptorhynchus*)
As the name suggests, these conures have an elongated upper mandible, which is used for digging up roots and tubers; it is also said to be used for extracting nuts from the monkey-puzzle tree. They are quite large, measuring 16 inches (40.5cm) in length. These conures are real characters, very playful and intelligent. If kept as a group they can appear quite inventive with the types of games and mischief that they get up to. They exist very happily within a colony system and appear to derive great satisfaction from this, although they pair-bond strongly during the breeding season. This is much less apparent for the rest of the year, when mutual preening and affection is bestowed on any member of the community.

They are quite hardy, not appearing to notice the cold. Our own birds will bathe in dishes where the ice has just been broken, and will invent all sorts of games in the snow. They will accept almost anything in their diet and will be excited by the variety. Out of the breeding season, our birds never roost in nestboxes. They are extremely demonstrative in their feelings and show this by eye-blazing, which is when the iris of the eye dilates and constricts in rapid succession, and by head-bobbing. Interestingly, they appear to be one of the few parrots which appear to hover and at times even to go backwards.

As pets they can be quite enchanting and will quickly learn tricks and mimicry, and they very much like to be included in everything that is going on. They can be noisy, but this can be minimal in hand-reared specimens when the alarm call is seldom used. Many people unfortunately find the elongated beak quite sinister in appearance and it is probably for this reason that so few are kept, whereas in fact they can be extremely gentle with their beak. We have an aviary consisting of hand-reared youngsters, where they all appear to use their beak in a most gentle way as a form of greeting when we open the hatch to replenish their food and water containers.

They are not frequently available, as very few appear to be regularly bred. Their normal clutch consists of 4-5 and some pairs can be quite prolific. In an aviary situation they gain tremendous satisfaction from digging in an earth floor. This does have the disadvantage of making them very susceptible to worm-infestations; therefore regular worming programmes are essential. If unhappy they may feather-pluck or even mutilate themselves.

AUSTRAL CONURE
(*Enicognathus ferrugineus*)
These are similar in appearance to the Slender-billed Conure, but are smaller, their length being 14 inches (35.5cm). They lack the elongated upper mandible, their beak, however, being quite narrow. Care is similar to the Slender-bills, but digging does not have to be catered for. Behaviourally they appear more aloof. Normal clutch size is 5-6. Their normal range includes cold areas, so these are not truly a tropical parrot. They are not frequently available and when they are, they tend to be unpopular and are cheap to purchase.

LORIES AND LORIKEETS

This exquisite family of bejewelled gems boasts an iridescent sheen to the feathers, matched only by their personalities. Lories and lorikeets are vivacious, playful characters separated from the other parrots by their possession of raised papillae on the tongue, used in the collection of pollen as part of their varied diet.

Like other members of the lory and lorikeet family, these Black-capped Lories require very specialist care.

Although fairly small members of the parrot family, the lories, on the whole, are larger and short-tailed, whilst the lorikeets are smaller with longer tails. Natives of Australia, Papua New Guinea and South East Asia, there are some highly successful species on the mainland and some severely endangered island species, in line with the other parrots.

Perhaps more than any other group of parrots, these lories require specialist attention. This is not to say that their care is difficult – just different. Most species require a nectar substitute at least twice a day, and if this is not provided freshly at intervals it will sour in hot weather, freeze in the cold and attract unwelcome visitors such as flies and wasps. The composition of this nectar is as varied as the keepers of these enchanting birds. The fashion has swung recently to offering all or part of the nectar substitute in dry form along with unlimited clean water. This has been particularly popular with those keeping lories as pets, as it solidifies the droppings, making life easier for the keeper. Whether health complications for the lory will be shown in the future remains to be seen. However, to our minds, the large quantities of liquid ingested by lories offered nectar mix is not healthy either. Although in the wild they will drink nectar, it will certainly not be half-a-pint a day.

Pollen, fruits, flowers, leaves, insects and seeds will be consumed. As such a large variety of foodstuffs should be offered to captive lories. Nectar, wet and dry, fruit cut in half and spiked on a nail, sweetcorn on and off the cob should all be offered. Some lories will consume mealworms and a little sunflower seed and millet, including sprays. Offering a wide variety of foodstuffs will ensure that the lories get all they need nutritionally.

Housing for lories needs to be carefully considered. The copious amounts of liquid droppings – often directed at onlookers – will need to be easily removed from washable surfaces within the aviary. Suspended aviaries are often popular and easy to keep clean – but adequate space must be afforded to these highly active birds. Lories kept as pets can be housed in enclosed mynah bird-type cages. They have three sides enclosed and are made of easily washed materials such as plastic. Layers of newspaper can be placed on the floor, cheaply and easily replaced at regular intervals. Most of this family like to roost in nestboxes, and with the provision of these they are very hardy, with the exception of some of the smaller lorikeets who may need to be provided with gentle heat in indoor accommodation in the colder months.

Adult lories can be absolutely murderous towards other lories, or in fact any other birds in an aviary, so great care must be taken when introducing partners to one another. Lories can be kept communally if sexually immature and brought up together. As such, they make a marvellous display, particularly if given plenty of playthings, whereupon youngsters will swing, play, roll over and mock fight with an abundance of energy. Some zoos and bird parks keep large flocks of free-flying lories who make a wonderful spectacle as they descend on visitors proffering food. In these circumstances they get on well as there is plenty of space and no territorial aggression. It is usually the beautiful so-called Rainbow Lories used in these displays.

PROLIFIC BREEDERS

Most of the lories are prolific breeders, often raising two or more broods in a year. The majority have two eggs per clutch and rear both chicks with apparent ease. Lories seem to take a long time from hatching to fledging, but generally, once they are fledged, the parents will attend to them very well. A close watch must be kept on the nestboxes and the shavings changed regularly, with a minimum of disturbance, as they will become very wet with the liquid nature of the young ones' excreta. Lories will be very aggressive in defence of the nestbox and tame birds will show no fear of humans. Plucking of the youngster is a very common problem in lories, usually exacerbated by wet nestboxes. The parents perhaps pluck the youngsters in an attempt to line the nestbox, so the provision of softwoods nailed to the sides of the box will help to prevent this problem.

The voices of some of the large lories can be quite harsh, and are used regularly as the birds get excited. At the other end of the scale, the smaller lorikeets have quiet, pleasant voices and can be suitable inhabitants of aviaries with close neighbours. Considering the sticky nature of their diet it is perhaps lucky that the lories are avid bathers, often indulging in baths every day if not twice daily. This will result in them being absolutely saturated, followed by a spell of sunbathing if there is sun, although they will often bathe in freezing weather too.

GREEN-NAPED LORIKEET

(*Trichoglossus haematodus*)

One of the most freely available of the lories as well as a highly prolific species, the Green-naped is often a wise choice for beginners to lories. One of the larger lories at 10 inches (25.5cm), it also has a fairly harsh voice. The normal two-egg clutch will sometimes be repeated continually throughout the year, with some pairs re-clutching before the previous young have fledged. Great care must be taken to avoid cross-breeding between this and the other rainbow lorikeets. The Green-naped is widespread in its native New Guinea.

ORNATE LORIKEET

(*Trichoglossus ornatus*)

This beautiful lory is sadly infrequently kept these days. Any single specimens should be paired up and encouraged to breed to boost the captive population. It is differentiated from the other rainbow lorikeets by scarlet cheeks rather than an otherwise blue head. The green of the plumage has an olive tinge. It originates from the islands around Sulawesi.

The Ornate Lorikeet should be encouraged to breed to protect its numbers.

MITCHELL'S LORIKEET

(*Trichoglossus haematodus mitchellii*)

Another rarity in aviculture, the Mitchell's is a little smaller at 9 inches (23cm). A chest of solid scarlet and a yellowish tinge to the green nape distinguish it from the others. It originates in the islands of Bali and Lombok.

FORSTEN'S LORIKEET

(*Trichoglossus haematodus forsteni*)

Originating from the Indonesian islands of Sumbawa, the Forsten's is at first sight similar to the Mitchell's, but the nape is yellowish and the head bluer than the blackish Mitchell's.

EDWARD'S LORIKEET

(*Trichoglossus haematodus capistratus*)

From the Indonesian island of Timor, the 10 1/2 inch (26.5cm) Edwards is a beauty, resplendent in a yellow chest set off by orange scaling. Fairly infrequently bred due to limited availability, it normally lays two eggs per clutch like the preceding members of this group.

WEBER'S LORIKEET

(*Trichoglossus haematodus weberi*)

The green-headed Weber's, originating from the Flores Island of Indonesia, have never been well-established in captivity. A little smaller than its cousins at 9 inches (22.5cm).

ROSENBERG'S LORIKEET

(*Trichoglossus haematodus rosenbergii*)

Again from the Indonesian islands, the Rosenberg's is one of the larger members of the group (12 inches/30.5cm). As with all the island parrots it is highly vulnerable. It has only recently become available, in small numbers, to aviculture. The heavily barred scarlet breast and wide yellow nape-patch distinguish it from the other members of this group.

MASSENA'S LORIKEET

(*Trichoglossus haematodus massena*)

The dark Massena's Lorikeet hails from the Solomon islands and is rare in aviculture. Fine lines mark the breast and nape in brown.

SWAINSON'S LORIKEET

(*Trichoglossus haematodus moluccanus*)

Another large member of the group at 12 inches (30.5cm), the Swainson's was fairly common in aviculture as well as in the wild. Incorrectly identified specimens have been subject to hybridisation with other members of the rainbow lorikeets.

RED-COLLARED LORIKEET

(*Trichoglossus haematodus rubritorquis*)

The startling colours on this beautiful bird have to be seen to be appreciated. The broad collar is quite a striking feature. It is widespread in Northern Australia.

SCALY-BREASTED LORIKEET

(*Trichoglossus chlorolepidotus*)

The delightful Scaly-breasted is mainly green with, as its name suggests, yellow scale-like markings on the breast. Eastern Australian in origin, it is rarely seen in aviculture now. 9 inches (22.5cm) in length, it sometimes lays 3 eggs in a clutch.

MEYER'S LORIKEET

(*Trichoglossus flavoviridis meyeri*)

The diminutive Meyer's is one of the soft-voiced species that won't upset the neighbours, They also have the advantage of being willing to breed in less spacious accommodation than the previous species. At only 6 inches (15cm) long these little jewels weigh only a couple of ounces and might appreciate being kept frost-free in the winter. Usually free-breeding, it is hoped that newly hatched chicks would not need to be hand-fed, as they only weigh 3 grams (1/8oz).

PERFECT LORIKEET
(*Trichoglossus euteles*)
The 10-inch (25.5cm) Perfect is wonderfully elegant in its muted greens and yellows. Another unusual lory in that it has clutches of three regularly, and is fairly soft-voiced. The Perfect originates in Timor.

VARIED LORIKEET
(*Trichoglossus versicolor*)
Another tiny gem from Australia, the Varied is not seen outside its homeland. It has a red cap, yellow cheeks and striation over its 7½ inch (19cm) body. This species has been known to lay up to 5 eggs in a clutch.

IRIS LORIKEET (*Trichoglossus iris*)
The Iris is sadly not freely available to aviculturists; if it were, it would surely have a great following. With a slightly heavier bill than others, it is likely to consume more seeds than some of its relatives.

The Goldie's Lorikeet

GOLDIE'S LORIKEET
(*Trichoglossus goldiei*)
At only 1½ ounces (42.5g), the Goldie's is very popular with lory keepers. Mild-mannered and quiet, it can be sexually mature at only a year old.

BLACK LORY (*Chalcopsitta atra atra*)
The blackest of all the parrots, the Black Lory has a sheen of blue, green and purple when seen in a good light, and looks quite spectacular. Immature individuals may have small amounts of red coloration, particularly around the face, but this disappears usually in the first year. They are fairly commonly kept and bred in captivity and are not uncommon in the wild.

RAJAH LORY (*Chalcopsitta atra insignis*)
A cousin of the Black, the Rajah retains the red on the face and has a suffusion of wine-red through the tail. A friendly, intelligent lory, is it much less commonly seen in captivity than the Black and is also an inhabitant of Western New Guinea.

DUIVENBODE'S LORY
(*Chalcopsitta duivenbodei*)
Like other lories, the colour combination of the Duivenbode's is unseen in any other parrot. Caramel brown and rich yellow makes this a most striking parrot indeed. Like the Black, at 12½ inches (32cm) it is large, and has a voice to match. Due to their high popularity several are bred in captivity and they boast a fairly stable popularity in Northern New Guinea, their home territory.

CARDINAL LORY (*Chalcopsitta cardinalis*)
The 12-inch (30.5cm) Cardinal is adorned in reds, quite unlike the red of any other parrot – brick red. Virtually unknown in captivity until the 1990s, it is fairly well established already, since the Solomons permitted the export of a small number of its native birds. It is relatively common in the wild.

The Yellow-streaked Lory is a vocal member of the Chalcopsitta Group.

YELLOW-STREAKED LORY
(*Chalcopsitta scintillata*)
Another vivacious member of the Chalcopsitta group, the Yellow-streaked is a very popular member among lory keepers, despite its vocal capabilities. Usually a willing nester, it is being bred in several collections. It originates from Southern New Guinea.

RED LORY (*Eos bornea*)
One of the most popular of the lories and one which is suitable for newcomers due to its abundance, the Red Lory from Indonesia is a willing breeder. If keeping a lory as a pet is on your agenda, these birds usually have a pleasant temperament.

BLUE-STREAKED LORY (*Eos reticulata*)
Another red lory with striking electric blue streaks scattered among the nape and mantle, the Blue-streaked is a definite subject for concerned aviculturists who must breed it to maintain a stable population. Numbers in the wild were seriously depleted due to large-scale trapping.

VIOLET-NECKED LORY
(*Eos squamata squamata*)
Smaller, at 10 inches (25.5cm), than the preceding Red Lories, the Violet-necked from Indonesia is declining in captivity, having been fairly common, as well as in the wild. It sports a livery of red and purple broad stripes, a delightful combination. The Violet-necked also has a 9-inch (23cm) cousin from the Island of Obi, which as well as being smaller lacks the violet neck markings, which give it the name.

BLACK-WINGED LORY (*Eos cyanogenia*)
Mainly red with a purple face patch and glossy black wings, the Cyanogenia is indeed a stunning bird. Like the majority of its cousins the Black-winged is a fairly willing breeder in captivity, and should be cultivated as it is becoming endangered.

DUSKY LORY (*Pseudeos fuscata*)
A hugely popular lory, the Dusky has been bred in many collections worldwide. It is seen in two colour types, orange the most common, and yellow interspersed among the brown. The Dusky tends to have a well-defined early breeding season unlike a lot of the other lories who will breed all year round. We have also found them to be good foster parents to other species of lory. Another lory that is potentially a good pet.

BLACK-CAPPED LORY (*Lorius lory*)
At up to 13 inches (33cm), and 7 ounces (198.5g) in weight, this is one of the larger lories. Originating from New Guinea, it is less harsh-voiced than one might think for a lory of this size. The Black-capped may also take a little longer to reach sexual maturity, some pairs not breeding until their fifth year.

CHATTERING LORY (*Lorius garrulus*)
Very popular in the 1980s and early 1990s the Chattering is less commonly kept and

bred now. Basically red with green wings, a subspecies, *Lorius Garrulus Flavopalliatus*, sports a larger yellow patch on its back. As the name, both common and Latin imply, it can be an extremely vocal bird.

YELLOW-BIBBED LORY
(*Lorius chlorocercus*)
This lory, with the yellow crescent moon emblazoned across its chest, was virtually unknown in aviculture until relatively recently. It soon settled down to reproducing and there is now a reasonable population of them in captivity.

PURPLE-CAPPED LORY
(*Lorius domicellus*)
Believed to be rare in the wild, the captive population of this lory is also very small. Every effort should be made to encourage an increase in numbers.

PURPLE-BELLIED LORY
(*Lorius hypoinochrous*)
From South Eastern New Guinea where it is fairly abundant, this lory is almost unknown in captivity.

MUSSCHENBROEK'S LORIKEET
(*Neopsittacus musschenbroekeii*)
Unusually for a member of this family, the Musschenbroek's has a horn-coloured beak rather than the common orange-coloured mandibles. Fairly shy and retiring in comparison with the rest of this family, the Musschenbroek's also takes a slightly different diet: more emphasis is put on seeds – particularly millet sprays – and they enjoy nuts of all varieties. This is a lorikeet for the specialist.

MUSK LORIKEET (*Glossopsitta concinna*)
The delicately proportioned Musk lorikeet is only bred in a few collections outside its native Australia.

LITTLE LORIKEET (*Glossopsitta pusilla*)
An unusually black-billed lorikeet, the Little has not been established outside Australia, where it is also infrequently bred. The clutch size can number up to five.

PURPLE-CROWNED LORIKEET
(*Glossopsitta porphyrocephala*)
A tiny beauty with a sky-blue chest and purple and red patches on the head, the Purple-crowned is again unknown outside Australia. In its native homeland it is breeding well and is a popular aviary inhabitant. Maturing quickly and with clutches of up to four eggs, the Purple-crowned could soon become well-established.

RED-SPOTTED LORIKEET
(*Charmosyna rubronotata*)
The diminutive Red-spotted is one of the Charmosyna group, who will breed in large box cages as well as small aviaries. They will also always appreciate a little gentle heat in the colder weather. Probably uncommon in their native North Western New Guinea, reasonable numbers are being bred by a handful of specialist breeders. This species is sexually dimorphic, the females lacking the red forehead and blue purple cheeks of the male.

RED-FLANKED LORIKEET
(*Charmosyna placentis*)
A charming, quiet species, the Red-flanked has all the qualities of the previous species. These and the Red-spotted will also live quite happily in a planted aviary or conservatory with similar-sized softbills.

FAIRY LORIKEET (*Charmosyna pulchella*)
As the name indicates, the Fairy is a delicate species from New Guinea, where it is thought to be scarce. Specialists are breeding from a few pairs but it is still virtually unobtainable. The sexes can be distinguished, as the female

has yellow patches on the rump. These delightful little red birds do not weigh much more than an ounce and will not thrive if kept unheated in the winter.

WILHELMINA'S LORIKEET
(*Charmosyna wilhelminae*)
These aviculture rarities are comparatively drab for this family, being mainly an olive-green-winged bird with a brownish-green body. Some blue feathers adorn the nape, and the beak is orange. A tiny bird at 5 inches (12.5cm).

STRIATED LORIKEET
(*Charmosyna multistriata*)
Another rarely seen Charmosyna, the Striated is adorned with bright yellow and green feather streaking, and carries a disproportionately large beak. If ever these and the preceding species of this group become readily available to aviculture they will undoubtedly find a large following due to their small size and quiet voice.

STELLA'S LORIKEET
(*Charmosyna papou goliathina*)
Elegant in the extreme is probably the best way to describe these beautiful birds. The two central tail-feathers extend way beyond the rest and follow the bird like streamers as it flies. This species has a huge following and is successfully bred in many aviaries worldwide. It is unusual in having a melanistic form of the normal red-bodied bird – and these black species are as readily available as the reds. Easily sexed – the lower back and sides of the rump are yellow in females. Sadly this species is prone to liver failure, probably due to an inadequate diet. This can manifest itself by paling of the beak in a sick bird from the usual orange red to almost white. From South Eastern New Guinea, it is of course, the longest of the lories at 16 inches (40.5cm) – but a lot of this length is tail.

JOSEPHINE'S LORIKEET
(*Charmosyna josefinae*)
At 9-10 inches (23-25.5cm) this cousin of the Stella's is considerably smaller. It hails from Central New Guinea and is thought to be fairly stable in its population. The natives use feathers and skins from these two species to add to their head-dresses – hopefully not in such numbers as to seriously threaten the population. Seen less often in captivity than the Stella's, it is nevertheless bred fairly frequently in those collections which house it.

TAHITI BLUE LORY (*Vini peruviana*)
To our eyes the Blue Lory is quite outstanding. No other parrot, except the Ultramarine and mutations, sport a livery of blue and white, and certainly not the depth of blue that this bird carries. The bright orange of the beak and feet set these off beautifully to give it an almost unreal appearance. From the Society Islands it is sadly an extreme rarity, due mainly to predation from introduced pests such as rats who eat the eggs and young. Incubating adults are also at risk. A captive population is not established and it is seen in only a handful of collections worldwide.

ULTRAMARINE LORY (*Vini ultramarina*)
A cousin of the Tahiti, originating from the Marguesas Islands, the Ultramarine has been seen by very few people and is unlikely to become available even to lory specialists.

BLUE-CROWNED LORY (*Vini australis*)
The Blue-crowned is another of the Vini species represented in captivity by only a handful of specimens. These are mainly in zoos world wide, San Diego being one that has bred them in the past.

KUHLI'S LORY (*Vini kuhlii*)
The crowning glory of this exquisite gem is the elongated nape feathers of the deepest

blue. Along with the other Vini species it is never likely to be seen by the vast majority of birdkeepers.

POICEPHALUS PARROTS

These consist of a group of small parrots from Africa, the largest being the Cape Parrot (*Poicephalus robustus*) at 13 inches (33cm), and the smallest the Meyer's parrot (*P. meyeri*). All have short square tails. As a group these parrots could be described as ideal pet or aviary birds and, with the exception of the Cape Parrot, are not particularly noisy. Most make good companion birds and will learn to mimic odd words and phrases. If obtained young or captive-bred they soon become confiding, when their characters and individuality soon become apparent. Wild-caught birds are often shy, retiring to the nestbox if intruded upon.

Most will eat a variety of seeds, nuts and fresh foods. Breeding this group of birds can be problematic. Most remain winter breeders, that is they lay and rear their young in often the coldest months of the year. Most appear to manage laying their clutch of eggs and the incubation period with few problems. However, problems frequently occur from the time that the young are about a week old, when the parents may stop brooding the young at night, which can result in the youngsters dying from exposure. If young are removed for hand-rearing, another clutch is frequently laid.

Because of this problem, some specialist poicephalus breeders use nestboxes with a false bottom; this enables a low-wattage bulb to be inserted under the false bottom; this when illuminated produces enough heat to keep the nestlings warm enough to survive, should the parents stop brooding. Poicephalus parrots will retire at night into their nestbox, and also if danger threatens, so it is important that they always have access to their nestbox.

SENEGAL PARROT
(*Poicephalus senegalus*)

This is by far the most commonly kept member of this group. It is a popular choice both as an aviary subject and as companion pet. Pleasing coloration as well as a very manageable size (9 inches or 23cm), the Senegal can be a very affectionate pet. They will learn to say a few words, but are generally fairly quiet. Senegals are imported regularly, but wild-caught they seldom become tame unless they are at a very early age. Hand-reared they do require some basic

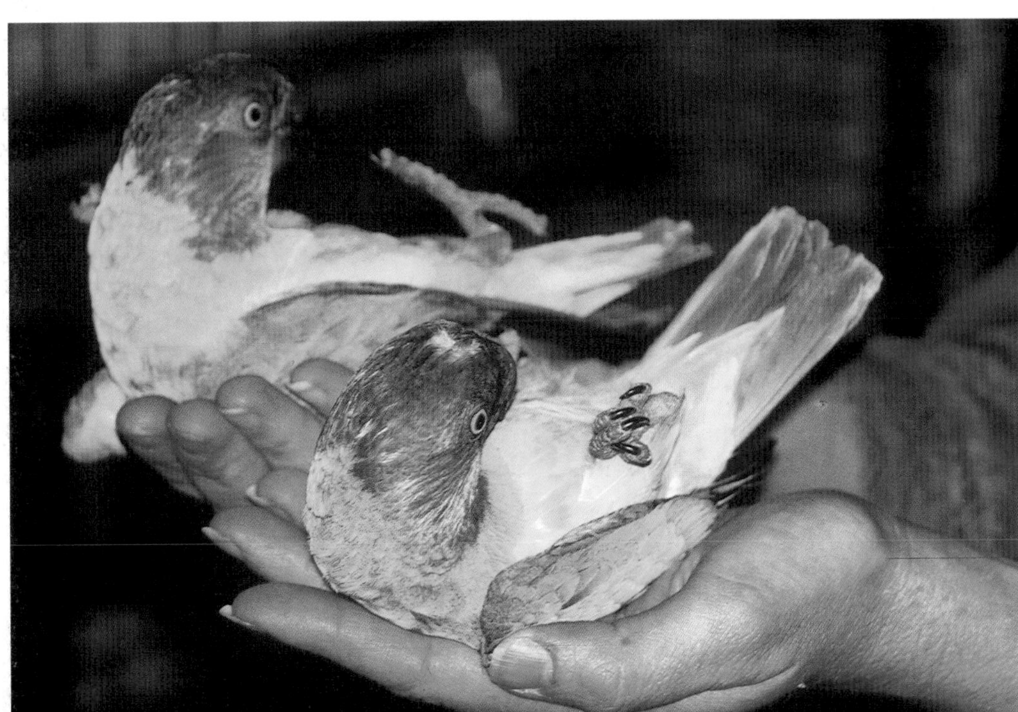

Senegals make affectionate pets.

training as they have a tendency to become rather domineering. A hand-reared Senegal is a good choice for the beginner. They breed well in captivity, usually having 3-4 young. Some parents will brood their young for the duration that the young are in the nestbox, others unfortunately will not.

MEYER'S PARROT (*P. meyeri*)
Not as common as the Senegal, but can also make a very good pet, and shares many of the characteristics of the Senegal. The main difference would appear to be ensuring that pairs are compatible. If not, one of the pair may be attacked, with fatal consequences. The likelihood of this happening is far greater if the pair are housed in a breeding cage rather than an aviary, where it is possible for the one being attacked to hide.

BROWN-HEADED PARROT
(*P. cryptoxanthus*)
Probably the most unpopular of the group. This is unfortunate, as Brown-headed Parrots have their own charm, which whilst not obviously apparent from first acquaintance will often grow on owners. If obtained hand-reared or very young they are usually quite captivated by their owners, always wanting to bestow affection and to be with them. In our experience young which have been hand-reared become quite humanised and we haven't found it possible to breed with them. It is therefore quite important to allow parents to rear some of their young. This is a parrot which could easily be lost to aviculture, unless more effort is made with it.

RUPPELL'S PARROT (*P. ruppellii*)
This is rare in aviculture and is seldom available, although is thought to be common in its native habitat. The few dedicated breeders of this species have made the observation that the parents consume live food in the form of insects and aphids when young are being reared. Given their precarious status in aviculture it would appear to be wrong at this stage to keep the Ruppell's Parrot as a pet. The hen is the more colourful of the pair.

RED-BELLIED PARROT (*P. rufiventris*)
In most parrots the sexes are alike (sexually monomorphic); however, this isn't the case with the Red-bellied parrot, where the male is usually much brighter in coloration (sexually dimorphic). They are colourful and handsome birds. Not frequently available, but well worth the effort. Again there are problems with hand-reared young becoming so humanised that they are reluctant to breed. There also appears to be a shortage of hens, as losses in hens appear to be greater than losses in cock birds. Their clutch usually consists of 3 young.

JARDINE'S PARROT (*P. gulielmi*)
Although the Jardine's Parrot couldn't be described as common, they have become more readily available, being imported fairly regularly and with more young being captive-bred. The young when hand-reared have proved to be affectionate and talented pets. This is a larger member of the poicephalus group, being 11 inches (28cm) in length. The clutch usually consists of 3-4. There have been some reports of imported birds' health being quite tender, especially during the first year, with some falling ill to respiratory conditions in the damp conditions of Britain. It would be pertinent to ensure that newly imported Jardine's have a dry frost-free shelter, especially in the first year following importation.

CAPE PARROT (*P. robustus*)
This is the largest member of the genus, $12^{1}/_{2}$ inches (32cm), and wouldn't necessarily be identified as part of the poicephalus group if seen in isolation. Cape

Parrots are not commonly available, with only a few being captive-bred, although it is claimed that once a pair have started to breed they will breed regularly. There would appear to be more hens than cocks; some of these 'spare' cocks are said to make good pets.

Cape Parrots are extremely handsome birds, with a large bold beak and head. Their large beak is put to good use as this member of the poicephalus group has a much greater need for nuts than the other members, and they are particularly fond of walnuts. The hen is more colourful than the cock; she also has an orange area above the beak which he doesn't generally possess. It is to be hoped that the Cape Parrot becomes more available in the future as they do have much to commend them. The main drawback is their voice which is loud and metallic-sounding, and which, although isn't unpleasant, may be irritating to close neighbours.

AMAZONS

When the average layman hears the word 'parrot', it conjures up the vision of a squat, broadtailed green parrot – the Amazons. This genus contains some of the most commonly offered pet parrots – Blue-fronted and Orange-winged amazons – and some of the rarest birds on earth, such as the unbelievably majestic Imperial Amazon. This gorgeous giant would dwarf the tiny White-fronted or Yellow-lored species, some of whom are not much bigger than a Senegal.

However, something they all have in common (apart from carrying varying amounts of green on the body or wings), is that they are big on character. Some amazons, most notably the Yellow-naped and Double yellow-headed are endowed with terrific prowess for imitating human speech and other noises around them, rivalling the king of talkers – the African Grey – on this front. But we have to concede that they probably do not possess the brain-power that their African cousins have. The natural call of some amazons is almost musical, and as such they appear to be able to pick up singing better than most other species.

Again, like the Greys, amazons tend to show a preference for human company of the opposite sex from themselves, although this is by no means always the case. When bonded with a person, an amazon can be very ferocious in his protection against all comers to his selected friend. We use the word 'he' advisedly, as it is normally the cock birds that are the most aggressive in this way.

Another peculiarity of this species is that in protection of the nest area, if on eggs or with

Amazons are big on character. Pictured: Blue-fronted Amazon.

chicks, ex-pet cocks will invariably fly to and attack the face of human intruders. This must be borne in mind when arranging housing for this species: consideration may be given to suspended flights, swing feeders, and outside nest-inspection hatches. As with the white cockatoos, some of this aggression can be vented on the bird's poor spouse, and it is not unknown for an amazon cock to kill his hen. For this reason, and because amazons are somewhat prone to obesity, they should be accommodated in large flights to encourage flying.

More than many of the other parrots, a diet high in pulses and low on fattening seeds should be offered to them: fruits, vegetables and favourites such as corn-on-the-cob and pomegranates can be offered in unlimited quantities and are usually relished. Outside the breeding season, we fly our amazons in large flights with macaws. In this way the macaws get first choice of the fattening food which suits them, leaving the slim pickings for the amazons. The resulting jostling for food all adds to healthy exercise and mental stimulation.

Rivalling the lories for a love of bathing, amazons should never be denied bathing facilities, and access to rain showers is a dream come true for them. Not as destructive to woodwork as some of the other large parrots, amazons will nonetheless greatly appreciate sprays of willow and fruit-tree twigs to chew, whether in the cage or aviary. Toys are a must for this playful family.

BREEDING PAIRS

Breeding pairs of amazons must be housed out of sight of the other pairs, otherwise all their time and energy will be spent trying to fight through the wire of the aviary. Housing several pairs of amazons in close proximity will result in a lot of noise, as on seeing the keeper approach one pair will start vocalising noisily to be followed by every other pair in turn. Disturbance of the nestbox with chicks in it can cause this excitable species to attack and even kill their offspring with misplaced aggression.

Very much seasonal breeders, the amazons will become sexually active at the onset of spring and most are in breeding condition by March or April. Often, the hen will be ready before the cock and will lay a clutch of infertile eggs. If these are removed, you may be lucky and get chicks from the second round, but of course there are no guarantees. Some pairs will only lay one clutch per year, whilst others will regularly lay two or even a third clutch, particularly if the first is removed for artificial incubation. Normally, if breeding hasn't commenced by June or July, there will be no breeding from that pair for the year.

Averaging three eggs in a clutch, some of the smaller species, in particular the White-fronted amazon, will lay up to six eggs. Many pairs make very good parents, rearing four chicks to fledging, without any noticeable difference in size between the siblings, unlike birds such as the macaws who may let a third chick waste away, or cockatoos who may only rear one and let the second perish. Because of this good parenting ability, amazons who have proved to be reliable in the past may be used for fostering with confidence – sometimes rearing two or three species in the same nest.

SPECTACLED or WHITE-FRONTED AMAZON (*Amazona albifrons*)

Hailing from Mexico and Guatemala through to Costa Rica, this tiny member of the genus is popular with aviculturists, being modestly priced and able to be housed in less spacious accommodation than some of the larger species. Despite its small size, the voice can still be fairly raucous. Fairly free-breeding, and with the potential to lay large clutches, this little gem would be an ideal pet if only it didn't have the tendency to be nippy, and even a little spiteful, as a hand-reared pet. Unusually for amazons, there are some sexual differences in this species, with the male usually showing more red coloration on the head, and having red alule and primary flight coverts. The wing is entirely green in the female with the exception of the flights.

YELLOW-LORED AMAZON
(*Amazona xantholora*)
Another Mexican, this bird is as rare in captivity as the Albifrons is common. At barely 9 inches (23cm) long, this is the smallest of the Amazons. It has a sexual dimorphism similar to that of the above, and as the name suggests, the brightest daffodil yellow coloration around the lores. Too rare to be considered a pet outside its native country, let's hope that the few aviculturists with pairs will be able to breed them and make up more unrelated pairs to boost their numbers in captivity.

YELLOW-BILLED AMAZON
(*Amazona collaria*)
This little beauty is rarely seen, as export from Jamaica, its native homeland, is illegal. Still smallish at 11 inches (28cm), it is unusual in the possession of a yellow tinge to the horn-coloured bill. Youngsters have dark patches on the upper mandible. A few specialist breeders are having success in breeding this species.

CUBAN AMAZON
(*Amazona leucocephala*)
Listed in Appendix I of CITES, the Cuban is now being bred in greater numbers than ever, but this hasn't affected the still rather high price. It is a moderate-sized bird at 13 inches (33cm). It is a very excitable Amazon and attacks by cocks on hens are unfortunately rather common. As always, pair bonding from an early age can prevent a lot of bloodshed later on, but attacks can be triggered in even the most compatible pairs.

The Cuban Amazon is a very excitable bird.

HISPANIOLAN AMAZON
(*Amazona ventralis*)
Another aggressive bird, precautions should also be taken with this highly excitable species when pairing, or during the breeding season, to avoid any damage to the female. The Hispaniolan is being bred by ever more amazon fans and is gaining a foothold in aviculture. At 11 inches (28cm) it is one of the smaller Amazons. The clutch consists of 3-4 eggs.

TUCUMAN AMAZON
(*Amazona tucumana*)
From Bolivia and Argentina, the 12-inch (30.5cm) long Tucuman is much more slender in appearance, and rather delicate-looking around the head and beak, than most Amazons. It is on Appendix I of CITES and was really quite rare and much sought-after in aviculture until recent years. Now it is being bred in fairly large numbers, with a resulting drop in value. Sexual dimorphism is apparent by the number of red primary

coverts on the wing – eight in the male and less, or even none, in the female. The normal clutch size is three eggs.

PRETRE'S AMAZON (*Amazona pretrei*)
Adjoining territory with the Tucuman, the similar but more highly coloured Pretre's originated from Northern Argentina and Southern Brazil. Slightly heavier in its body proportions, the beak is also darker on this bird. The males display more red on the head, as well as on the carpal edge of the wing and the underwing coverts. It has the normal incubation period of 27 days for the three eggs in a clutch and the young display much less red than the adults. The Pretre's is sadly suffering a decline in the wild, so happily it is being bred in a few collections around the world, and will possibly be secure in captivity.

GREEN-CHEEKED AMAZON
(*Amazona viridigenalis*)
The 13-inch (33cm) Green-cheeked has only recently been placed on CITES Appendix I, an indication of the declining numbers in the wild. Having always been fairly abundant in captivity it will now attract renewed interest due to this listing. A striking bird, the Green-cheeked is known to be a good pet and is very popular as such in the USA. It is one of the better mimics in this family. It originates from Northern Mexico.

LILAC-CROWNED or FINSCH'S AMAZON (*Amazona finschii*)
This subtle beauty is from Western Mexico and displays a muted similarity to Amazona vindigenalis. It has a huge following in the USA and is becoming more popular and frequently bred in Europe.

RED-TAILED AMAZON
(*Amazona brasiliensis*)
Having long been on Appendix I of CITES, this bird is sadly quite rare, due to the deforestation of its native Brazil. It is one of the larger amazons at 14 inches (35.5cm). It is not an unwilling breeder in the few collections who are able to keep it. Red-tailed Amazons usually have two eggs to a clutch, although sometimes three in captivity.

RED-CROWNED or RED-TOPPED AMAZON (*Amazona rhodocorytha*)
Another CITES Appendix I amazon, the rhodocorytha is sadly severely declining in its native Bahia. It is equally unusual in captivity but is being established in several collections in Europe – due, in no small part, to one outstanding British breeder, who has substantially built up the number of captive-bred unrelated young pairs.

BLUE-CHEEKED AMAZON
(*Amazona dufresniana*)
Like the Rhodocorytha, Dufresniana is a 14-inch-long (35.5cm) Amazon, but somewhat heavier and stockier in appearance than the former. We have found it to be quieter in both voice and temperament than many other Amazons – two points which should endear this species to aviculturists. Very little breeding activity has been recorded for this species; however, captive-bred youngsters were being offered from France at one time. As with many parrots, there appears to be a preponderance of males available.

FESTIVE AMAZON
(*Amazona festiva festiva*)
The appearance of this amazon always strikes us as rather fierce – and the males sometimes live up to this look. Not uncommon in Brazil and Peru, it is however quite scarce in captivity. A stunning feature of this bird is a scarlet rump and back, only discernible when the wings are open. Because of its scarcity the Festive and the subspecies BODIN'S AMAZON (*Amazona festiva bodini*) have rarely been bred in captivity.

YELLOW-FACED AMAZON
(*Amazona xanthops*)
Quite different in looks and behaviour from other amazons, the Yellow-faced is a small bird at around ten inches long. The skin around the eyes and cere is a blushing pink, which is not seen in other members of this genus. Some males, but not all, also display yellow and orange coloration on the belly. As a species they are also much less flighty than some of the small amazons, assuming a still posture for long periods. They have not found a great following as aviary birds, and are rarely bred in captivity.

YELLOW-SHOULDERED AMAZON
(*Amazona barbadensis*)
On Appendix I of CITES, the Barbadensis is a medium-sized amazon at 12 inches (30.5cm). Originating from Venezuela and Small Islands, it is declining due to loss of habitat. The Yellow-shouldered is popular with amazon specialists and pet keepers alike, being an entertaining and talented mimic. If intended as a pet, only males should be used, as this is another species with small numbers of females, due in no small part to the aggressive nature of the cocks. Sadly many hens have been attacked and killed, so every precaution should be taken to prevent this. Large aviaries and clipped males go a long way towards saving hens. Where possible, only parent-reared males should be considered for future breeding. Pairing a young male with an older hen, if youngsters are not brought up together, will be a good move.

DOUBLE YELLOW-HEADED AMAZON
(*Amazona ochrocephala oratrix*)
The 15 inch (38cm) Oratrix is one of the most popular kept and bred of the genus. There are several subspecies, differentiated mainly by the amount of yellow on the head and the lime of the green on the body.

BELIZE AMAZON
(*Amazona ochrocephala belizensis*)
This parrot (from west Mexico) is slightly smaller than the nominate race and the yellow of the head only extends to just behind the eye down to the chin.

The Oratrix is a chubbier bird with varying amounts of yellow extending down the hind neck and towards the chest.

TRES MARIAS AMAZON
(*Amazona ochrocephala tresmariae*) has most of the head, neck and throat a lighter yellow, and is a bulky bird.

MAGNA AMAZON
(*Amazona ochrocephala magna*) has yellow spilling down into the chest and neck, and the bed of the wing has yellow as well as large amounts of red. Youngsters of all subspecies fledge with a much less extensive amount of yellow than the adults – the area enlarges with each successive moult, until the sixth year or so. They are also quite late maturing, as some pairs do not breed until at least the fifth year, when the clutch may consist of three to five eggs.

The double yellow-heads are bred in fairly large quantities in Europe and the United States of America, where they fulfil a demand for pets. Their beauty, personality and talking ability will ensure they are always sought after and maintained in captivity.

YELLOW-NAPED AMAZON
(*Amazona ochrocephala auropalliata*)
This parrot has long enjoyed a great following in the United States of America. Now the Yellow-naped is growing in popularity in Europe as well. Large, garrulous parrots, they are fantastic mimics. The nominate race originates in Mexico, whilst the subspecies *PARVIPES AMAZON* (*Amazona ochrocephala parvipes*) occurs in Honduras and Nicaragua. The Parvipes

differs in having a lighter beak, more yellowing on the crown and in having red on the bend of the wing. As the present time there is talk of the possibility of a new subspecies (*Amazona orchrocephala hondurensis*) being identified.

Lastly there is the Caribbean subspecies, *Amazona ochrocephala caribae*, which has a very light horn-coloured bill reminiscent of the Oratrix. Unusually for the larger species, some pairs of Yellow-napes can be highly prolific, having upwards of three clutches annually. They usually prove to be good and able parents, but like others in the ochrocephalal group they can be extremely aggressive towards their keepers whilst they are breeding. Three or four eggs form the normal clutch. As pets, hand-reared Yellow-napes tend to be great performers, clowning, displaying and talking with great delight. Again this species is one which seems to pick up short songs and sing them with relish.

VINACEOUS AMAZON
(*Amazona vinacea*)
This gorgeously coloured bird has a wine-coloured breast, the amount and intensity varying from bird to bird. The beak of a healthy bird is unusual in being reddish with a horn-coloured tip. When excited they raise the neck feathers in a manner reminiscent of a Hawk-headed parrot. On CITES Appendix I, deforestation has speeded their decline in the wild, which is in small pockets of Brazil, Paraguay and Argentina.

Fairly excitable and noisy, they have grown in popularity over the last decade and are now established and breeding well in several collections. It was recently reported to us that a young pair had bred when the hen was only 20 months old, and although this is the exception rather than the rule, Vinacea do seem to mature quickly. If ever they are bred in sufficient numbers to warrant being kept as pets, they would probably make excellent companions, being inquisitive and bold, even if parent-reared.

ST VINCENT AMAZON
(*Amazona guildingii*)
From the island of St Vincent in the Caribbean. An imposing and enigmatic bird, at 16 inches (40.5cm) long, the St Vincent is perhaps the most striking of the amazons, being an autumnal mosaic of oranges, brown, green, blue and cream. It appears in three indistinct colour morphs with orange, brown or green predominating.

Like a lot of the island amazons, it is on CITES Appendix I. This vulnerability is mainly due to the fragile environment of an island where a small amount of deforestation could have a marked effect on the population. A hurricane could all but destroy the species. Captive breeding successes are limited due no doubt to the small captive population and a preponderance of males. They are also extremely aggressive towards one another in a confined space, and many pairs need to have separate accommodation outside the breeding season, when a careful watch must be kept upon them. Hopefully, with the few people who are breeding them,

The rare St Vincent Amazon – the head colour varies in this species.

this fantastic bird will cling on and increase in numbers.

RED-NECKED AMAZON
(*Amazona arausiaca*)
Another vulnerable amazon, the Red-necked is from the Island of Dominica in the Caribbean. With only a few hundred birds left in the wild, there are only a handful in captivity, and as yet no breeding programme has been established.

IMPERIAL AMAZON
(*Amazona imperialis*)
The giant Imperial (18 inches or 45.5cm) with a head and breast of the darkest purples is truly a treasure from Dominica. With fewer than one hundred individuals left alive, the future looks bleak for this breed unless drastic action is taken very soon.

ST LUCIA AMAZON (*Amazona versicolor*)
Found on the island from which it gets its name, the 17-inch-long (43cm) St Lucia Amazon is the last of the Caribbean amazons, and, again, it is declining, its numbers counted in tens rather than hundreds. A small group is held in Jersey, and captive breeding efforts there are slowly boosting the numbers of these parrots.

BLUE-FRONTED AMAZON
(*Amazona aestiva*)
One of the most popular pet amazons, the subspecies *Amazona xanthopteryx* is the most readily available. This is quite a large Amazon at 15 inches (38cm). The coloration is variable, but usually there is some blue above the beak, with a variable amount of yellow on the head and the bend of the wing. There is a scalloped pattern to most of the green feathers. It usually lays three or four eggs, and some pairs are quite prolific. Blue-fronts are quite extrovert, very inquisitive and at times noisy, although this does vary from bird to bird. This is a South American amazon.

A rare, wild-caught specimen of the blue mutation of the Blue-fronted Amazon.

YELLOW-FRONTED AMAZON
(*Amazona orchocephala*)
Yellow-fronts have huge personalities – if they decide that they love you. Their devotion will be constant and woe betide anyone who gets in the way of it. They can get a bit excitable, especially if they come across a noise, such as music, that they find particularly exhilarating. Caution has to be kept in mind at these times, as they will occasionally give a nip. These amazons originate from Northern Brazil and are 14 inches (35.5cm) in length. They normally lay three to four eggs and can be extremely aggressive in defence of their nest. Yellow-fronts are all green, apart from an area above the beak which is bright yellow, and flight feathers which contain, red, black and blue feathers.

ORANGE-WINGED AMAZON
(*Amazona amizonica*)
These amazons originate from South America and are 13 inches (33cm) in length. Their coloration is quite variable, with differing amounts of yellow and blue on their heads, extending to below their lower

The Orange-winged Amazon. Note: the sexing ring on the left leg indicates it is a hen.

mandible. There are orange feathers on their wings. This amazon is much quieter than many others, and often has a slightly nervous disposition. This would appear to be reflected in their reluctance to breed, often taking a few years before they feel secure enough to breed. Their clutch size is three to four. As pets they are less exuberant than many amazons, but can be very affectionate. Most people who have had close dealings with Orange-wings wouldn't be without them.

MEALY AMAZON (*Amazona farinosa*)
This is quite a large amazon at about 15 inches (38cm) in length, but is also quite broad and stout-looking. It originates from South America. These amazons are one of the most trusting of all parrots – even those which have been wild-caught respond very quickly to kindness and quickly become confiding. Their head is large, which they will often hold to one side in a quizzical manner. They are frequently referred to as 'gentle giants'. This amazon is hardly ever bred with any regularity. There is a great shortage of hens and even when sexed pairs are set up for breeding, it is seldom achieved. Their coloration is basically green, and some have a yellow patch above their beaks, in others this is mauve. Probably because of this simple coloration, this amazon is one of the cheapest to purchase.

PRIMROSE-CHEEKED OR RED-LORED AMAZON
(*Amazona autumnalis autumnalis*)
The Red-lored Amazon has a very attractive appearance, it is $13^1/2$ inches (34.5cm) long, the front part of the head is red, and this diffuses with primrose yellow on the cheeks. There is often a mauve patch on top of the head, and the feathers on the nape are bordered with black. We have found the disposition of this amazon to be gentle; they are not too noisy, and soon learn to talk. There are usually three eggs in a clutch, and they again originate from South America.

HAWK-HEADED PARROT
(*Deroptyus accipitrinus*)
The Hawk-headed parrots are not of the genus Amazona, but Deroptyus; however, it does share some of the characteristics of Amazon parrots. Several Amazon species can erect their nape and head feathers, producing a surprised or aggressive appearance. The Hawk-headed parrot has exaggerated this feature. In other ways it could be said to resemble Pyrrhura conures. The ruff of this parrot makes it quite unique amongst parrots. The neck feathers, which are a dark red edged with blue, are erected when the parrot is excited, which can include anger, fear or surprise. This does make the bird look much larger and quite menacing. This is further exaggerated by the bird swaying from side to side, and the uttering of a high-pitched whining sound. This parrot also blazes the eyes, with the iris of the eye contracting and enlarging in quick succession. The feathers of the head above the beak are white, which then becomes dark brown

edged with white. It has a distinct periorbital ring, and the cheeks have white streaks against a brown background.

There is a subspecies, *Deroptyus accipitrinus fuscifrons*, where the dark brown colour is replaced by a dusky brown. The chest feathers are dark red with a large edging of pale blue, and the back is green. The tail doesn't have the characteristic wedge shape of the amazons but is longer, and the underside of the tail is black.

The length of the Hawk-headed parrot is 12 inches (30.5cm). It originates from South America and Guyana. Hawk-headed parrots have a nervous disposition and can be extremely noisy. Those that are hand-reared are said to be good pets but one has to wonder if they become aggressive when sexually mature. Hand-reared Hawk-heads that are breeding are extremely aggressive and must be approached with extreme caution. Probably because of their nervousness, they often prove difficult to breed, with a normal clutch size consisting of three to four eggs. Consequently they are much sought-after and are expensive. Hawk-heads use their nestbox for roosting and can be sensitive towards strangers visiting their aviaries.

KAWALL'S AMAZON (*Amazona kawalli*)

The most recently discovered of the Amazons, the Kawall's, unbelievably, was unknown to man until the early 1980s. It was found by the Brazilian collector, Nelson Kawall, after whom it was named. Amazona kawalli is a large squat amazon reminiscent of the Mealy Amazon (*Amazona farinosa*). This 14-inch-long (35.5cm) bird is generally green in coloration, and it sports a very distinctive patch of bare white skin adjacent to the bill. This is proportionally similar to that which is found on the Anodorhynchus Macaws. The Kawall's was found and is only known in the region of the Rio Jurua, Amazonas Province and Southern Santarem, Paraguay. The habits

The rare Kawall's Amazon has only been seen by a handful of people.

and status of this parrot are still unknown and at the time of writing it has yet to be bred in captivity.

SCALY-NAPED OR MERCENARY AMAZON (*Amazona mercenaria*)

Although it has been known for some time, the Mercenary has never been traded or kept in any numbers by aviculturists. This is due no doubt to its rather drab and sombre appearance. A principally green bird, with a black and grey beak, the 14-inch-long (35.5cm) parrot is also rather sedentary in its habits. We do not know of any records of captive breeding of this bird, but it is likely that odd birds have been bred in specialist collections. The species originates from the Andes of Peru to Northern Bolivia.

BLACK-BILLED AMAZON (*Amazona agilis*).

Not dissimilar in appearance from the preceding bird, the Black-billed hails from Jamaica. A smaller bird at only 10 inches (25.5cm), Agilis sports blackish ear coverts. As with so many island species this amazon is endangered due to commercial logging and trapping for trade. Isolated breeding attempts have occurred but, for the same reasons as the preceding species, these have been few and far between.

PUERTO RICAN AMAZON
(*Amazona vittata*)
Hugely endangered with a world population of only one hundred birds or less, this amazon from Puerto Rico is teetering on the edge of survival. This 11-inch-long (28cm) amazon is kept in captivity in a breeding station on the island, and also in Maryland USA where attempts are being made to increase numbers in the hope that one day suitable habitat will be available for a re-release programme. Vittata is similar in appearance to its cousin the Tucuman Amazon (*Amazona tucumana*), only being a little larger and sporting less red on the head than the Tucuman.

KAKAPO
(*Strigops habroptilus*)
The Kakapo is surely the most unusual of all the parrots. Like several of the other feathered inhabitants of its native New Zealand, the Kakapo is flightless. The birds of New Zealand fill ecological niches which are occupied by mammals elsewhere. The Kakapo, whilst not the largest by length, is certainly the heaviest parrot, with males weighing up to 3.5 kg (7lb 2oz).

The females reach 2 kg (4lb 2oz). Uniquely these birds may double their weight in times of plenty, to be called upon when times are hard or when they are breeding.

The breeding performance of the Kakapo is also quite extraordinary. They may not breed for up to five years, whereupon all the birds on the island come into breeding condition at the same time. Uniquely for parrots they have a lek mating system, whereby the males form a clearing and announce their presence by uttering a booming call. To enable them to do this, the Kakapo has another unique (for parrots) adaptation – inflatable thoracic air sacs. A solitary bird, once mating occurs both parties go their own separate ways, and the cock takes no further part in the rearing of the young.

Unusual also in being nocturnal, apart from the booming display cries these are silent creatures. They also sport an owl-like facial disc of hair-like feathers, and the body feathers are also extremely soft. Entirely herbivorous, the Kakapo has the bill adapted to grind food more thoroughly than most other parrots and therefore the gizzard is relatively small.

Before human settlement occurred on the islands, the Kakapo's nocturnal habits and green, yellow and black camouflaging coloration ensured it avoided heavy predation from its only enemies, the raptors. However, with man came cats, rats and stoats, and these flightless birds were powerless against them. Now there are only approximately fifty birds alive. Their survival is due in no small part to Don Merton and his team. These people have eradicated pests from small offshore islands and relocated vulnerable birds to these. This, along with supplementary feeding and constant management, has given these fascinating birds the opportunity to cling to existence, but the struggle is by no means over yet.

VASA PARROT
(*Coracopsis vasa*)
These are highly unusual parrots which are behaviourally quite fascinating. What the Vasa parrots lack in colour, they certainly make up for in character and behaviour. The Greater is 20 inches (51cm) in length; this compares with the Lesser Vasa's length of 14 inches. Both species originate from Madagascar. It is thought that the Vasa parrots are the most primitive of parrots, and may be the link between pigeons and parrots. If you observe the shape of the Vasa parrot, excluding the beak, the similarity is immediately apparent.

The Lesser Vasa (*Coracopsis nigra*) has the

The Lesser Vasa has the shortest incubation period of any parrot.

shortest incubation period of any parrot – only 14 days – the young developing rapidly and leaving the nest at about 5 weeks. In some collections they are bred successfully using trios of one hen to two cocks. When observing the three of them, you can't but be surprised at the vigorous nature of the hen begging from the cocks and the cocks feeding the hen – it all seems extremely rough. The cock has a melodious whistling song, which he repeats as he purposefully struts along the perches or floor of the aviary. All their actions when in breeding condition appear so robust and healthy. Highly unusual is the fact that both cocks and hens have large protruding sexual organs when in breeding condition; to people unaware of this the immediate belief would be a prolapse – but for the Vasas this is entirely normal.

The other behaviour which is different to all other parrots is their sunbathing antics: whilst many birds sunbathe, the Vasas adopt highly unusual postures, which in other birds would suggest an injury. They give the appearance of wanting to soak up every drop of sun possible. If you have a natural earth floor the Vasa won't hesitate to lie on this, almost luxuriating in the feel of the soft grass on their bodies. In the Greaters, the female when in breeding condition loses the feathers on the top of her head. The skin becomes bright yellow, and a yellow patch is also evident beneath the male's beak. In the Lesser, the hen loses several of her feathers but the effect is not so dramatic, and doesn't include the colour change. The clutch size is 3-5, and unfortunately egg-eating appears to be quite a problem.

Coloration of the Vasa would be described as either black or dark brown; however, when the sun catches the larger feathers they can take on an almost metallic blue-green. It must be hoped that a greater interest will be taken in Vasa parrots, as they could be so easily lost to aviculture. They appear to be quite susceptible to Psittacine Beak and Feather Disease, which incidentally changes their colour ultimately to white, and which has the potential of further reducing the rapidly declining avicultural stock. In their native range, deforestation is diminishing their habitat, which may eventually put them on the endangered list.

The Vasa may provide the link between the pigeon and the parrot.

13 RARE AND ENDANGERED PARROTS

With more than 350 species of parrots worldwide, nearly a third of them are endangered and are facing extinction. This is a huge proportion of the whole, and there is a multitude of reasons for this. Here we will look at these reasons, and at what can and is being done to help the situation.

LONGEVITY

In general, parrots are long-lived and therefore have slow reproductive rates. Some of the larger species will only fledge one chick every two or three years, and will struggle to maintain their populations, even without natural disasters or predation.

PREDATORS

Nesting parrots are fair game to a high number of predators. By the very nature of most parrots' nests – a hollow in a tree bough or trunk – they are easy prey to every climbing or flying predator looking for a meal. Many parrots have evolved these nesting techniques in the absence of predators in their habitat. Then man has introduced predatory mammals either deliberately or accidentally. Rats have invaded many islands where they were previously unknown. They have probably entered via ships docking on these islands, with a family of rats aboard along with cargo. Being

Conservation programmes have been successful at slowing the decline of Leadbeater's or Major Mitchell's Cockatoo.

Opposite page: Senegal Parrot.

Habitat of some pionus, amazon and conure species, around the Iguacu (CIDA) Falls, Brazil.

opportunists, the rats will climb and explore every nook and cranny, and soon discover a ready food supply in the form of parrots' eggs or chicks.

Cats are another alien visitor, introduced as escaped pets that have become feral. They then breed quickly and soon there is a whole colony of voracious predators. If they enter a nest, cats will eat eggs and chicks as well as the incubating parents, which is a big loss to any breeding hope. Sometimes parrots will re-clutch if they lose eggs or small chicks, but often the nest site will be abandoned as a result of the disturbance.

Measures have been taken to eradicate these introduced pests, by extensive trapping programmes. These are largely completely unsuccessful, although some of the New Zealand islands have been made predator-free by conservationists protecting the Kakapo (*Strigops habroptilus*). Known nesting sites are surrounded by a circle of live traps which are checked every day by those who are studying these intriguing birds.

Possums are experiencing a population explosion in southern North America, spreading to central and South America. Again these agile climbers are able to exploit every food source they come across.

Some of the smaller parrots and parrakeets will nest in hollows with the smallest entrance hole that they can squeeze through. This will often deter the larger predators, but some snakes are pencil-thin and can enter the smallest crevice.

With heat-seeking sensors on the head, some snakes specialise in robbing nests for eggs and chicks, and the larger ones will consume adult parrots of any size. In Australia, Goannas (large lizards) are hugely responsible for the demise of many parrots. A tree-tinning programme has been initiated there. This involves banding the trunks of nesting trees with shiny metal, which stops Goannas and other climbing predators gaining access to nests. Major Mitchell's Cockatoos (*Cacatua leadbeateri*) have been assisted greatly in this way, having previously fledged very few young successfully in some areas. As well as the tinning of the trunks, branches from adjacent trees are lopped off to prevent access from the neighbouring trees. These measures and the trapping both aid in prevention of attacks from crawling and climbing predators, but there are also a huge family of winged hunters which prey on parrots – the raptors.

Otherwise known as birds of prey, the raptors have populated the world in various forms. Hawks, Falcons, Kites, Eagles and Owls fill niches in every corner of the globe. Smaller parrots and parrakeets flock in large numbers as a defence against these aerial attacks. It is confusing for the attacker when a number of birds break and wheel in every direction, and the chance of survival is greater when you are one of many. Once again, nests are not safe from raptors. Some of the long-legged kites will put a foot into a nest hole and grope around until they secure a chick in their talon, whereupon it will be pulled out and consumed. Being vocal and in many cases gaudy, the parrots of every size are fair game to a suitably-sized raptor. Even the magnificent Hyacinthine Macaw (*Anodorhynchus hyacinthinus*) is predated upon by the huge and powerful Harpy Eagle that also attacks and eats monkeys. Most attacks come from the air, when the swift-flying raptor overcomes the prey with sheer speed. Forest-dwellers are safer from these attacks, but some raptors are highly agile and make amazing manoeuvres to swipe an unsuspecting bird from its perch.

DEFORESTATION

The worldwide destruction of forests is well documented. Opening up tracts of forest affords these birds of prey easier access to the parrots. Fewer hiding-places are only one effect of this. Parrots are wasteful feeders and will naturally forage over a wide area, allowing much of the food to fall to the ground where it is utilised by other animals. With fewer available food trees, the resources soon run out. However, replanting schemes can replace both cover and food sources in a relatively short time. Such a scheme has been initiated by planting palms for the Lear's Macaw (*Anodorhynchus leari*), as one of the main reasons for its decline is the lack of its natural food source, the liluri palm nut.

But the major problem facing the larger parrots due to deforestation is the lack of large trees to nest in. It would take many, many years for a tree to grow big enough and to decay internally to allow a hollow to be created which is large enough to house a pair of macaws and their offspring. Palm trunks are utilised by some of the smaller parrots, but even these can take twenty years to grow to a suitable size. These open-topped nests are also liable to flooding. The macaws have not developed an anti-flooding strategy as have the Palm Cockatoos (*Probisciger aterrimus*), who build a platform of twigs in their open topped nests and continuously top them up as a precaution against flooding.

In the South American rainforest a nestboxing project is in place, whereby artificial nestboxes are raised high into the canopy and secured to a tree that is sturdy enough to hold them but not yet mature enough to provide a nesting site itself. Some initial reluctance to use them was overcome by making the nestboxes look more natural with a bark effect fashioned on them.

Another problem occurs whereby the nestboxes which should be utilised by the macaws are taken over by unwelcome visitors such as Africanised Honey Bees. These extremely aggressive insects swarm and nest in the boxes to the exclusion of the rightful occupants.

Another insect that increases the mortality of chicks is a form of bot-fly that lays its eggs on the unfortunate parrot chick. The resulting larvae burrow into the skin and make a meal of the hapless creature. Regular inspections of the nestboxes by the intrepid conservationists help to eliminate some of these problems. Removal of the angry bees whilst suspended high in the canopy would not be a priority but the conservationists do in fact do it. Dusting the nest litter with a Pyrethrum-based insect powder is helping to control the bot-fly invasion.

We can see the long-term and far-reaching effect that human interference with the rainforests can cause, but natural deforestation also occurs in the form of hurricanes. Some small islands are host to species consisting of numbers counted in tens rather than hundreds and a hurricane can cause unprecedented damage to a species and its habitats in these small areas. This makes a very good case for the captive propagation of species away from their natural habitat. Then, if such a natural disaster did occur, the species could be salvaged with these captive-bred specimens.

SMALL POPULATIONS

Many of these island dwellers are Amazons and their population is restricted naturally by the lack of space a small island affords. Fewer acres mean fewer trees, less feeding and nesting opportunities so these are limiting factors for these parrots. Historically only small populations have ever occurred of three species of macaw from the enormous continent of South America. The Blue-throated Macaw (*Ara glaucogularis*), Lear's Macaw (*Anodorhynchus leari*) and Spix's Macaw (*Cyanopsitta spixii*) have only ever boasted small populations in pockets of their native homeland. This is probably due to the fact that they fill a niche of specialised dietary requirements and face competition from their larger or more boisterous cousins. Obviously these species lead a fragile existence and need every bit of help we can offer.

The Blue-throated Macaw's existence is threatened due to competition from its larger cousins.

CAPTURE

In developing countries where hunger is rife, every available food source is utilised by the natives. Parrots are captured and eaten where they are able to catch them. As repulsive as this may appear to us, it does not have a huge overall effect on the population of stable species. Many Macaws, Lories, Pesquet's Parrots and other brightly coloured birds are also caught and killed to have their feathers used as adornments for beauty, tribal head-dresses and even to sell as ornaments to tourists.

Aviculturists can be of some help in this situation by donating all moulted large feathers back to the country of origin. They can be kept in good condition by sealing them in plastic bags with the addition of mothballs to protect from deterioration.

By doing this, and by the education of the native peoples to be proud of and protect their birds we may be going a long way towards perpetuating many species. Conservationists worldwide stress the importance of letting the natives know how valuable ecologically their parrots are, as well as educating us, the consumers to help protect the species. We, as consumers, are totally responsible for the parrots in our care. Even though your parrot may have been fourth or fifth generation captive-bred, somewhere along the line wild-caught birds have been involved and suffering has been inflicted upon them. For many years mass-importation of parrots has occurred and for every one that survives the trauma of capture, being held prior to export, the journeys and quarantine, many have perished.

Stress is a killer not in itself, but in that the stressed bird becomes open to disease and infection, so many wild-caught birds died months after being installed into their new homes as a result of this stress. Wild parrots are caught in a number of ways. Some hunters will survey nest sites and collect the fledglings when they are a suitable age – not so small that they require many feeds, not so large that they fly before the hunter has a chance to bag them. The collectors will then crudely pump-feed the chicks until they are old enough to go to the buyers. Nest trees that cannot be negotiated will sometimes be felled and if any chicks survive the felling they will be collected – and a valuable nesting tree is lost.

Another method these trappers use is to utilise a bait bird. This unfortunate bird has its wings clipped and is tied to a perch. The surrounding perches are coated with a glue-like substance. The distress calls of the bait bird bring others to investigate and they become adhered to the sticky branches. They are then removed by the captors, and usually have their flight feathers roughly chopped off to prevent further escape.

Nets are also used. Mist nets are very fine and suspended in the flight path of birds returning to the roosting area. They do not see them until it is too late, and they are tangled in the net rather like a fly in a spider's web. Cuts and injuries are common in these birds, as they are disentangled. Similar nets are spread on the ground in areas where ground feeders proliferate.

Some hunters even shoot the parrots out of the sky, hoping to just wing them so that they fall to the ground and their injuries are hoped not to be so severe as to make them unsaleable. Inevitably, bad shots mean that many are killed. Once the unfortunate birds have undergone such trauma, they are overcrowded in holding pens and fed a totally unsuitable and alien diet. It is no wonder that so many species have been captured to the point of extinction. However, without the original wild-caught parrots we would not be fortunate in being able to keep and enjoy these birds in our aviaries as we do now. It is therefore our duty to try ourselves, and encourage others, to purchase only captive-bred and reared stock.

Many of the species are completely self-sustaining in captivity and it is unthinkable that they should still be imported. But imports are still cheaper and ignorance prevails. Educating the public about the diseases wild-caught parrots may carry and the fact that, for example, an adult wild-caught Grey will never tame down, despite the dealer's promises, may help to prevent even more suffering. Who knows which species may next come onto the endangered lists? Earlier this century the Carolina Parrakeet was so numerous that great flocks would swarm like locusts. Now it is extinct.

WHAT IS CITES?

CITES stands for the Convention on the International Trade in Endangered Species. This is a collaboration between participating countries to govern the trade in endangered birds, animals and plants. Those parrots which are most endangered are placed on Appendix I of the CITES list. These include:

The St Vincent is listed as one of the most endangered Amazon species.

Amazons
Red-Necked (*Amazona arausiaca*)
Red-Crowned (*Amazona rhodocorytha*)
Red-Tailed (*Amazona brasiliensis*)
Yellow-Shouldered (*Amazona barbadensis*)
St. Vincent (*Amazona guildingii*)
Imperial (*Amazona imperialis*)
Cuban (*Amazona leucocephala*)
Green-Cheeked (*Amazona viridigenalis*)
Red-Spectacled (*Amazona pretrei*)
Tucuman (*Amazona tucumana*)
St Lucia (*Amazona versicolor*)
Vinaceous (*Amazona vinacea*)
Puerto Rican (*Amazona vittata*)

Macaws
Hyacinthine (*Anodorhynchus hyacinthinus*)
Lear's (*Anodorhynchus leari*)
Caninde (*Ara glaucogularis*)
Buffon's (*Ara ambigua*)
Military (*Ara militaris*)
Scarlet (*Ara macao*)
Red-Fronted (*Ara rubrogenys*)
Illiger's (*Ara maracarna*)
Spix's (*Cyanopsitta spixii*)

Cockatoos
Goffins (*Cacatua goffini*)
Red-Vented (*Cacatua haematuropygia*)
Moluccan (*Cacatua moluccensis*)
Palm (*Probisciger aterrimus*)

Others
Red and Blue Lory (*Eos histrio*)
Queen of Bavaria's Conure (*Guaruba guaruba*)
Forbes Kakariki (*Cyanoramphus auriceps forbesi*)
Norfolk Island Kakariki (*Cyanoramphus novaezelandiae*)
Night Parrot (*Geopsittacus occidentalis*)
Orange-Bellied Parrakeet (*Neophema chrysogaster*)
Double-Eyed Fig Parrot (*Opopsitta or Cyclopsitta diopthalma*)
Yellow-Eared Conure (*Ognorhynchus icterotis*)
Ground Parrot (*Pezoporus wallicus*)
Red-Capped Parrot (*Pionopsitta pileata*)
Hooded Parrot (*Psephotus chrysopterygius dissimilis*)
Golden-Shouldered Parrot (*Psephotus chrysopterygius*)
Paradise Parrot (*Psephotus pulcherrimus*)
Mauritius (Echo) Parrakeet (*Psittacula eques*)
Principe Grey Parrot (*Psittacus erithacus principe*)
Blue-Throated Conure (*Pyrrhura cruentata*)
Thick-Billed Parrot (*Rhynchopsitta pachyrhyncha*)
Maroon-Fronted Parrot (*Rhynchopsitta pachyrhyncha terrisi*)
Kakapo (*Strigops habroptilus*)

The convention is implemented by means of licences issued in member countries. No species on Appendix I can be traded without documentation. It prohibits international commercial trade in species which are threatened with extinction and which may be threatened by trade.

Appendix II is applied to species whose survival is not yet threatened but may be unless trade is controlled.

Appendix III is used to reinforced the protection of species already protected by national legislation. This appendix is rarely used in connection with parrots.

Some of the Appendix I birds which are being bred in captivity become available for sale to other breeders. To be able to apply for an exemption certificate to sell an Appendix I parrot, the breeder must closed-ring it as a chick or insert a microchip for identification purposes. In the UK the breeder can then apply to the Department of the Environment for the permission to sell the bird in question.

If the buyer wishes to resell the bird in the future, he must re-apply for an exemption certificate with proof as to where the bird was obtained. All breeding birds must be registered as proof that they are the parents of any chick you may wish to sell. If any doubt arises, DNA matching can be used to prove relationships.

Rarity usually increases the value of parrots and some of those listed are very expensive indeed. Therefore some people want them as status symbols, but it is vital that parrots with a small gene pool are put into breeding programmes and used effectively. These birds should only be obtained if you are confident that you have the time and experience to do them justice.

The Purple-bellied Parrot is much sought-after for its looks and its whistling voice.

UNUSUAL SPECIES

PURPLE-BELLIED PARROT

(*Triclaria malachitacea*)

If it were more freely available, the charming Purple-bellied would be highly sought after by Psittaculturists. As well as being beautiful they have a melodious whistling voice. Although they are twelve inches (30.5cm) long, they only weigh five ounces (142g) so they are fairly slender birds. Sexually dimorphic, only the males have the purple coloration on the belly. They are otherwise all green with a startling whitish beak.

With a graceful fluttering flight these birds will appreciate a large aviary and are less destructive to framework and plant life than many other parrots. Purple-bellies seem to appreciate a long and fairly narrow nestbox for the security it affords. However, with a clutch size of up to six, enough space must be afforded at the base to accommodate a potentially large brood. They are rarely kept in captivity and therefore have only been bred by a handful of keepers. Originating from South Brazil, they are shy and retiring in lightly forested areas.

RED-CAPPED PARROT
(*Pionopsitta pileata*)
An attractive small parrot, and another one with a lovely voice. Thought to be declining in the wild it is on CITES Appendix I. Another sexually dimorphic species, only the males have the red caps which give them the name. They originate from pockets of South Eastern Brazil, Paraguay and North Eastern Argentina. Once available to aviculture quite frequently, the only birds available now are being captive-bred. There is one prominent breeder in the UK and several on the continent. The clutch size varies from two to four, and on the whole Red-caps are very diligent parents. Enjoying the security of flocks, the Red-caps appear to breed more freely when there are several pairs in the vicinity.

VULTURINE PARROT
(*Pionopsitta vulturina*)
The extraordinary Vulturine parrot is one of only two psittacines almost exclusively lacking head feathers – not just bare cheeks like the macaws and greys. This would indicate that the diet is quite messy, and the birds probably delve into very ripe fruits. An enigma to ornithologists, the Vulturine has not been studied in the wild and is almost unknown in aviculture. Those who have tried to keep this species in the past have sadly been defeated in their attempts to maintain it alive. Perhaps with the knowledge available to parrot keepers now, attempts would be more successful.

SHORT-TAILED PARROT
(*Graydidascalus brachyurus*)
At nine inches (23cm) long, the short-tailed is a square, chunky little parrot. It tends to sit quietly amongst the foliage, and freezes if it is threatened, taking flight at the last minute if necessary. Fairly common along the rivers of the Amazon, it has not been sought after by the Psittaculturists and so has not been traded freely in the past. We have knowledge of only one breeder in the UK who has persevered with this species and has enjoyed moderate breeding results. The birds were given a secluded aviary and minimum disturbance. Due to the short-tailed's sober appearance and retiring habits, it is unlikely to become popular with parrot keepers in the future.

THICK-BILLED PARROT
(*Rhynchopsitta pachyrhynchus*)
At around fifteen inches (38cm) long, the macaw-like Thick-billed is sadly suffering a steep decline in the wild. Originating in Mexico, the destruction of its pine forest habitat is causing the drop in numbers. The pine trees offer this specialising species both food and nesting sites. With its macaw-like appearance and habits, it is probably only the lack of bare facial patches that have prevented this species being classified with the macaws. With a clutch size of two to five eggs, a few Europeans and several breeders in the USA have been successful with this species. A captive breeding and re-introduction programme has been implemented in Mexico but to date it has been fairly unsuccessful. Released birds were fitted with tracking devices and followed. Sadly the majority were found dead, either from predation by raptors or from starvation, being unable to find adequate amounts of the correct food. Hopefully, with increasing captive breeding and habitat re-development a better release programme will occur.

YELLOW-EARED CONURE
(*Ognorhynchus icterotis*)
An extreme rarity, the yellow-eared Conure is another macaw-like parrot with a rectangular patch of bare skin running from the upper mandible to the chin. An Andean bird it is only now the subject of study in its natural habitat – maybe too late to save it from the brink of extinction. In captivity only a couple of birds have been kept, to our knowledge, and sadly have not bred.

RED SHINING PARROT
(*Prosopeia tabuensis*)
As the name suggests, the shining parrot has iridescence to the feathers quite different from the other members of the genus. From the Fijian Islands there are several subspecies ranging from fifteen to eighteen inches (38-46cm) in length. All sport green wings. The largest subspecies have scarlet-red head, chest, sides and undertail coverts. These areas darken to maroon in the smaller subspecies. Like so many island species they are all teetering on a knife edge at the mercy of human intervention and the elements. Having not been imported for many years, there are only a handful of these gorgeous birds in captivity and sporadic breeding results have occurred over the years. As with so many of these rarities, a breeding programme needs initiating to increase the numbers and avoid another species falling to extinction.

PESQUET'S PARROT (*Psittrichas fulgidus*)
In its striking livery of black and red the Pesquet's also has a near-featherless face and crown adapted, like the Vulturine, to a messy diet. Highly frugivorous in captivity, guava, mango, kiwi, passion and other such exotic soft fruits should be offered, in addition to the more usual bananas, apples, carrots and so on. If given whole fruits, Pesquet's will derive great pleasure in digging out the soft flesh from within them. Rather like members of the family Loridae, many of this species have perished due to an inadequate, mainly seed, diet given to them before their true needs were understood and catered for.

A few breeding successes have been recorded at some of the larger collections. Many observations have been made that digging out and hollowing a nest log has stimulated the birds to breed. Two eggs form the normal clutch. Males are distinguished by a patch of red on the ear coverts; however, all juveniles have a few red feathers here. In its native New Guinea, the Pesquet's is highly prized by the natives for its feathers that are used to adorn head-dresses. Sadly this poses a very real threat to the species.

THE FIG PARROTS

This family of small (five to seven inches, or 12.5 to 18cm, in length) stocky parrots is another one of the dietary specialists. They do need a high proportion of figs in the diet, supplemented by a vitamin K additive, along with other fruits, berries, small seeds and insectivorous foods. Mealworms will be taken by some pairs and must be offered when chicks are in the nest. Some breeders have found that withholding seeds and increasing the fig and live food portion of the diet brings about success when chicks hatch. Several breeders have hatched chicks only to lose them during the rearing stage and the diet has often been indicated as the problem. All species lay two eggs. In captivity fig parrots seem to suffer from overgrown beaks much more than many other species, and a plentiful supply of twigs, cuttlefish bone and mineral blocks will help to alleviate the problem.

DOUBLE-EYED FIG PARROT
(*Opopsitta or Cyclopsitta diophthalma*)
This five-inch-long (12.5cm) bird is from

New Guinea, with subspecies from Indonesia, Northern and North Eastern Australia. The male has full red cheek markings whereas they are beige yellow in the female. This is probably the most frequently kept and bred of the fig parrots.

ORANGE-BREASTED FIG PARROT
(*Opopsitta or Cyclopsitta gulielmiterti*)
Another five-incher (12.5cm), although fairly common in the wild it is very rarely seen in captivity and we are not aware of any successful breedings.

DESMAREST'S FIG PARROT
(*Psittaculirostris desmarestii*)
A beautiful parrot with subtle blending of colours on the head. The Desmarest's is larger than the preceding two at seven inches (18cm). From New Guinea and surrounding islands, it is not uncommon in the wild. The difference in sexes is slight, with the females having less yellow on the neck than the male. A few have been bred in captivity but, as with all the fig parrots, breeding has been fraught with difficulty.

EDWARD'S FIG PARROT
(*Psittaculirostris edwardsii*)
Unusual, with the outstanding feather shafts around the cheeks and throat, the Edward's are of similar proportions to the other Psittaculirostris. Sexual dimorphism in this species is seen in the male's red breast, contrasting with the female's light green.

The Edward's Fig Parrot.

SALVADORI'S FIG PARROT
(*Psittaculirostris salvadorii*)
Not dissimilar to the Edwards, with yellowish cheek feather shafts rather than the red of the former, again this species presents a challenge to the breeder and few have been successful. The female lacks the red band on the chest of the male.

BLUE-RUMPED PARROT
(*Psittinus cyanurus*)
Importations have occurred recently of this mild-mannered, shy little parrot. At around 7 inches (18cm) long, it will remain frozen still, hoping to remain undetected, if alarmed. Despite its being unusual and quiet, not much interest has been shown in it, which is a shame as it may die out in aviculture if not propagated by some serious breeders. The clutch numbers 3-5 eggs and are more likely to be laid in a quiet corner of a secluded aviary. A varied diet, including small seeds such as millet sprays and canary seed can be offered along with the usual fruits and vegetables. The sexes are unmistakable, with the male having a powder blue/grey head and an orange-red upper mandible. The female has a brown head and a black upper mandible.

GREAT-BILLED PARROTS
(*Tanygnathus megalorhynchos*)
Unusually in captive parrots, there seems to be a surplus of females in the few specimens available of this species. Although a largish parrot at 16 inches (40.5cm), with enormous mandibles, its quiet disposition belies its appearance. The Great-billed is a female-dominant species, as is its relative the

Eclectus. Similarly, it also lays two eggs in a clutch. However, unlike the Eclectus, it has not become established in aviculture and so is rarely bred. It originates from Indonesia.

BLUE-NAPED PARROT
(*Tanygnathus lucionensis*)
Although only 12 inches (30cm) long, this species is very similar in appearance to its cousin, the Great-billed: slightly duller in coloration, it also has the blue hind skull and hind neck. Originating in the Philippines where it is fairly stable in population, it again is unpopular in captivity and so will remain unavailable unless more interest is shown.

MULLER'S PARROT
(*Tanygnathus sumatranus*)
Another Filipino, the Mullers has not got the black wing markings of the preceding two species, but nonetheless has attractive light edging to the wing feathers. The beak is red in the male and light horn-coloured in the female. Although common in the wild, the same lack of interest is shown in these as in the other Tanyghathus species, and so few people have seen them in captivity. A great pity – as all of these are quiet birds, with noise being a deciding factor to many when choosing which birds are kept.

KEA (*Nestor notabilis*)
At 19 inches (48cm), the New Zealand Kea is a quite extraordinary bird from the mountainous ranges. Although once slaughtered as a sheep killer, it has climbed back to be fairly common once more. It does indeed scavenge around sheep, and will devour the afterbirth from lambing ewes, feast upon the carrion of stillborn lambs and on the naturally occurring deaths of adults. The mischievous birds will peck a wounded adult, and they will eat the fat around the wound. Great opportunists, Keas will eat almost anything that is edible, and play with that which is not. They have even been seen to enter the burrows of nesting sea-birds to remove and kill the unfortunate fledglings. The high fat content of the diet is essential to these birds living in the snowy, cold areas that they do.

The Kea is starting to increase its numbers once more.

Keas also nest underground, in abandoned burrows or cracks in rock faces where they will lay up to four eggs. In captivity trying to replicate an underground nest has met with success in the case of several breeders in Europe, where the breeding of these birds is increasing. Few parrots will use the space of an aviary as extensively as these birds, and every dimension should be as large as possible. The roof will be swung from, the sides flown to-and-fro from, and hours will be spent on the ground playing, searching, digging and feeding. Every conceivable toy should be added to the aviary, as swings, ropes, boxes, balls, pebbles and logs will be explored, tossed around or played upon.

Although quite soberly coloured in browns and olive greens, the feathers are beautifully scalloped and the underwings are a beige shade of orange – enjoyed most whilst watching the bird in flight. Few animals have time to play for very long in the wild, but these birds seem to think the world is their playground. Tourists who venture into their territory will find that their cars will be set upon, with birds sliding down the roof and knocking at the windows, and any items found will be stolen.

KAKA (*Nestor meridionalis*)
At 18 inches long (45.5cm), and 2lb (900g) in weight, the Kaka is 8 ounces (227g) lighter than its cousin the Kea. This species has shown a marked decline in the wild with deforestation and the introduction of alien predators. Much more shy and retiring than the Kea, the Kaka prefers to remain in the forest where it will supplements its seed and berry diet with grubs and insects that bore into the wood. In aviculture it is only found in a few zoos in its native country and one or two outside of it.

CONSERVATION PROJECTS

Annette De Saulles

Thirty-nine parrot species in the Far East, Australia and New Zealand have been identified as being under threat. The situation has been intensified in the Far East in recent years with out-of-control forest fires destroying large tracts of land.

In the Latin American countries and islands 47 endangered species are at risk; some of them are in imminent danger of extinction in the near future. It is believed that 27 species worldwide have already disappeared over the last four centuries.

Major building schemes for dams, gas pipelines, power grids and roads are cutting through dwindling forest habitats, and 26 hectares (8 acres) of forest are being lost every day. With more than half the world's forests already destroyed, along with their vital tree-hole nesting sites and the fruits and seeds parrots depend on for food, conservation groups and projects are on the increase.

One approach to the problem is to discourage poachers from taking parrots from the wild by showing them that their income can be obtained from other sources, such as involvement in eco-tourism. This gives local peoples a reason to protect and conserve the birds rather than hunt them for the pet trade. Educational initiatives in schools are in place in several areas. However, old attitudes and customs die hard.

Two of the major organisations committed to changing the situation are the World Parrot Trust and World Wildlife Fund. These organisations cooperate with various other conservation schemes based throughout the world to:

- raise funds;
- carry out research into endangered species and the specific threats facing them and their habitats;
- stop the trade in wild-caught parrots;
- oppose habitat destruction;
- liaise with and educate local people to preserve wild parrots and their natural habitats;
- support captive breeding programmes;
- organise rehabilitation into the wild where possible.

THE WORLD PARROT TRUST

The Trust has been in existence since 1989 and now has 12 national branches in the UK, USA, Canada, Benelux, Denmark, France, South Africa, Italy, Switzerland, Germany, Australia and Spain, with many supporters worldwide.

ECHO PARRAKEET
The first species to be targeted by the World Parrot Trust (WPT) was the Echo Parrakeet, native to Mauritius and considered at the end of the 1980s to be the world's rarest parrot. Support was given to an existing recovery programme team by the provision of a new four-wheel-drive vehicle. Funding has been ongoing and the WPT is now joint sponsor of the project with the Jersey Wildlife

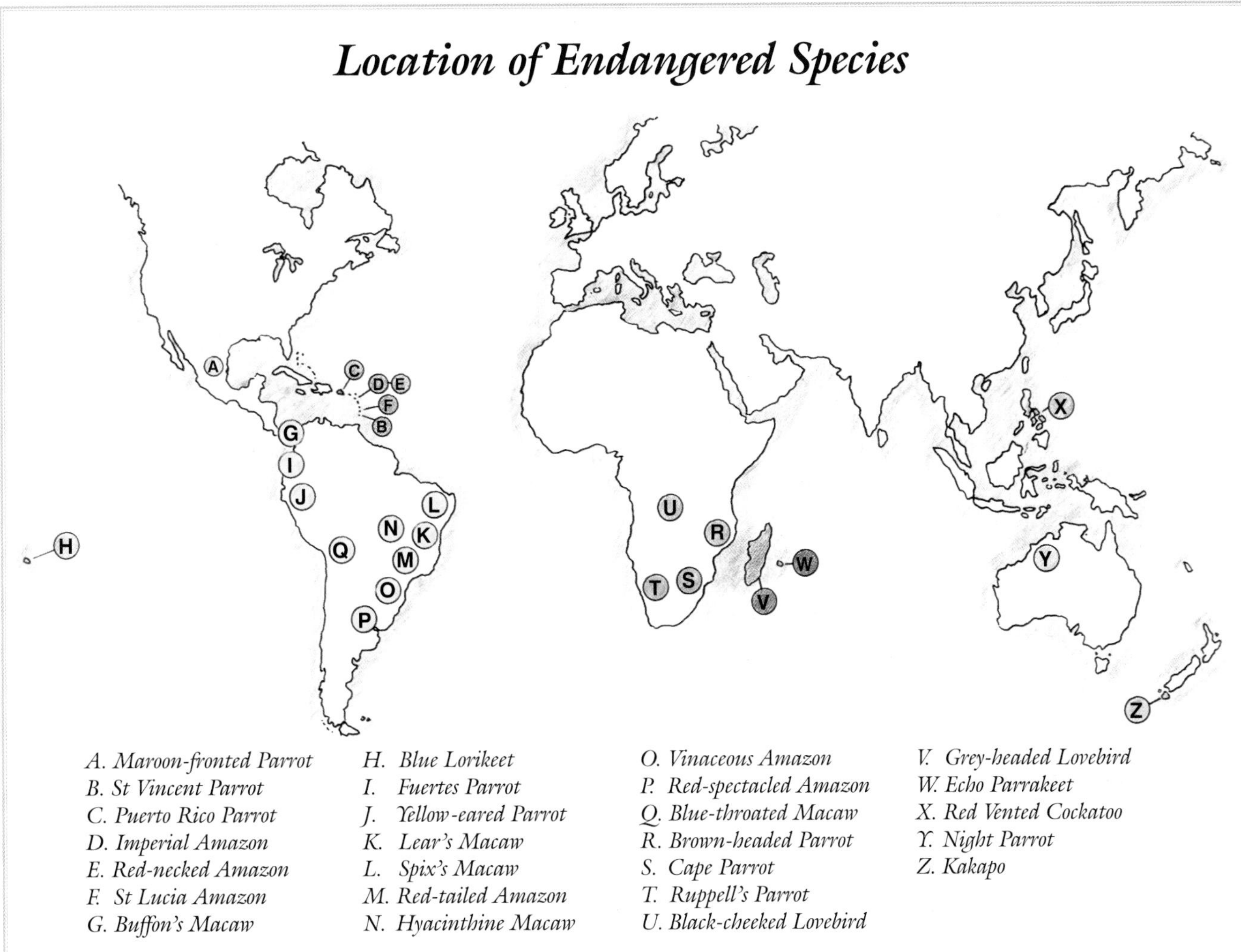

Preservation Trust, based at Jersey Zoo. There is a captive breeding programme in place for the bird on Mauritius.

Ten years on, the Echo Parrakeet has been brought back from the brink of extinction with over 100 birds now living in the wild and captive-reared birds continuing to be released.

LEAR'S MACAW

The 'Palm for a Parrot' campaign raises funds for palm-tree planting in Brazil. The rare Lear's Macaw depends for its food on Licuri palm nuts, which are becoming increasingly scarce due to deforestation.

HELP FOR CARIBBEAN PARROTS

Several species are severely depleted in numbers on the islands of the West Indies, where habitat conservation is vital to the birds' survival. The St Vincent, Imperial Amazon, Red-necked Amazon and St Lucia Amazon are all under close scrutiny by the WPT in conjunction other conservation programmes. Funding has been put into the captive-breeding of St Vincent Parrots, both at the WPT headquarters in Cornwall and on its native island.

Specially equipped and painted Caribbean buses tour the islands, with the aim of bringing accessible conservation education to local people.

COCKATOOS

Conservation work takes many forms and is always costly. In the early 1990s, the WPT managed to get 319 illegally held Goffin's cockatoos released back into the wild on Tanimbar, Indonesia. It was several months before this was achieved and meanwhile, the Trust had to finance the care and feeding of more than 500 birds.

GLOBAL ACTION PLAN

One recent UK initiative, a 'Global Action Plan for Parrots' has been launched by the World Parrot Trust in conjunction with the World Wildlife Fund (WWF) in the UK. Eighty-nine highly endangered parrot species are being targeted for help, with recovery teams being set up for each threatened species.

Actor John Cleese, well known for the Monty Python 'Dead Parrot' sketch, is supporting the campaign. He points out that: "A pet parrot can need as much attention as a human baby – and for up to 50 years. So think carefully before you bring a pet parrot into your home."

For the Action Plan to succeed, cooperation from the relevant governments is vital to halt further habitat loss and illegal trading. The Brazilian government has agreed to triple the area of protected Amazon forest, which now covers 25 million hectares (62 million acres). Amongst the parrots that will benefit from this is the magnificent Hyacinth Macaw, which is thought to number no more than 3,000 individuals in the wild.

Following the devastating forest fires in Indonesia and elsewhere in the Far East, WWF is highlighting the responsibility of commerce for what is happening there. The WWF has set up over 300 forest conservation projects in vulnerable areas, their long-term aim being to halt and reverse the destruction. Cleared forest is used for cattle grazing, but the soil is too thin for sustained grassland, with the result that the slashing and burning of forest is continuous.

CITES legislation is supported and enforced by *Traffic*, a WWF programme that monitors and investigates the wildlife trade. Illegal capture can be disastrous to a species under threat. Seven hundred Red and Blue Lories – thought to number less than 2,000 in their wild habitat in Indonesia – were illegally exported in the early 1990s, before *Traffic* were able to intervene and stop the trade.

Smuggled birds that have been confiscated by the authorities can be reintroduced into the wild, although this requires careful planning. CETAS is one Brazilian organisation that rehabilitates smuggled parrots. The birds are treated for stress and possible disease before being released into their new habitat. Food is provided initially until the parrots can fend for themselves again.

THE LORO PARQUE FUNDACION

Loro Parque has an extensive captive breeding programme, at its base in Tenerife, for many endangered parrot species. It has

There is just one Spix's Macaw in the wild.

also initiated several long-term projects to protect species in the wild, such as that for the Red-tailed Amazon (*Amazona brasiliensis*) in southern Brazil, which now numbers fewer than 4,500.

The most endangered wild parrot – and the symbol of the Loro Parque Fundacion – is the Spix's Macaw (*Cyanopsitta spixii*). This bird was thought to be extinct until rediscovered a decade ago. Just one lone male remains in its native north-eastern Brazil. Its mate is a female Illiger's Macaw. The Fundacion has been working painstakingly for years towards their goal of re-establishing the Spix's Macaw in the wild, but this is proving very difficult. A captive-bred female Spix's was carefully prepared for release into the vicinity of the male, but the hoped-for pairing did not happen. She vanished a few weeks later and was reported killed. Although only one Spix's remains in the wild, there are more than 40 individuals in captivity and the recovery project to re-establish this species in the wild is continuing.

JERSEY ZOO

The Wildlife Preservation Trust at Jersey Zoo has a captive breeding programme for several species of endangered parrots. One bird they have been involved with is the St Lucia Amazon (*Amazona versicolor*). At one time it was thought that only about 50 of these birds remained on their native Lesser Antilles islands in the Caribbean. Now the numbers run into several hundred. Jersey Zoo has been successful in breeding these parrots in captivity and releasing some of them back on to St Lucia. Together with legislative and educational support from local government and conservationists, awareness of the St Lucia Amazon has been raised and its future now looks a little brighter.

AFRICAN PARROTS

The University of Natal's Research Centre for African Parrot Conservation has been studying numbers and habitat status of several declining species.

Once considered a pest, the Cape Parrot is now an endangered species.

- The Brown-headed Parrot is seriously depleted in some areas of its range along the east coast of Africa.
- The Cape Parrot is at risk from extensive logging in its native forestland of eastern South Africa. The trees it depends on for fruit and nesting holes are disappearing. In the past, Cape parrots were shot as pests.
- Ruppell's Parrot: native to north-west Namibia, fewer than 10,000 of these birds remain in the wild. Although a protected species, illegal poaching is an ongoing threat.

HYACINTHINE MACAWS

Projeto Arara Azul is an ongoing project in the Hyacinth Macaw's native Pantanal, Brazil. With vast areas of forest cleared for cattle-

The nesting hollow of a Hyacinthine Macaw in Pantanal, Brazil.

grazing, nesting sites are at a premium. One dedicated woman, Neiva Guedes, has been working in the area for ten years, monitoring natural nest holes used by Hyacinths and putting up nestboxes to encourage further breeding. Other parrot species have inevitably moved into some of the nestboxes, but as Hyacinthine Macaws prefer natural tree holes, it does at least mean more of these are left for them.

The good news is that the population of *Anodorhynchus hyacinthinus* in that area is now growing.

TAMBOPATA

In south-east Peru, a 3.7 million-acre (1.5 million-hectare) reserve and research centre at Tambopata was set up in 1990. The forests here are sanctuary to 32 parrot species – 10% of the total worldwide. At a huge clay lick on the reserve, many species of parrots and macaw can be seen nibbling at the clay, which has a detoxifying effect.

FUNDING

The US-based ABC Small Grants Program provides support for projects benefiting parrot conservation in Latin America and the Caribbean. It considers proposals from conservation groups and has teamed up on projects with the World Parrot Trust, the Disney Wildlife Conservation Foundation and the Kaytee Avian Foundation, among others.

- In north-west Mexico, ABC is involved in work to save the Thick-billed Parrot, contributing funds to help establish a conservation base in the area.
- In Belize, a conservation site is being set up for the Scarlet Macaw. The aim is to promote eco-tourism and thus help parrots and local people alike.
- ABC is involved in a population assessment of the Blue-winged Macaw in south-east Brazil, with a view to future action.
- On the island of Dominica, it is assessing crop damage by Red-necked and Imperial Amazons. The conflicting interests of parrots and farmers will then be addressed.
- At Belize Zoo, 1,000 students have been involved in a nestbox project for the Yellow-headed Amazon.
- A local community 'honorary reserve warden' scheme has been set up where Green-winged Macaws have previously been hunted.
- Projects for endangered Amazons in the wild include the Cayman Brac, Yellow-billed, Black-billed, Blue-fronted and Red-tailed.
- The Yellow-eared Parrot in Colombia is the subject of an emergency programme to avoid imminent extinction.

EDUCATION

Raising awareness amongst local populations is considered vital in the fight to save parrots in the wild. One example of this is The Bay Island Conservation Association's project. This was launched to save the island's severely depleted population of Yellow-naped Parrots. 'Promote Protection through Pride' was the motto of the campaign, which recognised the fundamental part the islanders themselves would have to play if it was to be a success. Thousands of leaflets, posters and bumper stickers were distributed to local people, telling them about the bird and the threat to it from trapping and habitat destruction.

Schoolchildren were closely involved, with songs about the Yellow-naped Parrot being produced, recorded and taught, an environmental puppet show touring the schools, and environmental comics distributed. Books on the 'Birds of the Bay Island' were also produced and Yellow-naped Parrot T-shirts sold.

Churches were targeted, with environmental sermon sheets distributed throughout the island, and a legislation booklet for the policing authorities was produced.

Questionnaires sent out pre- and post-project showed a marked increase in awareness of the Yellow-naped's plight. The project also succeeded in raising awareness of the need to protect the island's environment. This would promote tourism and reduce the need to make a living from trapping wild parrots.

THE GREEN PARROT PROJECT

One of the problems facing customs officers when attempting to intercept illegally smuggled birds, animals and eggs is that of being able to accurately identify the creature in question. To the inexpert eye, one parrot may look much like another – but it might also be highly endangered, with a ban in operation against exports.

'Green Parrot' is an innovative computerised identification system aimed at stopping wildlife smugglers. Pictures and detailed information enable even inexperienced customs officials to quickly and accurately identify the bird (or animal, fish, reptile, skin or animal part) from the computer screen.

NOT ALL BAD NEWS

Identifying a species at risk, setting up a recovery project and finding the funds for what is likely to be many years' work, is no easy task. Progress is usually slow and setbacks are common. But there are already several success stories where a parrot species has been brought back from the brink of extinction.

The Red-fronted Macaw is on the CITES endangered list.

New Zealand's ground-living Kakapo was once very common, until imported cats and rats decimated its numbers. Despite its flightless condition and slow breeding rate, the Kakapo is now making a hesitant comeback, with numbers very slowly increasing, due to a concerted effort on the part of conservationists.

THE NEED FOR AVICULTURE

Before the advent of captive-breeding and hand-rearing, taking birds from the wild was accepted practice. Nowadays, with a few exceptions, there can be no excuse for it. Great advances have been made in aviculture in recent years, with plenty of breeders now hand-rearing baby parrots for the pet market. If carefully raised, these birds are relaxed and happy in human company and make excellent companions. A wild-caught bird rarely becomes fully tame and may never recover from the trauma of capture and exportation.

Conservation successes inevitably rely on captive breeding where populations are severely diminished. Bird parks, zoos and private individuals throughout the world are involved – notably such organisations as Loro Parque in Tenerife (see above).

To establish a compatible pair of birds, provide the right environment, accommodation and diet, and build up a stock of birds can take many years. Releasing into the wild involves very careful preparation, as well as monitoring after the event. The parrots need to be made aware of natural dangers and predators, they have to be taught which foods can be eaten and where to find them. Nest sites need to be available in the area of release.

The success of aviculture and captive-breeding has brought its own problems, however. Some species – such as the Peach-faced Lovebird, Budgerigar and Cockatiel – are easily and quickly bred, and this has reduced their monetary worth. Consequently, the value placed on them by some owners is also reduced and the bird is regarded as unimportant and dispensable.

Species that are in decline in the wild may also not be popular with aviculturists, perhaps because they are slow or difficult to breed, or not in demand as pets. However, by studying the individual needs of these birds and following the natural conditions that would trigger breeding condition in the wild, success can be achieved. A real contribution can be made to the conservation movement by the breeding of rarer species by committed individuals.

WHAT CAN I DO?

Although we may feel the problems of deforestation and trapping are beyond our control, there is in fact a lot that the individual can do. The Kaytee Avian Foundation in the States list the following ways in which we can make a difference:

- Don't buy woods from the rainforest, such as mahogany or ebony
- If you want to keep a parrot, only buy a captive-bred, hand-reared bird
- Write to your member of parliament or congressman to let them know your views
- Join a conservation group dedicated to helping birds and their environments.

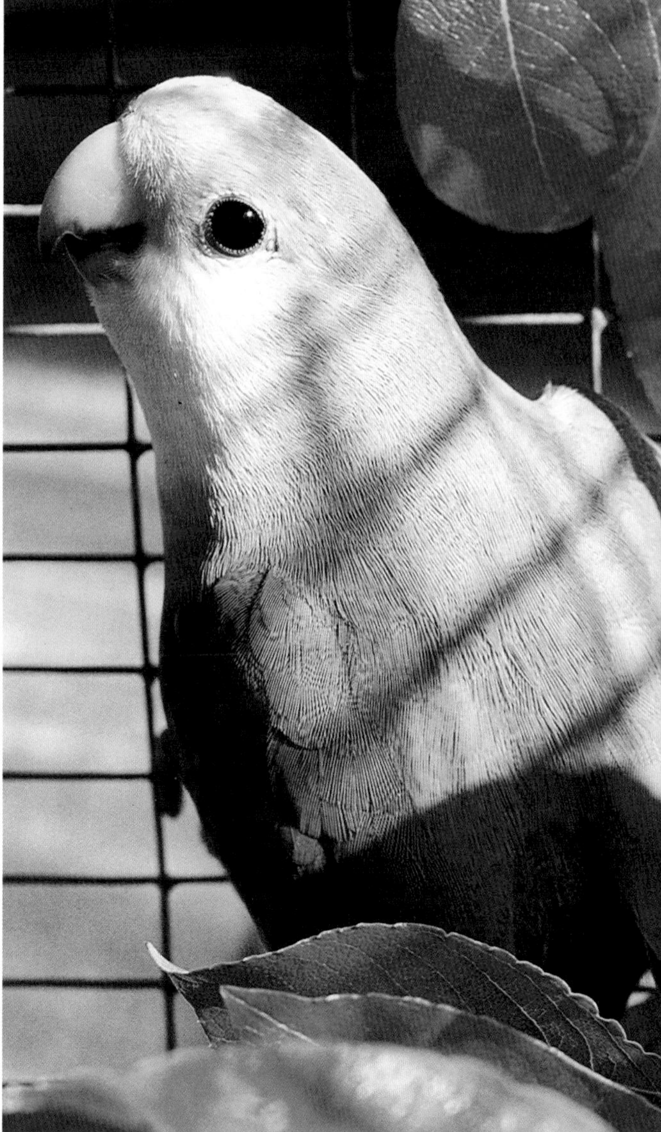

Budgerigars, Cockatiels and Peach-faced Lovebirds (pictured) face their own welfare issues caused by their popularity.

World Parrot Trust
Tel: + 44 (0)1736 753365

WWF-UK
Tel: + 44 (0)1483 426444

Loro Parque Fundacion
Tel: + 34 922 37 40 81
Website: www.loroparque-fundacion.org